MORE GENTLE HEROES

GARY B. BLACKBURN

INTRODUCTION BY LONNIE M. LONG

NEWMAN SPRINGS PUBLISHING
320 Broad Street
Red Bank, NJ 07701

First originally published by Newman Springs Publishing 2023

ISBN 978-1-68498-697-2 (Paperback)
ISBN 978-1-68498-698-9 (Digital)

Printed in the United States of America

One of the most wonderful and unexpected rewards to come from my book-writing journey has been the opportunity to meet and work with men who are truly heroes in every sense of the word. In most cases, I have found such men to be introspective, humble, and self-effacing. Those qualities are likely a result of what they have seen and experienced, at least in part, and those traits tend to make mere mortals (such as I am) even more appreciative of their accomplishments. I feel so humbled to be in their company and honored by their friendship.

One such man helped me with the first story in this book. Without his help and expertise, my tale would be much less accurate and far less interesting. We worked continuously for several weeks, emailing copy back and forth, writing and rewriting Green Beret training episodes and Vietnam battle scenes. We had friends in common, and in the process of our correspondence, we too became friends. He never expressed to me any hint that he was terminally ill. It came as a great shock when I was informed he had passed away twenty-nine days after my last note from him. Marcie, his sister, said, "He wanted so much to finish the job that he worked tirelessly to make it happen. Thank you for giving him the opportunity as well as the purpose to finish strong, for being his friend and for giving him such a worthy task to complete."

In one of our mail exchanges, I asked Hamp about his military experience, and this was his reply:

> I retired from the Army in 1988 having served as an NCO in the 6th, 7th, 5th and Training Group [Special Forces]. I went to Infantry OCS

in '72 and enjoyed serving as a commander in the 1st Cav and 2nd Infantry Div. I also commanded at the National Training Center (NTC), Fort Irwin [California]. I returned to Special Operations in the 80's, with assignment to a Tier 1 [Special Missions] unit, US Army Intelligence Support Activity. I was fortunate and blessed to serve with and among some of our nation's greatest soldiers.

It is my great honor to dedicate this book to my friend Maj. Hampton Dews II.

Hamp Dews, 1947–2020

And in that time when men decide and feel
safe to call the war insane, take one moment to
embrace those gentle heroes you left behind.
                    —Maj. Michael Davis O'Donnell

CONTENTS

FOREWORD

From Gary B. Blackburn
Coauthor of *Unlikely Warriors: The Army Security
Agency's Secret War in Vietnam 1961–1973*
Nominated for the Henry and Ann Paolucci Book Award (2014)
Author of *Those Gentle Heroes—A Tribute*

The stories in *Those Gentle Heroes* and *More Gentle Heroes* recount actual events that occurred during the Vietnam War. The stories are true. The main protagonists and other primary figures were and are real people. Some of the peripheral characters, dialogue, and scenes, however, were created to preserve the integrity of the story line. The names of some characters have also been changed to protect the identities of those involved in the stories.

Technically, that makes these stories works of historical fiction, but this should in no way detract from the heroism of the main characters. Their deeds, their medals and awards, and the main details surrounding their heroism are factual. Some events may not correspond precisely with the memories of all those involved. Like witnesses to a crime, individual people can remember the same event differently and may have seen it from a dissimilar perspective. And time has a way of distorting the past, especially memories of traumatic events. I have used a variety of sources including personal interviews with family members, friends, and/or witnesses, news articles, official records, medal citations, and after-action reports. In some cases, the research varies significantly regarding the sequence of specific actions, the importance of particular episodes, the timelines when the events took place, and even the individuals involved. I have simply tried to weave the stories together in ways that seem to be the most logical and make the most sense.

PREFACE

Reader response for *Those Gentle Heroes* was phenomenal. One of the stories in the book is about an Army helicopter mechanic named Jimmy Warr. His brother, David, helped me write the story. Upon receiving his copy of the book, David wrote, "Banksy said: 'You die twice. One time when you stop breathing and a second time, a bit later on, when somebody says your name for the last time.' *Those Gentle Heroes* certainly ensures their names may never be spoken for the last time."

Mildred Skidgel, the sister of MOH recipient Sgt. Donnie Skidgel said, "I want to thank you. Your book answered so many questions I've had all these years. My daughter said your book touched her heart. She knew Donnie had been awarded the Medal of Honor, but she never knew any details because my parents could never stand to talk about his death. Now we're so proud to tell his story."

Sam Braaten wrote, "I thank you for doing the research and taking the time to write the book. I am looking forward to reading all the stories, especially the one of my cousin Sparky [Ellis] who was a special friend all my life. He was a kind and gentle person full of life and so fun to be around. We had some great times together. Born the same year, we were very close. I am proud of his service and the price he paid for our country. He was for sure an American hero."

Rev. Andy Lambert said, "Powerful stuff. There is real heartache in the stories of these unknown heroes, but their courage eclipses the sorrow. Thank you for telling their stories."

Former ASA pilot and Vietnam veteran, WO1 Harry D. Locklear said, "This is damn well written, even stirring. You bring these men back to life."

That was my intention for the first book, and also for *More Gentle Heroes*—to remember and symbolically embrace those gentle heroes we left behind—to keep their memories alive and never permit them to die that second final time. I have heard it said dying for your country is not the worst thing that can happen—being forgotten is. Our sacred duty in these uncertain times is to remember, and those memories are our legacy for our children and grandchildren. As George Santayana said in 1905, "Those who cannot remember the past are condemned to repeat it."

Former Cobra pilot, Jim Kurtz, who helped me write the heroic attack portions of the Kenny Luse story, said, "In the forward of your book, you describe how some of the peripheral characters, dialog, and scenes were created to preserve the integrity of the story line, and you observe that 'technically, that makes the stories works of historical fiction.' I guess technically it does, but I am glad you did it. I can dig around in the archives and find message traffic and after-action reports that were written deliberately in 'officialese,' with no emotion. Your stories tell the story of the *Gentle Heroes*. In doing so, you tell the story of those times so many of us lived through. I would not change a thing."

We must never forget these heroes. In this era of noneducation, miseducation, diseducation, rewritten history, cancellation, censorship, and "wokeness," we must find ways to educate future generations. That is another sacred obligation we must fulfill. We cannot rely on others to do it for us, or past history as we know it—our past, which may not be "socially correct"—will cease to exist.

—Gary B. Blackburn

THANK YOU

It has been said "behind every successful man is a great woman." It can also be said behind every successful military book is a team of veterans who are willing to give freely of their time, expertise, and experiential knowledge.

I wish to honor and thank former active-duty Marines Lee De La Garza, John Burkett, and Lief Ericson (known to some thirty thousand Vietnam-vet followers as "Que Son Valley Contractors"), former US Army Green Berets Hamp Dews and Ed Woody, former US Army Cobra pilot Jim Kurtz, and former US Army Security Agency operators Lonnie Long, David Hewitt, Richard Schlies, Harry Locklear, and Jon Swayze for their input, advice, and constant support during the writing of *More Gentle Heroes*.

Regarding the "great woman" portion of the original quote— as always, I must thank my resident proofreader, grammarian, and punctuation expert Myra Meadows Blackburn for her expertise and continual support.

Myra Meadows Blackburn

INTRODUCTION

Fifty-Eight Thousand Notifications

On a dark December night in 1961, a cab driver made his way toward the Clarence Davis residence in Livingston, Tennessee. The merry feeling of Christmas was in the air, but on this wintry evening, the family was celebrating another happy occasion. It was December 22, the birthday of Janie—the fourth of five children born to the Davis family. Adding to the festive mood was the anticipated return of their eldest son, Tom, who was serving with the Army Security Agency in Vietnam, a place none of them had ever heard of before. From what they could tell in his letters, Tom seemed to be serving his overseas tour in a tropical paradise. He was due home any day.

"Tom didn't even have a uniform when he got over there," younger brother Jack said. "They were required to wear civilian clothes." Jack remembered the taxi arriving and the driver bringing a telegram to the door. "It was the last day of school before Christmas vacation, and I was sitting at the dining room table. Dad went to the door and mumbled something and turned around. Then he called, 'Mother, something bad has happened.'"

It was a tragedy no one expected. The family was waiting for their son to come home. After all, America was not at war—not yet. There had been nothing in the news, but that would change soon enough. Tom Davis was the first American serviceman to die in ground combat in Vietnam.

Carried over from WWII in the early years of the Vietnam War, death notifications were delivered by cab drivers with Western Union telegrams; however, in the aftermath of the Battle of Ia Drang Valley in 1965, that practice changed. The efforts of Julia Compton Moore (wife of Lt. Col. Harold "Hal" G. Moore) prompted the Army to establish casualty notification teams in March of 1966.

The Ia Drang Valley battle was the first major ground engagement involving US forces in Vietnam, and those forces were under the command of Lt. Col. Moore. As the numbers of US casualties increased, Mrs. Moore concluded the Army had not established an adequate system of notifying the next of kin. She did not actually assume responsibility for the delivery of the telegrams, but she did follow the cab drivers and assisted in the death notifications. She often grieved with the widows and families of men killed in battle and attended the funerals of those who fell under her husband's command. Her efforts were noticed at the highest levels of the Department of Defense, and the example she set prompted the Army to set up notification teams.

There are thousands of stories—tens of thousands of memories of the officers, NCOs, and chaplains who were tasked with delivering the life-altering message: "The Secretary of the Army (or Navy or Air Force) has asked me to express his deep regret…"

"I never knew a man who refused to do it," one former commander said. "They all hated doing it, but each man knew it was his duty to do it, and he would want it to be done in the right way if he were the one who was killed."

The impact of those thousands of notifications across the country cannot be over emphasized. From neatly groomed cottages in New England to the crowded streets of New York and Chicago, the green hills of the Carolinas, to the beaches of Florida and the Gulf Coast, the sprawling farms of Iowa and Nebraska, the limitless horizon of Texas and the majestic Rocky Mountain states to the golden coast of California and the misty Northwest; no state was spared. Even the smallest towns and villages lost sons and occasionally daughters to the ravages of the war in Vietnam. Midland Park, a 1.5 square mile borough in Bergen County, New Jersey, lost eight of its sons in three years in the late 1960s, and the mayor fired off a letter to President Nixon begging him to spare the community any further loss.

A retired Army chaplain said, "There was a period of time when I was stationed at Ft. Benning. We were just overwhelmed, so I was tasked with making a notification alone. I drove out into rural Georgia to notify a young wife. She was living with her in-laws while her husband was in Vietnam. The wife answered the door—she was pregnant and had a toddler in her arms. I had to tell her that her husband had been killed.

"I was invited in, and ten minutes later, a dozen neighbors were on the porch. Soon, their pastor arrived, and I've never seen such an outpouring of love and support. After giving the family the required information and contact numbers, I got ready to leave. There was quite a crowd out on the porch, and ladies from their church were already bringing in food. As I left town, I stopped at a little store for gas and a soft drink. The storekeeper saw my Army uniform and figured out why I was there. He told me someone had ordered all the chicken he had on hand for the dinner that night, so I paid for the chicken. When I got back to Benning, I turned in the receipt to the first sergeant, and he just processed it for payment without comment. I guess I had worse days during my Army career, but I can't think of one right now. I will never forget that young widow standing in the doorway with her baby."

The *impact*—the impact of those fifty-eight thousand notifications was multiplied not only by other family members who were affected but also by family affiliations, their workplaces, church congregations, schools, and the local communities the spouses and families were part of. Like concentric circles spreading out from a stone thrown into a lake, the repercussions of each of those thousands of deaths were felt by thousands of other people. There was hardly a family in the US who was not impacted to some degree, in some way, by those fifty-eight thousand notifications during the twenty-year conflict that was the Vietnam War. And five or six decades later, much of the nation still grieves for those young heroes who died so many years ago.

—Lonnie M. Long

A TRIBUTE TO TWO
GENTLE HEROES

Bruce Allen Crosby Jr. and
Gary Patrick Westcott

Bruce Crosby Jr.   Gary Westcott

In early 1972, across the remote fringes of northern South Vietnam, a handful of Army Security Agency intercept operators began to hear signs of an enemy buildup. From secret underground bunkers in the most isolated and dangerous locations, in barricaded firebase rabbit holes where even generals were forbidden to tread, highly skilled, unlikely warriors were intercepting North Vietnamese communications that reflected increased infiltration by enemy troops; NVA artillery units were moving south through the DMZ; and there was increased activity by surface-to-air missile crews moving down from the north.

Regular US military units had also seen large numbers of refugees moving south. The Vietnamese rural population always knew when the shit was about to hit the fan. If it got quiet and there was no one around, you'd better get out'a Dodge, and you'd better do it fast. Something was about to happen, and you'd better not be in the way.

Further south, another secret US installation monitored vehicle traffic crossing the DMZ. By the end of the month, monitors were recording heavy traffic twenty-four hours a day. That had never happened before. However, the generals at MACV in Saigon did not find it reason for concern. They were too focused on the continuing US troop drawdown and the "Vietnamization" of their ongoing operations to be concerned with a little thing like the North Vietnamese Army.

As Easter neared, many generals and senior officials decided it was time to take a little vacation. The US Ambassador to South Vietnam, Ellsworth Bunker, left for Nepal; Gen. Creighton Abrams, commander of Military Assistance Command-Vietnam (MACV), was visiting family in Thailand; MACV J-2 Maj. Gen. William Potts was on R&R in Hawaii; and Col. Donald Metcalf, adviser to the South Vietnamese Army 3rd Division, left for the Philippines to visit his family. Even the Secretary of Defense, Melvin Laird, was preparing to play golf in Puerto Rico. Some ARVN generals stated they had sent out a country-wide alert, although no one seemed to have received it (neither South Vietnamese nor Americans). Essentially, the upper echelon was not asleep at the switch; they were not even in the country with the switch.

The 407th RRD (Det A-Eighth RRFS) was located north of Quang Tri City. It was the direct support unit for the 1st Brigade, 5th Mechanized Infantry Division and consisted of their headquarters and intercept sites at various exotic locales across the northern rim of South Vietnam: Fire Support Base Fuller on Dong Ha Mountain, Charlie-2 (north of Dong Ha), FSB Barbara (south of Quang Tri City), FSB Sarge and Con Thien (Alpha-4). Con Thien was located on the eastern edge of the DMZ and Sarge was located farther west on Dong Toan Mountain in the Cam Lo District.

Rocket attacks had been occurring regularly but were not of sufficient force to warrant concern until March 29. That afternoon, the firebases were hit at least hourly. The 407th commander, WO2 Larry Wilson, talked with his superiors about evacuating Sarge and Alpha-4, but no final decision had been made. Wilson and his team waited and watched.

There were only two ASA soldiers on duty at FSB Sarge on March 29: Sgt. Bruce Crosby Jr. and Spc.5 Gary Westcott. Crosby was a terminal receiving system repairman and charged with maintaining Explorer III, a highly classified remote communications-intercept system NSA had deployed to Sarge and Alpha-4 in November 1971. Crosby had been stationed at Sarge since November and helped build the bunker housing the system. Westcott was a Vietnamese linguist and Explorer technician who had helped set up the Explorer equipment when it arrived in Vietnam. The technology was so advanced, it required a lot of tweaking to keep it working. Technologically, Explorer was fifteen years ahead of anything the Russians or the Chinese had on the drawing board. Westcott made frequent trips to the two outposts to check the equipment and happened to be onsite at that time. He had just returned from leave, having been married three weeks before. The only other American at Sarge was Maj. Walter Boomer, a US Marine adviser to the 4th Vietnamese Marine Corps Battalion, which was assigned to protect the firebase.

Crosby (L) and Westcott (R)
Camp Carroll, January 1972

Before noon on March 30, 1972, an intense artillery barrage began at Sarge, and it did not let up. The shelling continued to build in intensity, convincing Boomer the predicted offensive had begun. What he and other US commanders did not know was that the small remote outposts along the DMZ were under attack by two NVA Divisions, the 304th and the 308th, with some thirty thousand regular North Vietnamese infantry, five artillery regiments, and two tank regiments fielding over four hundred tanks and APCs.

Hunkered down in his dust-filled command bunker, Boomer contacted headquarters and advised Sarge was being shelled. "The NVA's fire is as accurate and heavy as we've ever experienced up here," Boomer said. "We're all okay now, but there's probably a big battle coming our way. Looks like this could be their big push." With artillery rounds slamming into his underground post—red dirt and dust filtering down through the cracks between the logs—Boomer contacted Crosby and Westcott and told them to "remain in the Explorer bunker where they'd be better protected." He also told them to keep in radio contact with him and Alpha-4.

The Explorer system was housed in a ten ft. x sixteen ft. steel and precast-concrete shelter with several other pieces of top-secret

NSA/ASA crypto equipment. The shelter was partially buried in the mountain top and surrounded by a reinforced bunker made of sandbags, several rows deep. A steel roof covered the container with another five feet of sandbags on top of that. For ventilation, there was one small opening set high in the side of the bunker wall.

Below Sarge, the NVA was firing Soviet 130mm guns (M-46) the size of telephone poles, along with 122mm rockets. With sweat stinging his eyes and soaking his dust-covered uniform, Boomer again contacted headquarters demanding to know why there was no response from allied forces to stem the incoming enemy barrage. He received no satisfactory answer. Shells and rockets continued to bombard his bunkers and the fortifications at Firebase Sarge.

Maj. Walter Boomer, USMC
His job was to protect Fire Support Base Sarge.

Thirty minutes after the attack began Boomer and the radioman at A-4 lost contact with Crosby and Westcott. The major continued his attempts to contact the two men over the roar of the artillery, but there was no response. He heard only dead silence on the other end. Disregarding his own safety, Boomer left his command bunker and made his way toward Explorer. The noise from the massive barrage was deafening; the air was thick with smoke, clouds of red dust, and the bitter tang of cordite. He felt no particular danger from machine gun or small arms fire, although he could hear it. NVA troops were still well down the mountain, and his Vietnamese Marines, the "Killer

Sharks," had a well-earned reputation for combat prowess. However, it would only take one artillery round or rocket to end his sortie.

Looking west from old ASA bunker (L) and "narrow walkways" on Sarge (R)

Making his way quickly along the narrow walkways lined with vicious concertina wire, the Marine approached the old ASA intercept bunker. It was now used as living quarters for Westcott, Crosby, and ASA techs that flew in to work on whatever was in the new bunker. He had never been permitted to go past the sign that read, RESTRICTED AREA—KEEP OUT! He could not speculate about the bunker's contents, but it was obviously important and highly classified—his job was to protect it. Crouching low, Boomer rounded the corner past the old bunker and could only stare at the total destruction before him.

Shortly after noon, a 122mm rocket had scored a direct hit on the vent in the Explorer bunker. The rocket exploded inside, collapsing the steel roof laden with tons of sandbags and igniting the thermite destruction panels attached to each piece of secret equipment. The result was a fire of solar intensity (five thousand degrees F) that burned for two days.

Boomer ran toward the conflagration, searching for any sign of life, any way he might get inside. He had spent a year in combat in Vietnam, earning a Silver Star, so he had seen his share of fire and flame, but this was unlike anything he had encountered. Artillery continued to rain down on the mountain as the Marine tried repeatedly to reach the two soldiers trapped inside. Each time, he was repulsed by the extreme heat. Walt Boomer later received his second Silver Star "for conspicuous gallantry and intrepidity in action" from March 30 to April 3, 1972.

FSB Sarge was abandoned on April 1. The devastated Explorer bunker still smoldered. Crosby and Westcott were initially listed as MIA, but on June 27, 1972, their status was changed to KIA/BNR. The 407th had manned its dangerous outposts along the DMZ for four years; Westcott and Crosby were the unit's first and only combat fatalities. Over ten years, after Spc.4 James Davis became the first ASA soldier to die in combat, Westcott and Crosby were the last.

Gary Patrick Westcott was from Pomona, California; Bruce Allen Crosby Jr. was from Springville, New York. JPAC made three trips to Dong Toan Mountain to search for them. The last time was 2013, but no remains were ever found of either soldier. The two had become one with the mountain. Both men were twenty years old.

At dawn the ridge emerges massed and dun
In the wild purple of the glowering sun,
Smoldering through spouts of drifting smoke that shroud
The menacing scarred slope; and, one by one,
Tanks creep and topple forward to the wire.
The barrage roars and lifts. Then, clumsily bowed
With bombs and guns and shovels and battle-gear,
Men jostle and climb to meet the bristling fire.

"Attack"
Siegfried Loraine Sassoon

CHAPTER 1

BENEDICT MAHER DAVAN

Cicada Song

Ben Davan

For young Ben Davan, nothing was ever halfway. It was always "all or nothing." When your father is a sports legend in the state where you live, you are always going to be compared to him—that is a fact of life. First and foremost, he was "Paddy Davan's son," and he had to learn to deal with it.

John Patrick "Paddy" Davan was born in England, the only son of Irish immigrants who would eventually make their way to the US in the 1920s. They settled in New England, and Paddy was introduced to American sports during his high school years in Waltham, Massachusetts. With typical Irish wit and versatility, young Davan quickly became a high school star and moved on to Coburn Classical Institute, a college preparatory school in Waterville, Maine. There he bolstered his fortunes as a two-sport athlete. He then moved on to Colby College where his skills became legendary. He was captain of both the football and baseball teams in the early 1930s and gained national recognition for his athletic talent and leadership skills.

After graduation in 1933, Paddy Davan began teaching and coaching at Livermore Falls High School. In 1940, his teams won the state baseball championship, along with the Western Maine Class-B Basketball title. He also taught five subjects. He had married Rachel Maher, and their first child, John Patrick Davan Jr. was also born in 1940.

After ten years in Livermore Falls, Davan and his family moved to Westbrook, Maine, where he would gain his greatest fame and remain the rest of his life. Westbrook was a much larger city. There had been championship basketball teams there in the 1920s, and Paddy Davan was hired (with a big raise in salary) for the sole purpose of bringing back the glory years to Westbrook High School. It would take several years, but no one doubted Paddy Davan could do it. His second son, Benedict Maher Davan (named for his maternal grandfather), was born in Westbrook, on February 10, 1946.

Over the years, it was said Paddy Davan nurtured the burgeoning careers of hundreds of young athletes looking to advance to college and perhaps professional careers, but of greater importance—he encouraged thousands of those with lesser talent, steered them in the right direction, and they adored him for that. It would seem the much beloved history teacher and coach may have been father to every child but his own. Neither Jack (John Jr.) nor Ben could possibly compete athletically with the mythological image that was their father. Each son made an effort, but with only a modicum of success and (though unspoken) much to the disappointment of their father.

Ben Davan graduated from Westbrook High School in June 1964 and was unsure what he wanted to do in the future. Paddy wanted Ben to go to Colby, his alma mater, and he certainly had enough influence to get Ben enrolled. The school would have loved to admit the son of their legendary alumnus, but Ben had lived in his father's shadow his entire life. He was eighteen years old and had no intention of continuing that practice. Colby would have to get along without "Paddy Davan's son." It would have been a nightmare for him, and he knew it.

Like most young Irish Catholics in the 1960s, Ben Davan idolized Jack Kennedy. He was seventeen when Kennedy was assassinated, and the trauma of that event haunted him. One of Kennedy's special interests had been Army Special Forces. Kennedy had been a strong supporter and the primary force behind their official adoption of the green beret headgear. The more Ben thought about it, the more the idea of becoming a Green Beret appealed to him. He talked to an Army recruiter about his options and discussed it with his mother, Rachel. The war in Vietnam was heating up. He had registered for the draft on his eighteenth birthday in February, and if he was not going to college, he might be better off to enlist. He considered his choices throughout the winter months, and then signed up. He was nineteen by then and on his way to boot camp at Fort Pickett, Virginia.

All Special Forces candidates began their careers with nine weeks basic combat training. After basic Davan attended advanced individual training and then went on to infantry school to learn how to use small arms, anti-armor, and weapons such as howitzers and heavy mortars. Before he could advance to special operations training, he also had to complete the basic airborne course at Fort Benning, Georgia, and he loved it. He never thought he would jump out of a perfectly good airplane at 1,250 feet, but the adrenaline rush was awesome. He could not wait to do it again.

After airborne graduation, Special Forces training began in earnest. It was administered by the training group and was broken into three phases. Davan packed his duffel bag and moved to Camp Mackall, North Carolina, near Southern Pines. Phase One was a six-week course, which included patrolling, land navigation, other small unit operations, and advanced-level physical training. A plus-side of being Paddy

Davan's son was being in great physical shape. His father had insisted on it. The training was intense and resembled a mini Ranger School. Upon completion, students were issued their green berets.

Phase Two was MOS (career field) training in the skills needed on an A-Team, the primary operational element of a Special Forces company. (An A-Team consisted of twelve SF soldiers: two officers and ten sergeants.) The career fields were operations and intelligence, communications, engineers, and medical. The various MOS-producing schools varied in length based on the MOS the soldier was selected for. The process of completing those schools could take several months to a year and covered the various specialties needed to support a Special Forces A-Team in the field. Davan's MOS was 11F4C: Special Forces Operations and Intelligence Specialist, and the O and I course was taught at Fort Bragg in Fayetteville, North Carolina.

Phase Three, called "Branch," was a six-week advanced unconventional warfare course. It was also taught at Fort Bragg and included direct action missions such as raids, ambushes, and reconnaissance. The culmination exercise was a two-week field training exercise (FTX) called Cherokee Trail. This was for enlisted personnel. Officers were put through a separate exercise titled Gobbler's Wood. Students had to form their own twelve-man operations detachments and put the training and experience they had gained during the past months to the test. This was a realistic training setting dealing with indigenous personnel, counterinsurgency, and was tested in the mission of training a mock guerrilla force in a hostile environment in the Uwharrie National Forest in south-central North Carolina.

Ben loved the dense woods and clear lakes in the Uwharrie Mountains. It was some of the most beautiful country he had ever seen. He would lie awake at night in their encampment and listen to the night sounds—crickets would chirp, peepers peep, and bullfrogs croak. During the hot afternoons, cicadas in the hardwood trees would sing so loudly; it was unlike anything he had ever heard, and he didn't want it to end. Rachel Maher Davan, Ben's mother, had graduated from the prestigious Lesley School in Cambridge, Massachusetts, in 1934, and adored Henry David Thoreau. One of her favorite poems was Thoreau's "Anacreon's Ode to the Cicada." She had read it to Ben frequently when he was a child, and he still remembered much of the poem: "We pronounce thee happy, cicada, for on the tops of the trees, sipping a little dew, like any king thou singest…" Ben missed his mother.

Completing Branch successfully, Davan became a confirmed member of the Special Forces family. His rank was E-4. He and his fellow new Green Berets were then deployed to their duty stations. In 1966 and 1967, that usually meant South Vietnam or at least Southeast Asia. Ben Davan went home to Maine on thirty days leave and then shipped out for Vietnam. Flying from Boston to Seattle/Tacoma via Chicago, he arrived midafternoon and caught a military transport to McChord AFB, some thirty-five miles south of the airport. A few hours later, he boarded a Pan Am Airways government charter headed for Anchorage, Alaska.

There were two hundred young men on board the Boeing 707. The aircraft had been converted to all-coach, with no smoking or alcohol on board, but few of the soldiers stayed in their seats after the plane took off. Most were Army infantry. Many of whom knew each other from various training camps they had recently graduated from. Their general attitude appeared to be they were off on some great adventure. At the ripe old age of twenty-one, Davan was two or three years older than most of the other passengers. He'd had over a year more additional intense training and had a markedly different view of the "adventure" they were heading for.

About an hour into the four-hour flight, sack lunches and soft drinks were served by the half-dozen Pan Am flight attendants on board. The ladies, dressed in their sky-blue uniforms, probably had children the age of these conscripts. With bright smiles, they bravely endured the whistles, catcalls, and various marriage proposals from the "boys" as they efficiently made their way down the aisle. Then they quickly retreated back to the relative security of the galley area.

Arriving in Anchorage later that night, Davan was surprised there was still snow on the ground, and the passengers were allowed to deplane. Walking out into the frosty air, the men stretched their legs, smoked their cigarettes, visited the terminal for a snack or magazine—and then made their way back to the plane. They departed for Yakota AB, Japan, about 10:00 p.m., Alaska-time. Bone-tired after a very long day, Ben settled in, pulled his beret down over his eyes, and tried to sleep. They were flying the polar route. They would cross the International Date Line, and due to the time difference, arrive in Yakota at 10:00 p.m. the following night, Japan-time.

Upon arrival in Japan, everyone boarded waiting Air Force blue buses and was taken to a dining hall for a hot meal. The night was dark and muggy, and a thick drizzle was falling. The summer monsoon would begin in earnest in two or three weeks, and this was a "warm-up" for the rainy weeks to follow. The aircraft would receive a maintenance check, be refueled, and a new crew would board the aircraft for the remaining five-hour flight from Yakota to Cam Ranh Bay.

After a hearty Air Force breakfast of real scrambled eggs, hash-brown potatoes, pancakes, bacon, sausage, and several mugs of black coffee, Davan thought he might survive the remainder of the long trip. Leaving the dining hall, Ben walked alone under a covered walkway. The rain had ceased, and he strolled slowly, smoking a cigarette and enjoying the peace and quiet of the warm, misty night.

The walkway was dimly lit and bordered by miniature Japanese rock gardens and beautiful, red Suminagashi maples. Suddenly he heard a familiar sound as cicadas in the trees began their paean. This was a rare treat, usually only heard during the day. The sing-song grew louder, then softened, then grew louder again. It reminded him of those hot afternoons in the Uwharrie Mountains, and a slight smile crossed his face. "Like any king thou singest," he whispered to himself. He had a hunch there'd not be many quiet nights or days during the coming year. He had worked so hard through the long months in Carolina. It was difficult to believe he was within a few hours of arriving in Vietnam.

The passengers reboarded; seatbelts were fastened, and the plane taxied out to take off at 1:00 a.m. They would arrive at Cam Ranh AB at 8:00 a.m., Vietnam-time, Thursday, May 18, 1967.

PART 2

Emerging from the Pan Am plane, Davan blinked his eyes in the bright sunshine and surveyed the huge base. He saw rows of

F-4C Phantom II fighter-bombers, C-130 cargo transports, CV-2 Caribous, and many other types of aircraft parked wherever he looked. The heavy air was thick with aircraft exhaust, the smell of jet fuel, and a strong dose of malathion.

A young lieutenant standing at the bottom of the steps directed the soldiers to waiting buses for the short trip to the replacement depot where Davan handed over copies of his orders. The men were issued anti-malarial tablets, given instructions on what to do in case of an attack, and then the infantrymen were provided with bed linens and shown to a nearby barracks to wait for their unit assignments. Davan walked outside of the building to await transport to Nha Trang.

Stretching to get the kinks out of his joints from the long plane trip, Davan saw a jeep careening toward him across the parking area. It was driven by a young man wearing "tigerstripe" fatigues and a bright green beret.

Sliding to a halt, the young sergeant called out, "Hey! Are you Davan?"

Since he was the only Green Beret in the area, he was pretty easy to spot.

"Yes, I am," he said. "Ben Davan, here."

"My name's Waugh," the sergeant said with a smile. "Call me Jimmy!"

Ben retrieved his duffel bag, hoisted it into the back of the jeep, and the two were off, heading up the coast on Highway 1 to Nha Trang. It was about twenty miles but could take an hour, depending on the traffic, which consisted of heavy pedestrian traffic, wagons filled with produce and cages full of ducks and geese, ox carts loaded with huge bags of rice, an occasional Army jeep, military truck, or bus, and all moving at a snail's pace. Jimmy went as fast as was humanly possible, which was much faster than Ben was comfortable with. Laying on the horn, careening in, out, and around whatever was in his way, the pedestrians fled for their lives.

Ben held onto whatever he could grab hold of as the jeep veered north, and Jimmy never stopped talking (and swearing). "At least we've got sunshine this morning," Waugh said. "We've had nothin' but f***in' rain for days, man. We go from one goddamned monsoon to the next goddamned monsoon. Give me Iowa any day, man. It rains, it floods, and then it dries out for a while, man. I am so goddamned sick of the f***in' mud and rain. I hope we get to Nha Trang before the next round of rain 'n' shit moves in, man, or we're gonna get soaked!" Ben just smiled and held on to his seat as they narrowly missed a water buffalo with a small child on its back. "Get outa the damned way!" Waugh screamed at the top of his lungs as he hit the horn.

Arriving late in the morning, they drove through a gate with a huge sign over it that read, HEADQUARTERS, 5TH SPECIAL FORCES GROUP (AIRBORNE), 1ST SPECIAL FORCES, and Waugh delivered Davan to the Group Adjutant's office to report and turn in his records. From there, he was sent to report in at the headquarters building for A-503, the Mobile Strike Force company. It held the tactical operations center, the team dayroom and bar, and the team mess hall. Davan signed in and Jimmy showed him to the team house where he would sleep, so he could stow his baggage. Then the two soldiers made their way back to the mess hall for lunch. Ben had been traveling for over forty hours and was definitely in need of another hot meal.

After lunch, Waugh showed Davan around the compound. There were three U-shaped two-story troop barracks, another mess hall for the troops, a dispensary, and a communications shop. Last was the supply room where Davan was issued his camouflage uniforms, jungle boots, poncho with liner, additional paraphernalia he would need in the field, and his weapons. After carrying the equipment to the team house, Davan reported back to the headquarters building to meet with Capt. Lee Wilson, the detachment commander.

Davan was informed the commander was out in the field, but someone else wanted to meet with him. The B-55 compound was bordered on the north by group headquarters. Davan was ushered back across the compound to HQ for Fifth Special Forces in Vietnam and found himself outside the door of Col. Francis J. "Blackjack" Kelly, Commander of Fifth Special Forces.

Col. Kelly had taken over command in June 1966 and had become a legend in his own time. A WWII combat veteran, the colonel was one of those "old school" officers who believed in not ordering his men to do anything he was not willing to do himself. He frequently went on Special Forces missions behind enemy lines but loathed excesses of bravado that made it seem the Green Berets were not part of the regular Army.

Addressing a group of new Special Forces officers in Nha Trang in January 1967, Kelly had said, "This is no game for clowns. I haven't got time for boozers, cheaters or buglers." Kelly said a "bugler" was a Special Forces soldier who walked into a bar filled with GIs and sounded off about how the Green Berets were braver and smarter than anyone else in the Army. "That's a declaration guaranteed to start a brawl," the colonel asserted.

To avoid such spectacles, Kelly had declared Saigon off-limits for Special Forces. His men could wear their green berets but were to stop wearing unauthorized items like tiger-skin capes and elephant-hide boots. And he told them, "Shave off those goddamned handlebar mustaches."

Kelly was the man who had developed the Mobile Guerrilla Force, in which bands of some two hundred men—a team of two officers and nine enlisted Green Berets, as well as ARVN (South Vietnamese Army) and CIDG (Civilian Irregular Defense Group) soldiers set out on long-range patrols. They were expected to remain in the field several weeks at a time, springing ambushes, gathering intelligence on enemy movements, and generally creating chaos behind enemy lines. He had also given Special Forces an increased presence in the Mekong Delta.

And this was the man Benedict Davan was about to meet. Knocking on the door, he was told to enter and walked into a small outer office manned by a second lieutenant. The young officer was expecting him and immediately ushered him into the next much-larger office.

Saluting and reporting in to the commander, Davan was immediately put at ease and told to take a seat. Col. Kelly was an imposing figure seated behind a huge mahogany desk. Burly, but obviously in good physical shape, the colonel's hair was graying at the temples and his steel-blue eyes seemed to see right through you. He was almost as intimidating as Paddy Davan.

Col. Kelly began to ask questions, interspersed with information about the Special Forces mission. He talked specifically about what the unit at Nha Trang was doing with the Mobile Strike Forces and what Davan's role would be in that effort. The colonel explained he was looking for professionals, the sort of soldiers who could put into practice the Green Beret tactical doctrine for warfare in Vietnam. He had created most of that doctrine himself at the Army War College and the Special Warfare Directorate in the Pentagon. That was why he wanted to meet and interview a man who had just completed Special Forces training. He seemed pleased with the soldier he saw before him.

In the following weeks, Davan worked to become familiar with his Mobile Strike force company, and he was promoted to sergeant. Shortened to "Mike Force," the unit's mission was to act as a country-wide quick reaction force for securing and reinforcing CIDG A-camps, as well as to conduct reconnaissance patrols, search and rescue, and search and destroy missions.

Each of the MSF companies was commanded by a Special Forces NCO, with additional Green Berets to assist him. One was usually a medic, who served as both the company doctor and a platoon leader for one of the forty-to-fifty-man platoons. Each company had 180 to 200 soldiers, and they were volunteers from various indigenous minority groups who were recruited and paid by Special Forces. Each ethnic group was placed in a company of its own. The Nùng are ethnically Chinese, and the Degar people, native to the Vietnamese mountains, were usually referred to as Montagnards. (The Green Berets affectionately called them Yards.) The Rhade are also a Degar people but are a separate tribe.

During the ensuing year, Sgt. Davan spent most of his time in the field. The job was tough, but he learned to work with the men in his company. His initial training had been a starting point, but the real training began in Vietnam. His company was sent to one hot spot after another, supporting beleaguered Alpha-camps and Special Forces units that were in heavy contact with the enemy. Special Forces had gradually begun to hand over control of CIDG camps to their Vietnamese counterparts, the Lực Lượng Đặc Biệt (LLDB).

Both Camp and Mobile Strike Forces were also increasingly used in conjunction with regular US, ARVN, and Allied forces.

Davan with 6th Company senior medic Bill "Squirrel" Scruggs

During one such outing, a cordon and search operation was conducted against a village that was suspected of providing assistance to the enemy. As part of their psy-war operation, a planned deception contributed to their success. Davan and his fellow NCOs employed normal techniques to isolate the village during the hours of darkness; however, at first light a CIDG squad dressed as VC was sent into the village. The men were immediately greeted and presented with food by some of the inhabitants. Those villagers were later arrested as suspected VC sympathizers. Word of the operation would spread quickly to other villages. That would make their inhabitants suspicious and hesitant to make contact with other such parties, thus working to the disadvantage of the VC in the area.

Aside from the obvious danger, Davan enjoyed being on patrol in the countryside. Vietnam was beautiful, and in spite of the human conflict, wildlife was abundant. One evening in August, while preparing to spend the night in the mountains west of Nha Trang, Davan noticed a band of exotic-looking trees growing along the banks of a nearby stream. The trees had huge green leaves and were covered with clusters of trumpet-like lavender flowers. As dusk approached, the trees released a scent that was almost overpowering. It was a combination of vanilla and almond and was so strong; it tended to make the young soldier light-headed. Summoning Nguyen, one of the LLBD sergeants accompanying his platoon (who spoke excellent English), Davan inquired about the trees. The sergeant told him the trees were called dragon trees and were frequently planted in gardens for their flowers and scent. "It is also considered good luck to have one of the trees near your home," he continued, "because it is said to be favored by the mythical Phoenix who is drawn to its branches." As the two men stood by the stream talking, there was suddenly a strange buzzing sound that seemed to move from tree to tree, growing continually louder, until there was a cacophony of sound that drowned out the noise of the rushing mountain stream. Davan gave Nguyen a quizzical look. Leaning close to Davan's ear, he said, "Con ve sầu, con ve sầu, I do not know English word." Excusing himself, the Vietnamese sergeant left, returning in a few minutes as the noise continued. Cupping his mouth with his hands, Nguyen shouted, "*Con ve sau—Cicada! Cicada!*" and Ben Davan smiled.

PART 3

In November 1967, new leadership took over at Detachment A-503. The new commander was Capt. Larry O'Neil, and he brought with him, 1st Lt. (soon-to-be Captain) Joe Zamiara, as assistant commander, and 1st Lt. L.H. "Bucky" Burruss, the new operations officer. The new Mike Force Company was completing its training, and Burruss worked closely with Ben Davan to make sure the unit was prepared to take the field. The company had been recruited from among the Cham people who were concentrated around the coastal cities of Phan Rang and Phan Thiết. The Chams are descended from the Kingdom of Champa which once ruled all of Vietnam and much of Cambodia for over fifteen hundred years.

Religiously and culturally, the Cham people belong to two groups; Balamon Chams who subscribe to a form of Hinduism, and Bani Chams who adhere to a form of Islam. The new company was made up of Balamon Cham men. It was difficult to determine their age. Some were thought to be as young as fourteen, but they remained youthful looking well into their forties, so it was anyone's guess. It was irrelevant as long as they were in good health and ready to fight. Few spoke English, but some spoke a bit of French. The men were mild-mannered, honest, loyal, and not aggressive; however, they were staunchly anticommunist. That, combined with their salary (which was well above the local wage) created a waiting list of those wanting to join the Mike Force.

By Christmas, Davan had been promoted again. He was now a staff sergeant and in command of Fourth Company, the new Cham company. There was to be a holiday truce over Christmas and New Year's and then again over the Vietnamese lunar New Year (Tet) at the end of January. Most of the MSF companies were in Nha Trang and things were pretty laid-back. Some of the Vietnamese staff had put up Christmas decorations and decorated a tree in the Team bar. There were parties taking place somewhere almost every night. One of the team secretaries had an old Elvis Presley Christmas album with "Blue Christmas" on it, and she played it all day long. These were melancholy days for Ben. He was surrounded by friends and colleagues, but he suddenly felt lonely. He had picked out Christmas cards at the PX and mailed them to family and a few friends in Westbrook, but he missed home. He missed the snow and cold, salty air coming in off Casco Bay. Ben hated moping around. The Streamer Bar in downtown Nha Trang was the primary Special Forces watering hole, with its loud country music and bar girls. Ben normally did not drink, but he ended up there about every night, drinking shots of Crown Royal. He had never experienced these feelings before. For the first time in his life, Ben Davan was homesick.

S. Sgt. Benedict Davan with his Fourth Company Chams

The month of January 1968 was routine with the usual patrols, but there had been very limited contact with the enemy. Arriving back at the A-503 compound early on January 10, Davan showered, put on clean sweats, and walked to the dayroom for a Coke. Pop, the old Nùng-Chinese bartender, was manning the ornate stone bar and grinned, flashing a mouthful of gold teeth as he handed Ben a bottle of Coca-Cola and a glass filled with chipped ice. Reclining on one of the vinyl-upholstered couches, Davan took a deep breath and exhaled slowly. He was enjoying listening to Neil Diamond singing "Cherry, Cherry" on the old Sony turntable behind the bar, combined with the clatter of the old window air-conditioner.

A few moments later, Lt. Burruss walked in and sat down in a chair across from him. "Can I buy you a beer, Lieutenant?" Davan asked.

"Nah, thanks, Ben," Burruss said. Then reconsidering, he said, "Oh what the hell, it's my birthday." And he laughed.

"Well, in that case, let's do it up right," Davan said. "Pop, bring the lieutenant a large shot of Crown Royal."

Other team members drifted in, and at Ben's suggestion, kept buying Crown Royal shots for Burruss until the party was completely out of control. At that point, Davan grabbed another bottle of Coke and quietly left the day room ruckus. "My work here is done," he said, chuckling to himself. Then he strolled back to his quarters, crawled into bed, and was soon fast asleep.

Detachment A-503—Early 1968

On January 29, Davan, along with Jim Waugh and Ed Woody, "borrowed" a jeep and drove into Nha Trang. They planned to have dinner and celebrate Tet with the local citizenry. One of their favorite restaurants was La Frégate, a French restaurant (and hotel) that served the best food in all of II Corps. The chef de cuisine was Cambodian and had trained at the original La Frégate in Paris in the 1950s. Monsieur Tules Forse, owner of La Frégate-Nha Trang, had discovered the chef in Phnom Penh and persuaded him, at no small expense, to move to Nha Trang.

Before the Americans were seated, the maître d' had each diner pick out a grouper from the large tank in the front window of the restaurant. Then, as Ben and his friends were being shown to their table, they saw Lt. Burruss, Capt. O'Neil, Capt. Zamiara, and several other A-503 officers enjoying a lobster dinner across the restaurant and waved to them. The restaurant could only seat eighty diners, so Mike Force was well represented to welcome in the Lunar New Year.

Dinner for Davan's party began with fresh prawn steamed in coconut water and served with glass noodles. That was followed by a salad course of romaine lettuce, topped with brie, Dijon mustard, and red wine vinegar. The grouper, which was grilled French-style with ginger and coconut curry, was served with snow peas, followed by a selection of French cheeses and the dessert course, a classic chocolate mousse. Each course (of course) was accompanied with the appropriate French wine. Needless to say, the meal took hours, and no one was moving too quickly or too steadily as the magic hour approached.

The merrymaking outside the restaurant was nearing a fever pitch. The street was crowded with people blowing horns, beating cymbals and gongs, and shooting fireworks, which was typical of the Tet holiday. Davan and his friends paid their bill and strolled outside the restaurant to watch the festivities. The air was warm and sultry and smelled of sulfur and black powder from the firecrackers. Conventional fireworks displays high in the air were mixed with parachute flares and orange tracers as some of the ARVN troops joined in the celebration. That continued for some time but gradually began to die down. Then suddenly, the weapons fire began to increase again. And it was not being fired into the air, but in all directions, and it was accompanied by the sound of dull explosions. The orange tracers were soon mixed with green tracers and the explosions grew louder and nearer. The massive crowd began to scream and flee in every direction, and all hell broke loose. "Holy shit," Davan said. "We are under attack."

Running back through the restaurant and out a rear door, Davan and his friends jumped into their vehicle, escaped down a back alley, and fought their way through the crowded streets to the Mike Force compound. They were soon ordered out again with their MSF companies fighting to save the city and root out the communist attackers who had surreptitiously moved into various government facilities under the cover of darkness and holiday revelry. The MSF commanders assumed this was a local attack but soon discovered it was part of the communists' massive Tet Offensive of 1968. The attack in Nha Trang by the 18B NVA Regiment was primarily directed against the MACV Sector Headquarters, which was directly across the street from La Frégate Restaurant, and other government facilities in the city. The fight by Mike Force to regain control of Nha Trang lasted two full days. It was vicious—it was bloody, and A-503 paid a heavy price. Not only were many of the MSF strikers killed, fighting beside their SF commanders, but there were a number of Green Beret casualties, including the detachment commander, Larry O'Neil, who was medevaced to Japan, and the assistant commander, Capt. Zamiara, who was KIA. Joe Zamiara was twenty-four years old.

In February 1968, Ben turned twenty-two. The disastrous Battle of Lang Vei had taken place the previous week. Lang Vei Special Forces A-camp, which was a few miles from the Marine combat base at Khe Sanh, had been overrun by NVA infantry, led by tanks, which was a rare occurrence. With ten Americans dead or missing, eleven of the remaining fourteen wounded, and some two hundred of the five hundred CIDG troops dead or missing, two MSF companies left Nha Trang to assist the camp. After the survivors were rescued and transported to Khe Sanh, the decision was made to abandon the camp and the Mike Force companies returned to Nha Trang.

The detachment welcomed new commander Maj. Richard A. Clark, in March. Clark announced the detachment would expand to two A-Teams and two battalions of MSF strikers. Each battalion would have three rifle companies and a combat reconnaissance platoon. The commander of 1st Battalion would be 1st Lt. Bucky Burruss. Second in command would be 2nd Lt. Jack Cheatham. The NCOs would be Sgt. 1st Class Rick Reilly, S. Sgt. Ron Franklin, S. Sgt. Bob Skinner, S. Sgt. Sam Coutts, S. Sgt. Ben Davan, and Sgt. Todd Seaver. Sgt. Doug Baribeau was the medic.

1ˢᵗ Battalion Command—March 1968
(Top) Doug Baribeau, Sam Coutts, Todd Seaver, Bob Skinner
(Kneeling) Ron "Popeye" Franklin, Bucky Burruss,
Jack Cheatham, Richard Reilly, Ben Davan

The battalion was authorized one additional company, so Burruss sent Sgt. Franklin to the highlands to recruit Montagnards to fill it. Two days later, much to everyone's surprise, Franklin was back with his company. He had recruited a company of FULRO troops. FULRO was the Montagnard underground liberation movement and totally illegal in South Vietnam. The Montagnards had been well-trained in Cambodia, spoke passable French, and were willing and able to kill VC and NVA (and maybe a few ARVN troops while they were at it).

In May 1968, Davan had to decide if he was going to return to the States or extend his time in Vietnam. For most regular Army troops, Vietnam was a place to suffer through for a year, and then escape back to the "World." That was all they dreamed about, all they talked about, and they counted the days until time to leave. But it was different for Green Berets. For most of them, Vietnam was a second home. Ben talked to Lt. Burruss and made his choice. He agreed to extend six months if he could remain with his company of

Chams. Burruss agreed and Davan flew off to Bangkok for a few days R&R. In November, Davan extended again.

Davan on R&R—Bangkok 1968

PART 4

By the time his second extension was complete in May of '69, Ben Davan would have been in Vietnam for two straight years. He was planning to go home on leave and spend time with his family. Jack had married Diane LeFebvre in July 1965 while Ben was roughing it in North Carolina. He owed them a wedding gift. Maybe he, Jack, and Paddy could go fishing. It had been a long time since they had done anything together. And he definitely wanted to spend time with his mother. Then he planned to reenlist and return to his company at Nha Trang.

Deep in southwestern Vietnam stands a chain of mountains called the Seven Sisters or Bảy Núi (seven mountains). The southern-most of those mountains is a rugged peak called Núi Cô Tô. In February 1969, representatives from Fifth Special Forces and the Forty-Fourth Special Tactical Zone met and reached the decision that the Việt Cộng strongholds atop Núi Cô Tô and Tuk Chup, a lesser peak to the southwest, must be attacked and destroyed. As usual, there were conflicting opinions about how the mission could and should be accomplished. Most of the senior NCOs recommended a more conservative approach which entailed surrounding the peaks and starving the enemy out, thus saving the lives of many of their

Mike Force troops. They were, however, overruled by less seasoned officers who envisioned a glorious "charge up San Juan Hill"—a full frontal attack by hundreds of troops directly into the teeth of the enemy defenses.

In preparation for such an attack, inprocessing NCOs were asked by Fifth SF Group HQ to form a heavy weapons platoon. The platoon would field 106mm recoilless rifles and .50 Cal. M-2 machineguns, both mounted on M151 light utility Jeeps. The platoon also included two-man flamethrower teams. The recoilless rifles, utilizing "bee-hive" flechettes, would prove to be devastating weapons during the upcoming attack.

The Núi Cô Tô fortress was reputed to be the headquarters of Chau Kim, a notorious, almost mythic Cambodian communist. Chau and his troops had terrorized local farmers for years, demanding food and supplies for their camps.

In early March, Phase I of the operation called for CIDG troops from local Special Forces A-camps, South Vietnamese Regional Force units (Ruff-Puffs), and national police to cordon off and search local villages. That would cut off much of the enemy food supply, liberate the local populace, and help identify local VC who might still reside in the area. Phase II called for 1st and 2nd Battalions of the Fifth MSF (Nha Trang) to move in and seal off Tuk Chup ("chup" means knoll). The "knoll," covered with huge rocks and boulders the size of two-story houses, was riddled with caves used as storage facilities by the VC. The caves would be a source of resupply and reinforcements if not isolated from the main peak. In Phase III, Tuk Chup would be cleared of enemy forces before friendly elements moved in to clear and secure Núi Cô Tô itself. It was a simple plan, but there was nothing simple about Tuk Chup. Phases I and II were completed by March 14, 1969, and the Mike Force units were flown by choppers into positions west of Núi Cô Tô the following day.

Sgt. *1ˢᵗ Class Albert "Buddy" Belisle*
Núi Cô Tô—March 15, 1969

At 4:30 a.m. on March 16, an artillery barrage commenced. That was followed an hour later by the ground assault of Tuk Chup. Hidden within the eight-hundred-foot-tall pile of boulders, several hundred enemy troops waited. They were armed with AK-47s, Chinese hand grenades, CHICOM .51 caliber heavy machineguns, rocket-propelled grenades, rocket launchers, and a variety of other miscellaneous weapons. Well-trained Việt Cộng sharpshooters, armed with Russian Mosin-Nagant sniper rifles watched from their hidden lairs.

In the predawn haze, hundreds of MSF strikers guided by their Green Beret advisors moved silently across the paddies and marshland surrounding the ominous peak. Sgt. 1st Class Charles "Doc" Blanchard and the Rhade troops of 6th Company led the way. They were followed by S. Sgt. John Talley with 5th Company's Rhade troops, S. Sgt. Benedict Davan with his 4th Company of two hundred Chams and Sgt. 1st Class Albert "Buddy" Belisle commanding the 3rd Company of Montagnards.

The first troops arrived at the base of the rocky mass and began their ascent as weak sunlight filtered through the swirling mist.

The men began to scramble over and around the massive boulders. Surprised birds squawked as they were flushed from their nests, and rodents scurried for their holes as the legions of small, dark soldiers moved quickly and quietly upward. They did not speak as they tensely watched for signs of the enemy they knew were waiting for them. There was only the creak of their equipment and the swirl of wind through the ghostly rocks.

Initially the Mike Force troops encountered only scattered sniper fire, but at 6:45 a.m. the mountainside exploded. Grenades and B-40 rockets rained down on the advancing troops, followed by a hail of machinegun and small arms fire. The barrage came out of nowhere and from everywhere. There were dark holes, cracks and crevices wherever the soldiers looked, and bullets seemed to be coming from all of them. Some 20 percent of 6th Company was knocked out in minutes, and the onslaught had only begun.

The local Vietnamese called the rocky mass "Superstition Mountain" in their Khmer dialect. They believed its defenders were protected by spirits and "immune to death." ARVN troops believed the soul of every man killed there wandered the mountain forever because Buddha had abandoned the ugly crag. It was certainly true that in earlier efforts to attack the mountain, it seemed the mountain had won. In the prior six months to the current operation, the Fourth Mobile Strike Force had lost Joe Smith, Bobby Herreid, Gary Goudy, Roger Brown, and Bob Stec on Tuk Chup. The promontory was a natural fortress overlooking the surrounding paddies and the Plain of Reeds, and so far it had proven impregnable.

Sgt. Belisle said, "When we crawled over the big boulders, Việt Cộng snipers picked us off one by one. We tried to crawl forward under the rocks, but the VC came on top of us, throwing and rolling grenades down."

There were snipers everywhere; Belisle's company had lost two men to VC sniper-fire before they reached the foot of the knoll. As the MSF troops attempted to push beyond the massive rocks at the base of the mountain, they encountered even stiffer resistance. "We fought straight up the hill," Belisle said, "but every twenty yards another man fell. We crouched between the rocks with a grenade in one hand and the other hand free, listening for the sound of a grenade pin being pulled. When a grenade came clinking in your direction there were two choices—throw it back with your free hand or hunch between the rocks and pray." Neither choice was a good one.

Sgt. Davan said, "When my men crawl up the crevices and squeeze over the boulders, we catch the most accurate fire I've ever seen. It's screaming hell. Wounds are terrible. Charlie wastes no bullets on easy wounds like arms and legs. When a medic crawls after them, Charlie knows where he'll expose himself and drops the medic right on top of the wounded man."

Ben Davan, Yap, and Doc Blanchard

Doc Blanchard led his 6th Company Rhade troops from boulder to boulder with small arms and grenades. He and Sgt. 1st Class Richmond Nail, his understudy, additionally called in artillery and 106mm recoilless rifles to fire on cave complexes from which VC snipers and heavy machineguns were deployed. The fight on the sixteenth ended with 6th Company near the top of Tuk Chup where elements of Fourth Corps Mike Force had occupied a small helipad. Almost a third of 6th Company had been killed or wounded. Talley's 5th Company and Ben Davan's 4th Company had experienced similar losses. The major missions during the day had been evacuation of the dead and wounded and resupply of their dwindling ammunition and water supplies. The battle usage rate had been badly underestimated due to the fierceness of the fighting and the stifling heat of the day.

"We just swapped grenades with the VC most of the afternoon, tried to keep our heads down, and move forward," Davan said. "The one who was more accurate with the grenade lived. It was a hell of a day in a hell of a place."

PART 5

Early on March 17, a group of nine Hồi Chánhs defected to the Americans on Tuk Chup. "Hồi Chánh" was the term used for Việt Cộng who opted to take part in the Chiêu hồi Program (loosely translated as "Open Arms"). Chiêu hồi was a psy-war initiative to encourage defection within the VC ranks. Recent psy-war efforts in the Núi Cô Tô area, combined with the current successes of the Fifth Mobile Strike Force had convinced the group that Tuk Chup was going to fall, and they were willing to provide a wealth of valuable information in return for safe passage. The deserters pointed out the locations of weapons caches, gun emplacements, troop concentrations, and the tunnel entrances of the principle caves.

With the lead companies moving on up the mountain, the troops of Sgt. 1st Class Stan McKee's 1st Company was still at the foot of the rocky butte and were receiving the brunt of the enemy defenses. The company was comprised of ARVN troops with LLBD sergeants in charge. It was an early "Vietnamization" effort, and there were only two Americans assigned to the two-hundred-man company. The LLDB cadre had little control over their troops and discipline was lax compared to the companies of Montagnards, Rhade, and Cham troops. As machinegun fire intensified, the unit began to take casualties and halted. The men crawled behind rocks and cowered there, refusing to move, in spite of prodding and threats from their LLDB sergeants.

McKee was away from the company trying to rescue Sgt. Jack Greene, who had been hit by a sniper while dragging a wounded

ARVN soldier to safety. McKee was determined to reach Greene, but in his absence, half of 1st Company deserted. Even a litter detail he had brought with him to help rescue Greene had disappeared. It was not the ARVN company's finest hour.

Doc Blanchard and his Rhade troops

About mid-morning, Blanchard, Nail, and Sgt. Hampton Dews II, 6th Company's medic, along with John Talley, met near the top of Tuk Chup and the helipad to discuss movement in support of the planned sweep operation. They were joined by two combat photographers from the 221st Signal Company Spc.4 David Allan Russell, who had recently landed at the helipad with his assistant, was a young public information officer. Blanchard told them about a sniper that was located approximately three hundred feet ahead of the planned line of assault, and it was agreed they needed to take the sniper out before moving ahead. Blanchard, Nail, Talley, and three Rhade troops headed them forward upon Doc's command. The PIO immediately lobbied to go with the team, and they moved out about 9:30 a.m.

Dews got a call from Doc thirty minutes later: "We have a US down. Need you here ASAP." The medic grabbed his M-4 aid bag and headed in their direction. He stopped when he saw the team huddled in a rocky ravine dodging automatic weapons and sniper fire. Nail yelled for Dews to "get low and run like hell" down to their position. Without hesitation, Dews flew down the steep slope, grabbing a small scrub bush to stop himself. It was immediately shot out of his hand, and he rolled the rest of the way down into the ravine in a cloud of dust and scree.

"Arriving in the ravine, I found Russell, the PIO, had sustained a severe gunshot wound to the left side of his chest," Dews said. "CPR and an aggressive 'cut down' to establish intravenous fluids failed, and he expired within minutes from shock and internal bleeding."

The Special Forces team was in a desperate situation. The men were pinned down in a tight, restricted area very close to enemy forces, and unable to move due to the sniper. Rich Nail said, "I'm going back to the company and bring forces to outflank the snipers." As Nail spoke, he hunched over and moved toward the path Dews had taken coming into the ravine.

Dews yelled, "No!" and reached out to grab the sergeant as the enemy sniper opened up a fusillade of fire. Almost as if in slow motion, Nail fell back toward the medic shouting about his back. A round had gone through his ammo pouches and was exploding the .556 mags inside. Dews pulled out the hot mags and spun Nail to the ground where he saw Nail had sustained a massive head wound. His left eye had been removed from its socket and was suspended against his cheek. Not having a separate place to lay the injured man out of the line of fire, Dews had to lay him on top of the deceased photographer.

Dews placed Nail's injured eye back near its socket and bandaged his head, covering both eyes. He then bandaged Nail's back and administered an IV and morphine to keep the man from going into shock. During the sniper's barrage, Blanchard had also received ricochet wounds to both upper thighs. The wounds were not life threatening but were debilitating and very painful. Dews got Nail settled and then bandaged Blanchard's injuries.

As the day wore on, Fifth SF HQ called in napalm on the caves directly in front of the trapped team. The F-100 pilots were good enough to keep from dropping the flaming liquid on top of the Green Berets, although the men could feel the heat from each canister and smell the fumes. After every run, the sniper fired a few rounds at their position to let them know he was still in action. HQ tried artillery next, which literally rocked the trapped team's world as each man covered his ears and huddled deeper behind the rocks in the ravine. Then came the recoilless rifles, blasting away at the unseen enemy position.

By midafternoon, the team had run out of smoke to mark its position. More importantly, they had run out of water and were baking under the relentless Vietnamese sun. The 106s were able to continue firing, which kept the enemy at bay, or the team would have been immediately overrun.

Ben Davan and his 4th Company of Cham troops had been under intensive sniper and machinegun fire, and it was impossible to tell where the fire was coming from among the tall boulders. Davan was aware of the team from 6th Company that was pinned down near the summit of Tuk Chup. Between the Special Forces artillery and recoilless rifle attacks, he, along with Sgt. Manny "Speedy" Gonzalez, Sgt. 1st Class John Maketa, and Sgt. Mike Lunsford continued to search for the location of the sniper who had the group trapped.

Ben Davan and John Maketa

Several of Davan's men had been hit, and others in 4th Company seemed disorganized and confused. Ben sensed his troops were on the verge of panic. Leaving the company under the command of Sgt. Gonzalez, Davan led a handpicked team through withering machinegun fire to a vantage point where they could see one of the bunkers that had been harassing their company.

After instructing the team to lay down covering fire, Davan moved quickly through the field of boulders until he was within twenty feet of his goal. None of the VC soldiers in the bunker had spotted him from their narrow promontory, so he paused to get his breath and wipe the sweat from his eyes. The half-dozen Cham troopers he had brought with him continued to blast the bunker as they awaited their commander's signal to stop. Then, while the enemy troops still had their heads down, Davan charged. He single-handedly assaulted the emplacement with such ferocity, throwing hand grenades and placing such deadly fire on the gunners that the position was destroyed. The enemy soldiers who had survived the onslaught surrendered and were taken prisoner by the Cham troops.

Davan and his company regrouped and moved some distance on up the hill before once again coming under deadly sniper and machinegun fire. He surveyed the area, looked back down the rocky slope—then back up toward the cliffs where the sniper fire had come from. And suddenly he knew. This was the sniper he, Maketa, and Gonzalez had been searching for. This was the VC devil that had killed Russell, wounded Rich Nail and Doc Blanchard, and still had the Green Beret team trapped in the rocky ravine below.

Three more of Davan's troops had been wounded by machinegun-fire, and now they were pinned down by that same sniper. The injured soldiers were unable to move, and no one dared to try reaching them—no one except Ben Davan. With no thought for his own safety, the young sergeant handed his CAR-15 commando rifle to Speedy Gonzalez, stripped off his ammo belt and other gear, and crawled down through the rocks to assist his men.

Sgt. Manuel "Speedy" Gonzalez

The first man he reached was Jaka. Nicknamed Jackie, he was from a small fishing village on the coast of Ninh Thuận Province. Lifting Jackie slightly off the ground, Ben managed to drag him in a circuitous route to a sheltered location. Making sure the young soldier was still alive, Davan quickly returned for the second man named Jaya. The sniper's bullets were ricocheting off the huge granite rocks as the sergeant snaked his way back down through the boulders. Reaching Jaya, Davan helped him crawl back up through the rocks. The sniper emptied another five-cartridge magazine spraying the two men with chips of granite as the boy was delivered into the waiting arms of medic Doug Baribeau.

But now there was only one left, and this one was the most difficult—the young man named Dharma, who Davan called Donnie. He was one of Davan's favorite recruits. Donnie was probably about seventeen. He was so honest and reliable; Ben had come to depend on him in a very short time. The youngster was sprawled awkwardly in an open area of golden sand between two massive rocks. He appeared to be alive but unconscious. If he moved, he would die.

Once again, Davan made his way down the boulder-strewn hillock. He stared across the sandy expanse at his young friend and paused. Suddenly realizing how hot and miserable the day was, he tugged the green towel from around his neck, and took a deep breath. There was not a hint of breeze in the hellish bowl to which he had descended—only the proximity of death, and the heat which radiated oppressively from the surrounding stone edifice. It was so damned hot.

He removed his helmet, perspiration streaming down the sides of his face soaking his collar, and Ben realized he was very tired. "What a goddamned shit hole this is," he said, slowly shaking his head. Taking another deep breath to help clear his head and free his mind, he closed his eyes. "Boy, I wish I had an ice-cold Coke," he said to himself.

Wiping his face and clearing away the sweat from his eyes, Ben tucked the towel back in around his neck. Then, steeling himself, he placed his left hand on the boulder next to him, feeling the rough grained surface of the stone. With a strong push, Davan flew across the open expanse, crashing to the ground behind one of the huge granite stones next to Donnie. Several bullets blasted large pits in the earth, spraying out showers of sparkling golden sand, and the loud report of the Mosin-Nagant reverberated and echoed among the mammoth boulders.

Taking the sniper by surprise, Davan had made it across the first wide-open expanse alive, but now the gunner knew exactly where he was. Coiled like a deadly viper, the sniper was directly above him in a deep fissure in the rocky face of the mountain waiting to strike. Davan paused again and contemplated his next move. How could he get to Donnie and move him to a safe location without killing them both?

Hunkered in the shade of the massive boulder, Ben looked down and spotted a small gecko. It was about four inches long, olive-gold in color, and had white blotches along its back and tail. It had been flushed from one of the caves by the human battle and was seeking relief from the heat of the day. The gecko eyed the huge American warily and apparently concluded Davan posed less of a threat than the blazing sun. Scrunching its small body a bit deeper into the soft dry sand at the rock's base, the small reptile closed its eyes and resumed its midday nap.

Edging his way around the side of the rocky bulwark, Davan was careful not to disturb the dozing lizard. He could make out Donnie's head and shoulders and could detect ragged, shallow breathing. The boy was between him and the next large boulder. As Ben contemplated his next step, the youngster moved his head and groaned. He was regaining consciousness. If he rose up, he was dead.

Donnie spoke little English but did speak some simple French, so Davan called out, "Donnie! *Ne bougez pas! Je suis la pour t'aider.*" (Do not move! I am here to help you.) "Thank God for Mr. LaPierre's French class at Westbrook High," Ben thought to himself.

The boy was now fully awake. He turned his head toward Ben's voice but otherwise did not move. Ben could see the pain and fear in the young man's dark eyes. He had to save him.

Without pausing to think further, Ben threw himself around the boulder, landing on top of the boy, and the sniper blasted the area between the boulders with a thundering fusillade of shots. Davan felt as if he had been hit full force in the back with a baseball bat. There was no great pain—he just lost his breath. He could not move; he could not breathe; there was only a dull ache. As Ben stared down into Donnie's face, everything began to grow dark, and he saw tears well up in the young Cham's eyes.

The last machinegun in the area had been silenced, and the compatriots of the Green Berets trapped below had continued their effort to locate the hiding place of the sniper who had brought their operation to a halt. Each time the sniper fired, they had moved closer to the sound of the weapon. When the shots were fired that killed Ben Davan, John Maketa found himself directly above the sniper's location. He heard the rifle's report, and it had come from a deep, shadowed cleft in the rocks below him. Borrowing a flamethrower from the Special Weapons Platoon, Maketa strapped it on his back and rappelled down the rock face to a position that seemed correct. Taking a deep breath, he swung out in front of the gunman's hole, filled the cavity with a deluge of flaming fuel, and Tuk Chup was quiet.

Sgt. Doug Baribeau, 4ᵗʰ Company medic

As the sun began to sink behind the massive stone hulk, a squad of Ben Davan's Cham soldiers and Doug Baribeau descended into the grotto below to retrieve their commander and rescue the young man he had saved. Donnie was conscious but was pinned under the weight of Davan's body and could not move. He was seriously wounded, but he would survive.

The SF team that had been trapped below decided they must "escape and evade" back to friendly lines. There were still VC troops on the hill, but with the sniper gone, they had to make their move to survive. It had been ten hours since Nail was wounded, and the entire group had been without water for hours. Russell's assistant photographer, along with the three Rhade troopers, carried his body, wrapped in a poncho liner. Talley and Dews supported the amazingly tough Rich Nail—Blanchard limped alone with their radio. The team trudged down the length of the darkening ravine; then up and over to another gully leading to 6th Company and the helipad.

"The thirty-minute trudge seemed like a twelve-mile forced march with an eighty-pound ruck sack," Hamp Dews said. "We made it, but we were spent."

Once inside friendly lines, the men dropped to the ground in total exhaustion and in sore need of water. The Rhade soldiers quickly moved their wounded commanders and the dead PIO to the helipad, and by 7:00 p.m., all had been medevaced to Canto Field Hospital.

PART 6

At first light on March 18, Mike Force soldiers began the sweep south. The 1st Battalion secured the lower half of the mountain and the 2nd Battalion secured the top. Three 4th MSF battalions served as the rear guard, ensuring the 1st and the 2nd were not attacked from behind.

John Maketa replaced Benedict Davan as commander of Fourth Company, and the Cham troops continued to perform valiantly. John Talley was still leading his 5th Company Rhade troops, and Capt. Prince Powe, a newly arrived understudy of 2nd Battalion commander Capt. Henry Sturm, stepped in to replace Doc Blanchard as commander of 6th Company Sgt. 1st Class Larry Pease had replaced the seriously wounded Richmond Nail.

John Talley and Hamp Dews check a cave entrance—Tuk Chup

As midday approached, the MSF troops encountered heavy resistance and saw substantial casualties. Reinforcements were brought in, and the steady forward movement continued. Strikers cleared snipers, machinegun nests, spider holes, and caves as they went. Battery B of the 6/77th Artillery (9th Infantry Division) provided direct artillery support and helped to soften up the opposition ahead of the Mike Force troops, firing over fourteen thousand 105mm rounds. The MSF Special Weapons Platoon also supplied invaluable support, as they utilized the jeep-mounted 106mm recoilless rifles for precision fire on the well-hidden VC snipers and machinegun nests. Particularly devastating was the bee hive "timetable" flechette round. It could be delivered accurately into cave openings before exploding. After the battle, US troops found the bodies of enemy machine-gunners who had been chained to their rocky firing posts seemingly "nailed" to their positions by hundreds of the flechette darts.

Darkness settled over the unearthly landscape, and the attack slowed but did not stop. The moon, combined with occasional flares and illumination rounds, created a fantastic landscape of wildly distorted shadows and eerie phenomena among the giant boulders. The exhausted troops continued to push forward but had to wonder when they would catch the elusive foe that always seemed to remain one step beyond their grasp.

As dawn broke on the fourth day of their campaign, little had changed. The assault continued to move slowly around the massive pile of boulders; the opposition continued without abatement. There was still little physical sign of the enemy. Morale among the troops was low. They had seen many of their comrades killed and wounded and, in their minds, had little to show for it. Most of the Special Forces NCOs were hardened veterans who had returned tour after tour to work and fight with the Mike Force troops, but they had never dealt with an enemy that was so lethal and evasive. At midnight that night, the Americans declared a ceasefire until 7:30 a.m.

The break provided much-needed rest for the Strike Force soldiers who had pushed so hard for so long. It also allowed the Green Berets time to intensify their psy-ops campaign. Using loud speakers, they invited the VC units still on the mountain to surrender or come forward and fight, but there was little response. Chau Kim's influence was strong. At 7:30 the next morning, the mountain was hit with a barrage of artillery and air strikes, and the Mike Force assault resumed.

Somewhat refreshed, the two Strike Force battalions pushed forward for two more days, taking several large caverns and well-defended ravines in the process. There were more skirmishes with the VC on March 24 and 25; additional caves and tunnels with caches of weapons and documents were discovered, but most were deserted. Information from the Hồi Chánhs indicated the Strike Force was near the main communist complex and Chau Kim's headquarters. Defeating Chau would be a major blow to Việt Cộng prestige in the Mekong Delta. Most of the VC troops had slipped away, but hundreds of weapons, huge quantities of supplies and ammunition, and thousands of pages of documents and personnel records were captured. Numerous additional caves with stores of equipment and supplies were also discovered over the next ten days as the Fifth MSF, assisted by CIDG units and national police, mopped up the area.

Fifty-five Việt Cộng bodies were recovered, but the true numbers of enemy dead and wounded were never known. It was believed Chau Kim and two to three hundred of his troops escaped across the Cambodian border. The Mike Force strikers paid a heavy price for their bravery and determination. They suffered forty-five dead and 191 wounded in action. Hamp Dew's 6th Company had fifty-six functional Rhade troops remaining (out of two hundred) when it returned to Nha Trang. The Third, Fourth, and Fifth Companies fared about the same.

Special Forces casualties included twenty-four wounded and three killed. In addition to Benedict Davan, Master Sgt. Willis F. House of the Mike Force Special Weapons Platoon was killed by a sniper as the MSF forces moved into place during Phase II on March 13. Special Forces Sgt. John "Jack" Greene was rescued from the battlefield and medevaced to a hospital but died of his wounds six days later. Greene, of Charlotte, North Carolina, was posthumously awarded the Silver Star for his heroic effort to save his wounded man. Jack Greene was twenty years old.

B-55 was declared combat ineffective after Núi Cô Tô, and the next two months were spent recruiting and training replacement forces. The First and Second ARVN Companies in 1st Battalion were disbanded and the soldiers fired for deserting the field of battle. Those companies were replaced with Montagnard troops.

The Battle of Nui Coto (as it became known) received little note in the US media. The press was totally consumed with the story of the Chicago Eight, Abbie Hoffman, Jerry Rubin, Bobby Seale, Tom Hayden, et al. On March 20, 1969, they were indicted by a Chicago grand jury for crossing state lines to incite riots during the 1968 Democratic Convention. The media circus that followed dominated front pages across the US for months. The deaths of three Green Berets and forty-five indigenous tribesmen in South Vietnam could hardly compete with that.

In the Seven Sisters region of the Mekong Delta, however, the battle was a big story. For the first time in twenty years, the area was not under communist control. Tuk Chup had fallen.

S. Sgt. Benedict Maher Davan died on St. Patrick's Day, March 17, 1969. Two weeks later, he was laid to rest in the Davan family plot at St. Hyacinth Catholic Cemetery in Westbrook, Maine. It was a beautiful day, and the church was a sea of pink hyacinths and yellow daffodils. The cemetery was filled to overflowing with a few of Ben's friends, along with hundreds of adoring former students and athletes who had been taught and coached by his father. Paddy Davan's son had come home.

In July 1969, Paddy and Rachel Davan were ushered into the offices of Gov. Kenneth Curtis in Augusta, Maine. In a solemn ceremony, Gov. Curtis, who was a lieutenant commander in the US Naval Reserve, read the citation for Sgt. Davan's Distinguished Service Cross, second only to the Medal of Honor, for "extraordinary heroism...at the cost of his own life."

Davan's additional medals and awards included the following: Two Bronze Star Medals, the Air Medal, the Purple Heart, the National Defense Service Medal, Vietnam Service Medal, Vietnam Campaign Medal, and the Vietnamese Gallantry Cross.

Benedict Davan served in Vietnam for twenty-two months. He was twenty-three years old.

The cry of the cicada
Gives us no sign
That presently it will die.

"The Cry of the Cicada"
Matsuo Basho
Translated by William George Aston

Epilogue

Addendum for Other Warriors

A few weeks after the Battle of Nui Coto, the B-55 compound at Nha Trang was named Davan Compound in honor of Benedict Davan and his heroic effort to save his men.

Two months after capturing Núi Cô Tô, the Việt Cộng retook it from occupying ARVN forces. MACV in Saigon alerted Fifth Special Forces at Nha Trang to get prepared to retake it. In formation the next morning, the Mike Force strikers in B-55's two battalions stacked their weapons and said in their limited English, "Hell no!"

> *Per Hamp Dews: Sgt. 1st Class Richmond Nail's injuries included severe head trauma, the loss of an eye, the loss of a kidney, and the loss of his spleen. Not receiving hospital care for over ten hours would have killed most men, but he survived on pure toughness and determination to fight another day. Nail's long relationship with the JFK Special Warfare Center began in 1969, when he was hand-picked to perform duties as an instructor at Camp Mackall in Phase I of the Special Forces basic enlisted division. He served in this capacity until 1975. During that time, he personally wrote every lesson plan for Phase I training and set up a jungle lane and a RECONDO course. In 1982, Lt. Col.*

James Rowe requested Nail join him in creating the Survival, Evasion, Resistance, and Escape (SERE) Course in the Special Forces School. Sgt. Nail joined Rowe and lent his expertise to the SERE program. In June 2006, Sgt. Major Nail retired after thirty years in the Army and twenty-four years of service to the John F. Kennedy Special Warfare Center and School. This good and honorable man passed away in September 2020. Hamp Dews said, "Rich gave new meaning to the old saying 'tough as nails.'"

The first story I wrote about Nui Coto was posted on our "Unlikely Warriors" Face Book page in 2014, and I was ably assisted by E. L. "Shotgun" Woody. Sgt. Ed Woody also served as a medic and platoon leader during the Battle of Nui Coto, and was a legendary figure in MIKE Force circles. Ed provided many of the photographs I used in this chapter. My first story did not focus on Benedict Davan; however his death was mentioned and Ed made the comment: "Ben Davan was my best friend." Unfortunately, Ed passed away in May 2017. We extend our condolences to his family and his many friends around the world.

Presumably you have read the dedication in the opening pages of this book and know Hamp Dews passed away in November 2020, just a few weeks after helping me write this story. Hamp's assistance was crucial to the accuracy of my writing about Special Forces training and procedures. I was an Air Force Security Service Chinese Linguist, so you can conclude for yourself exactly how much knowledge I had of Special Forces training in the mid-1960s. As a Special Forces medic and platoon leader, Hamp was an indispensable and limitless source of information, not only on the Battle of Nui Coto, but anything and everything dealing with Special

Forces as it existed fifty years ago. That information is not readily available online or even in published books. Apparently no one has considered writing a book about Green Beret training in 1966. Without Hamp's help and advice, Ben Davan's story would be much shorter, far less factual, much less detailed, and let's face it, a whole lot less interesting.

When I asked for Hamp's help with my story about Ben Davan, this was his response: "Gary, I am happy to help you take on the challenge of documenting Ben's heroism and Nui Coto. I knew Ben well. He was a great soldier and teammate. I've often said to my SF compatriots that Nui Coto was probably the largest organic Special Forces operation of the entire war. Periodically I've been challenged by fellow Regiment members who've maintained that some A-Camp battles (like Duc Lap) involved more enemy forces and resulted in huge NVA casualties. What they don't account for is that the Nui Coto order of battle drew from almost every internal asset available to Special Forces. Those included two Mike Force units, local A-Teams with RFPF assets, MAC-SOG Teams, a volunteer Heavy Weapons Platoon, Special Forces C-Team support, and Command and Control elements from 5th Group HQ. Non SF assets included Close Air support from the USAF and a number of Big Army MAC-V signal, intelligence, and medical assets (and probably Army Security Agency support throughout, although we didn't know it).

"Bottom Line: Thank you for bringing back to life one of the biggest Special Forces battles of the war: The Battle of Nui Coto, and the cave to cave fight to dislodge the enemy on Tuk Chup, which was reminiscent of the Marines clearing the Japanese from Mt. Suribachi on Iwo Jima in March 1945.

Those who fought it have gone unrecognized for decades—even among the ranks of the Regiment." They must be remembered.

Sgt. Hamp Dews
Nui Coto, March 1969

In one final bit of tragic irony, Ben Davan's brother, John Patrick Davan Jr. enlisted in the US Air Force on September 21, 1975. Jack was killed in a plane crash on St. Patrick's Day, March 17, 1978, nine years to the day after Ben's death on the rocky slopes of Tuk Chup. However, to quote Winston Churchill, Jack's death "is a riddle wrapped in a mystery inside an enigma." It is a mystery why he would leave his wife and family to enlist in the Air Force at the age of thirty-five, and his military grave marker at St. Hyacinth is an even greater mystery. It reads,

JOHN P. DAVAN, JR., S. SGT., US AIR
FORCE, VIETNAM, 1940–1978.

The only action in Vietnam on March 17, 1978, was a simmering border war between Vietnam and Cambodia and a massive wave of Vietnamese "boat people" seeking to escape communism. If Jack Davan died in a plane crash in Vietnam, it was in some covert capacity. There were no US military personnel operating officially within the Socialist Republic of Vietnam in 1978.

CHAPTER 2

EMILIO ALBERTO DE LA GARZA JR.

Junior

Lance Cpl. Emilio De La Garza Jr.

East Chicago, Indiana, was originally swampland bordering the underbelly of Lake Michigan. The state of Indiana began selling plots of land to railroads and land speculators in the 1850s to fund the local school system. Settlement of the area was slow, and as late as the 1890s, the city had no proper streets or public utilities. The area was incorporated as a city in 1893 and was named for its location, east of Chicago, Illinois. The 1900 Census showed a total population of

3,011, but the arrival of the Inland Steel Corporation in 1903 transformed the city into an industrial powerhouse.

In the 1910s, several thousand Mexican citizens immigrated to East Chicago to work in the steel mills. There was a labor shortage in 1917 and 1918 due to US participation in World War I. Additional Mexicanos were also recruited to act as strike breakers during labor unrest in 1919. Most were single men (called *solos*) who hoped to return to Mexico, but many stayed on and eventually were joined by their families. That small Mexican community paved the way for later Latino immigration

By the 1950s, East Chicago had developed a reputation as a rough industrial city—plagued by pollution, organized crime, gambling, political corruption, and prostitution. However, the city continued to grow, and the population peaked in 1960 at almost fifty-eight thousand. At that point, the population began to decline as suburbanization, white flight, affordability of automobiles, and construction of highways meant workers no longer had to live in the city but could commute from less-polluted suburbs.

That grim overview of East Chicago does not begin to illustrate the close-knit Latino communities that existed within it. Anchored by its Catholic churches, authentic Mexican restaurants and local bodegas, the neighborhoods were filled with good families who resided there, worked in the mills, and thrived. One of those families was "la familia De La Garza."

Emilio Alberto De La Garza was born in a shack on a ranch near Austwell, Texas, on April 8, 1919. His parents, Guadalupe and Emilia De La Garza, were Mexican citizens, but Guadalupe was a talented mechanic and musician. Guadalupe went back and forth across the border performing mechanical jobs for the farmers and ranchers in the area, and they paid him with livestock. There was little in the way of public education available for Mexican American children in South Texas in the mid '20s, but Guadalupe and Emilia saw to it that Emilio learned to read, write, and speak English, so he could eventually attend public school.

Emilio's father was killed in a bus accident when he was thirteen, so his option of continuing a formal education ended. Emilia had three younger sons to care for, so Emilio had to manage their farm and ensure there was some family income. In his late teens, the young man moved to Laredo, Texas, which was on the Mexican border, and went to work as an upholsterer. Rich oil and gas finds in the grasslands surrounding Laredo had boosted the local economy and created good-paying jobs in the area.

While in Laredo, Emilio met a lovely young senorita named Carmen Castañeda. Carmen had been born in Monterrey, Mexico, in August 1923, and was now living in Laredo. She had come into the upholstery shop a few times and Emilio was interested in getting to know her. His grandfather, Pedro De La Garza, had stepped into the role of advisor after Guadalupe's death, so Emilio asked his advice. Abuelo (Grandpa) Pedro encouraged his grandson to go where Carmen would hang out with her friends, get to know her, and ask her out. Emilio followed his advice, and the two were soon dating.

Emilio began to save his money. He planned to build a small house in Laredo and ask Carmen to marry him, but when he confided his intentions to his mother, Emilia was opposed to the idea. She thought Carmen was too young and did not approve of her son's choice, but Emilio was not dissuaded. The issue continued to deteriorate until, in an ultimate act of parental authority, Emilia took the money her son had saved and hid it away. She reasoned that if Emilio had no money, he could not marry; however, Abuelo Pedro provided the money his grandson needed, and the two were married in 1940. Emilio was twenty; Carmen was seventeen.

Within a few months, Carmen became pregnant, and the young couple eagerly awaited the birth of their first child. With the help of his grandfather, younger brothers, and Carmen's brothers, Emilio built a small house. Carmen spent her days decorating the house the way she wanted it and preparing to become a mother. In the spring of 1941, with the assistance of a local midwife and Emilia, Carmen gave birth to a beautiful daughter, and they named her Adriana.

For the first few months, everything was wonderful. Carmen had wanted a daughter and Adriana was a delight, bright-eyed, precocious, and always smiling; however, by fall, she began to fail. Chronic diarrhea set in, and none of the local doctors seemed to be capable of finding a solution to the problem. At Christmastime, the baby was listless and slept most of the time. Adriana died in January 1942, and the new parents were devastated.

Carmen was heartbroken, refusing to eat for days and immersing herself in hours of prayer and penance. Emilia stayed with Carmen during the day, afraid to leave her alone. Emilia was trying to pull her daughter-in-law through those terrible days while suffering herself—mourning the death of her first grandchild. She seemed better equipped to deal with the young mother than Emilio, who felt totally helpless in the face of such abject desolation. Carmen gradually returned to some state of normalcy, but she would never be quite the same as the vivacious, young mother who had so joyously welcomed her new daughter only a year before.

Emilio enlisted in the US Army on December 21, 1943. He served as a gun crewman and surgical technician. In 1945, De La Garza saw combat in the Po Valley and the final Allied attacks of the Italian campaign. He also saw combat in North Africa, earning the European African Middle Eastern Campaign Medal with one bronze star and the WWII Victory Medal.

Emilio De La Garza, 1945

Emilio received his discharge from the Army at Fort Lewis Washington on March 12, 1947. He was a sergeant and had the added specialist rank of technician fourth grade (T/4), which increased his salary. Sgt. De La Garza was a talented linguist. He had quickly picked up Italian and also Polish from some of his Army buddies. His superior officers were impressed and had wanted De La Garza to reenlist. The Army offered him a bonus and the possibility of language school, but Carmen wanted no part of it. Being an Army wife was not her idea of marital bliss, and whatever Carmen wanted, Carmen usually got.

Returning home to South Texas after his years in the Army, De La Garza was no longer willing to subject himself to the prejudice and segregation he had endured there his entire life. He needed to find a good-paying job with some long-term stability. Carmen's brother, Severo Castañeda, was living in The Harbor, an area of East Chicago, Indiana. Severo worked for Inland Steel, as did most of his neighbors, and he told Emilio the mill was primarily hiring WWII combat veterans. Now was the time for him to act. Emilio, Carmen, and Oscar Castañeda, another of Carmen's brothers, packed the De La Garza's old Chevy, and on December 26, 1947, the three headed north for a new beginning and a new life.

Hitting US Highway 83 out of Laredo, the trio planned to drive to Shamrock, Texas, which was near the Oklahoma border. From Shamrock, it was Route 66, The Mother Road, all the way to Chicago. It was almost six hundred miles from Laredo to Shamrock, but Carmen had packed enough food to last them several days. Barring problems with the car, they should be able to drive straight through, only stopping for gas. Then they would take a break and get some rest.

From Shamrock to Oklahoma City—Tulsa to Joplin—Springfield to St. Louis and on to Chicago, the De La Garzas hoped to complete their trip in five days. The roads were narrow and the weather not the best, but traffic was light between Christmas and New Year's Day.

Meanwhile, in the Chicago area, New Year's Day dawned with steady rain and temperatures hovering around the freezing mark. The rain had started about 1:00 a.m. and continued, mixed with sleet, adding to the icing woes. Utilities were devastated as strong northeast winds gusted to more than 60 mph and downed ice-covered trees, telephone lines, and power lines. Entire metropolitan areas were soon without power and communications. As winds gusted to near hurricane force, radio towers were toppled, windows were blown out, and twenty-foot waves from Lake Michigan crashed onto Lake Shore Drive. Hundreds of accidents resulted in numerous deaths, and all traffic was ordered off the roads. Chicago and its suburbs were at a complete standstill. After eleven hours of freezing rain and sleet, the precipitation changed over to heavy, wet snow, accompanied by thunder. Almost five inches of snow fell on the half-inch of ice, and the temperature plummeted. This was the worst ice storm ever recorded in the City of Chicago, and it was just the opening round for 1948.

Delayed by bad weather and icy roads, the De La Garzas and Oscar Castañeda did not get to Chicago until after the storm was over. Most of the ice and snow had been cleared from the main thoroughfares, but everywhere they looked was a winter wonderland. Carmen and Oscar had never seen snow before, except in pictures. They were enchanted with the scenery, but the temperatures were bitterly cold. Arriving in East Chicago, the three drove to Severo's home. A few days later, Emilio and Oscar applied for work at the mill, and they were hired.

Within a few weeks, the De La Garzas had found an apartment of their own. The weather continued to be miserable with below-zero temperatures and bone-chilling winds blowing in off Lake Michigan. Emilio was working long hours at Inland Steel, and Carmen was helping cook in a nearby restaurant. Carmen was happy to be someplace new, and by October, she was expecting their second child. Emilio Alberto De La Garza Jr. was born on June 23, 1949. With a thatch of dark hair and sparkling eyes, Mi'jito (my little son) was a born charmer, just like his father, and (like Adriana) he was the love of Carmen's life.

Emilio Jr. was soon nicknamed Junior (with Spanish pronunciation and a rolled *R* at the end), and he started kindergarten in

1954. Carmen had come from a large family, and she wanted several children, but fate was not kind. Over the ensuing years she had two miscarriages, and each one was a devastating disappointment for both her and Emilio Sr.

As Carmen grew older, the probability of her successfully carrying a child to full term became less and less likely. When she became pregnant in 1959, Carmen was thirty-seven years old. In the late '50s, that was considered to be an "older" age for bearing children, even for a woman having had no problem with miscarriages. For a woman who'd had two or more miscarriages, the chance of her having another one was about 40 percent.

Carmen was a devout Roman Catholic, so she dedicated the new baby to the Virgin of Guadalupe, and she began to pray to the virgin saint every day. She had a small shrine in her bedroom, and before retiring each night, she would light a candle and say one last prayer for the life of her baby. She promised that if the baby was born alive and healthy, she would name it Guadalupe. Regardless if it were a boy or girl, the name would be Guadalupe.

Junior's younger brother, Guadalupe Lee, joined the family May 14, 1960. Junior was nine years older, but he adored his baby brother Lupe. They loved to play together, and anytime Lupito needed a big brother, Junior was always there. He took Lupe with him everywhere he went. The boy even hung out with Junior and his buddies on the rooftops on Main Street in The Harbor. The buddies drank Bud. Lupito drank root beer. The family had moved from their apartment on Deodar Street and was now living in a house on Fir Street.

The De La Garza home was usually a happy place for the boys. They shared a bedroom with twin beds, and Lupe would help Junior workout in the basement. Junior took welding classes at EC Washington High School and had made a weight bench for himself. Papi De La Garza had bought Junior weights to train with, and Lupe would sit on his feet when he did sit-ups.

When the boys left the house, Mama Carmen would make them stand in front of her. She would make the sign of the cross in front of their faces and say, *"En el nombre del Padre, hijo, y Espiritu Santo, que Dios te bendiga."* (In the name of the Father, son and Holy

Spirit, may God bless you.) She was always concerned about their welfare, but everyone knew who the De La Garzas were, and the close-knit neighborhood provided a refuge from the crime and corruption rampant in other parts of the city.

Junior graduated from high school in June 1968 and went to work for Inland Steel. He had become involved in a relationship with Rosemary Rejón during his senior year, and his parents did not approve of it. More importantly, Mama Carmen did not approve of it. Junior was street smart, but when it came to the fairer sex, his experience was limited (at best). He had an innocent quality about him—an honest, straightforward charm that made him very attractive to everyone he met, especially some of his less savory friends, who loved to tease him and were determined to "save" him from himself (and his mother). Rosemary had a somewhat questionable reputation among The Harbor community elders. The older women felt she was "not as modest as she should be around boys." Carmen did not think she was the appropriate girlfriend for her son, but Junior would sneak Rosemary into their house when his parents were not home. Lupe knew about it, of course, but being the loyal little brother, he kept Junior's secret.

Junior and Rosemary Rejón—December 1967

Lupe said, "One day, Junior asked me if I could keep a secret from Mom and Dad. I said 'Yes.' Then, he asked me if I wanted to be an uncle. I laughed and told him I thought I was too little to be an uncle. He laughed, hugged me around the neck and said, 'Well, it's our secret.'"

"This was in the summer," Lupe continued, "They were expecting a baby in October, but Junior didn't tell Mom and Dad. He and Rosemary got married in secret because our parents were both against them getting married."

Lupe continued, "One time Rosemary's parents came looking for Junior, and they were very angry. My brother was hiding in the basement. My dad told them he did not know where Junior was. I think this was when Rosemary's parents found out my brother was the father of Rosemary's baby. Gosh, it was awful."

PART 2

Junior had long considered becoming a US Marine, but he had kept it to himself. He knew his mother was opposed to the idea. He admired his father's WWII record but had no desire to go into the Army. Many of his friends were receiving draft notices every week. Junior knew it was only a matter of time—when his draft notice came in the mail, he tore it up. On February 4, 1969, Junior enlisted in the Marine Corps. Carmen was still against it, but Junior's father supported him. If Junior thought the Marines was the best course for him to take, then Papi would stand by his son, much to Carmen's dismay. Carmen always demanded deference to her point of view and was not pleased if she did not receive it, especially from her *esposo*.

"Before my brother left for boot camp, I believe my parents found out something about Rosemary and the baby. They had a big fight with Junior. My brother told me later he was leaving, but not to worry, he'd come back."

The family took Junior to Ohare Field in Chicago two days later, and it was a difficult scene. Papi had charge of Lupito and tried to lighten the mood. He laughed and joked around. He had such a kind and loving heart. He wanted Junior's departure to be as peaceful as possible.

For Carmen Castañeda De La Garza, watching Mi'jito leave "convertirse en soldado" (to become a soldier) was much more visceral. Junior had discussed his decision with his mother at length.

She understood his reasons. She saw the logic in controlling his own destiny. She looked at him, nodded her head seeming to agree when he told her he did not want to be drafted into the Army. However, this was her mother's heart being torn from her body. This was her firstborn son beginning a journey that would lead him inevitably to war, and all that came with it—and every bit of logic went out the window. It was more than she could bear to think about.

Carmen's relationship with Junior had been special from the day he was born. She and Emilio had wanted many children, but with the loss of Adriana, and then two more babies after Junior, Carmen's hopes began to diminish. Eventually, she had been blessed with Lupito, whom she loved dearly, but Mi'jito would always have her heart. By the time he was a teenager, Carmen had put on a few extra pounds. Junior would come up behind her, hug her around the neck, call her "mi gordis" (my chubby one), and kiss the back of her head. She loved it when he called her that, but only Junior could get by with it. Carmen was a tough woman, and no one else would dare to face her wrath, but Junior held no fear of his mother—nor did he need to.

As they began to board his flight, Junior spoke individually to each member of his family and kissed each of them. Papi had tears in his eyes and wished blessings on his journey' "Adiós, Junior," he said softly. "Go with God." Carmen was struggling to keep her emotions in check. She gave Junior her usual blessing, made the sign of the cross, and then prayed with him. Finally he knelt on one knee and spoke to Lupe, "*Hasta luego, hermanito* [little brother]." Then, he boarded the plane for California.

Junior received his recruit training at MCRD San Diego with the 2nd Recruit Training Battalion, Recruit Training Regiment. Upon completion of basic training, he was ordered to the Marine Corps Base, Camp Pendleton, California, where he joined the 2nd Infantry Training Regiment (ITR) and underwent individual combat training and weapons training with the Basic Infantry Training Battalion. After graduation, De La Garza flew home for ten days leave, then returned to San Diego and shipped out for Camp Courtney, Okinawa—headquarters for the 3rd Marine Regiment, 3rd Marine Battalion.

Promoted to private first class on July 1, Emilio arrived in South Vietnam on July 25, 1969. He was assigned duty as a machine gun-team ammo carrier with Company H, 2nd Battalion, 3rd Marine Regiment. On September 29, 1969, he was reassigned to the 1st Marine Division and served with Headquarters and Service Company, 2nd Battalion, 1st Marines, until the following December. He was meritoriously promoted to lance corporal on February 1, 1970, and joined Echo Company, 2nd Battalion, serving as an M60 machine gunner.

Junior wrote to Lupe frequently. He would tell him about boys his age who were working all day in the rice paddies and with water buffalo or oxen in the fields. "They beg for cigarettes and candy from us," he would tell him. "The boys here smoke all the time, but it's not good for boys your age to smoke in the US. It's not good for you."

After Junior deployed to Vietnam, Emilio Sr. had a business opportunity to purchase an apartment building in The Harbor. There were five apartments, and Lupito helped him remodel them so they could be rented. Papi had always had a secret desire to be in construction. He loved to build things and had a real talent for it. Downstairs was a large open room, and the De La Garzas converted it into a bingo hall to raise money for poor families in the area. They put Lupe in charge of the concession stand, which kept him busy all day and out of trouble. Carmen was concerned he might get in with the wrong crowd without Junior to watch over and guide him.

Emilio on a Đà Nẵng beach with one of his compadres

Throughout early 1970, both sides in I Corps (US and NVA) adhered to the patterns of operation they had established during the previous year. The North Vietnamese Army continued their small-unit attacks, terrorism, and infiltration. Threatening a resumption of large-unit warfare, the communists massed troops and supplies along the DMZ in the first months of the year and opened new bases along the Laotian border in northwestern Quảng Trị Province.

In February, the focus of enemy activity began to shift to CTZ I (the northernmost area of South Vietnam) and attacks increased steadily. Hostile forces staged their heaviest attacks in the Central Highlands near Civilian Irregular Defense Group camps at Dak Seang, Đắk Pék, and Ben Het. The enemy also conducted numerous attacks by fire and several sapper attacks against US fire support bases. Marine ground operations were limited largely to Quảng Nam Province where the 1st Marine Division conducted continuous small-scale battles in defense of Đà Nẵng.

For Emilio, daily life consisted of long marches through thick jungle or tall elephant grass, struggling with a heavy pack along with his M60 machine gun. With a continual stream of sweat running down his face and into his eyes, he kept an olive green towel slung around his neck to wipe it away. And then there was the never-ending series of day patrols and night ambushes in the tree lines, rice paddies, and sand dunes south of Đà Nẵng. He was always worried the next bend in the road or the next turn in the path might reveal an ambush or a booby trap that would take him or one of his buddies out of action or worse. High stress was a regular part of the job.

And the f***in' booby traps. "God damn the booby traps," Emilio thought to himself. They were everywhere, just waiting for the unlucky bastard who happened to step on one or hit a trip-wire. Some guys volunteered to walk point. They knew they were good at spotting the traps and wanted to look out for their buddies, but the best point man in Nam could have a bad day. "It only takes one bad day," Emilio said, "and you are screwed."

De La Garza had been in Vietnam almost nine months. He'd made good friends and lost good friends. These guys were his brothers. There'd never be another time in his life like what he was going through now with his brothers. He wrote Rosemary and his parents as often as he could, but he couldn't tell them the real story of what he was seeing and doing. They'd never understand. Only his brother Marines knew, and many wouldn't make it back home alive.

On Easter Sunday night, March 29, 1970, Lance Cpl. Jackie Lundell, the radioman for Echo Company, was mortally wounded in a Việt Cộng grenade attack while on patrol. The VC came out of nowhere, firing AK-47s and tossing grenades. Radiomen were frequent targets in order to disable communications and prevent the Marines from calling for help. Lundell was rushed to First Med-Danang but died the next day. He was nineteen years old and from Ohio. "Jackie was a good guy and always careful," Emilio said, "but it only takes one bad day."

"I've never seen a Marine cry," Emilio said. "We are Marines after all," he continued with a slight smile, "but there were nights alone on watch in a fighting hole, all alone except for my buddy, who was sleeping next to me [and snoring loudly], that it just got to me— and goddammit, I cried, because I'd lost a friend, someone who'd had my six in a fight, someone I'd drunk beer with, eaten chow with, lived with—someone so young and full of life was now gone—gone forever. Shit!

"Then I remembered a prayer mi Mami had taught me. She is one tough lady, but she has a strong faith. She had given me a St. Christopher's medal to wear, and I know she prays for my safety every day. '*Angel de mi Guarda, dulce compania, no me desampares ni de noche ni de dia. No me dejes solo, que me perderia.* [Guardian Angel, sweet company, do not abandon me by night or by day. Do not leave me alone, for I would lose myself.] I recited the prayer to myself. I felt a sense of calm come over me, and I knew everything would be okay."

Emilio De La Garza Jr.

PART 3

All US military personnel serving in Vietnam were eligible for one R&R (rest and recuperation) period out of the combat zone during their tour of duty. The duration of R&R was five days leave to Bangkok, Hong Kong, Kuala Lampur, Penang, Manila, Seoul, Singapore, Taipei, or Tokyo (as well as in-country at China Beach). Due to their greater distance, seven days leave was permitted for Hawaii and Sydney. Hawaii was the most popular destination for married GIs planning to holiday with spouses. It was the cheapest place for their wives to get to.

Junior and Rosemary had never had a honeymoon. They had no money. Both had to find work, and neither family wanted them to marry. Each one had continued to live with their parents. Junior had been sending Rosemary money every month, so they could get a house when he got out, but now he told her to purchase a plane ticket from Chicago to Honolulu. The young father longed to see his baby daughter. Renee was now eighteen months old, but she had been ill, so the decision was made. She would stay home with her abuela (grandmother). It would be just the two of them in Hawaii. Junior and Rosemary would have their honeymoon in paradise.

Emilio put in for R&R in February and received his orders for the first week of April 1970. On March 31, he was pulled from the field and sent to the 2/1 Marines base area to turn in his weapons and gear, shower, and get some sleep. Early the next morning, he was flown to Tan Son Nhut Air Base. Later that day, he changed into his C uniform, boarded a chartered Continental Airlines plane ("freedom bird"), round-eyed stewardesses and all, and flew to Honolulu.

There were special rates for wives meeting their husbands on R&R, and Rosemary was able to purchase round-trip coach tickets for under $300. Ironically, she was also flying on Continental Airlines from Chicago to Honolulu, via Los Angeles. She had not flown before, so the long trip was thrilling, and she was excited at the prospect of seeing Junior. It had been so long since he left Chicago. She had been advised to arrive in Honolulu the night before Junior's aircraft was due from Vietnam. As her plane descended over the startling blue waters surrounding the island of Oahu, she thought she had never seen anything so beautiful in her life.

The US Army authorities in Hawaii, striving for efficiency, had created a military-style reunion for the family members. Dependents were told to stay at the R&R center in downtown Honolulu and not try to meet the charter flight. The standard elapsed time after opening the airplane door, taking the troops through immigration, giving them a fifteen-minute briefing, busing them from Fort DeRussy into town, and sending them away in taxicabs with their families was one hour. When the servicemen were ready to be released at the center, wives were lined up on both sides of a corridor, and the men were sent through so their women could grab them.

Junior could see Rosemary as he moved down the crowded hallway. She was wearing a bright yellow dress with a bolero jacket and looked beautiful. Running the last few feet to meet him, she threw herself into her husband's arms, and he held her for a long embrace. Someone had handed Junior a lei made of purple orchids. He placed it around her neck, kissed her again, and said, "Aloha, Mrs. De La Garza. Welcome to Hawaii."

Gathering their bags, Junior hailed a taxi, and they headed for their hotel. They were staying at the Surf Rider on Waikiki Beach. It was a luxury hotel, but there were discounts on almost everything from hotels to car rentals for the visiting servicemen and their families. The De la Garzas were on the eleventh floor, and they had spectacular views of Waikiki Bay and Diamond Head to the north. Junior gave Rosemary an opportunity to freshen up, and after a couple hours of intimate time, the two got dressed and headed up Kalakaua Avenue looking for a place to eat.

Drifting lazily along the avenue, enjoying the warm, tropical breezes and the wonderful scent of plumeria and jasmine, Junior and Rosemary moved with the crowd, looking at the sights, and refusing to think about the hours that would quickly slip through their fingers. They would have about 140 hours to try and make up for the months the war had stolen from them. Rosemary found it difficult to take her eyes off of the tanned, young Marine walking beside her. With his short-cropped hair and the slightly haggard look around his eyes, Junior appeared very young and vulnerable. He had grown a mustache since she had seen him last, which made him look a bit roguish—like a young Pancho Villa. She reached out to touch his face, and he laughed, his dark eyes twinkling in the streetlights.

Junior De La Garza in Hawaii—April 1970

The ensuing days flew by in a whirl of activity. They hiked and spent time on the beach. They attended a luau at the Moana Hotel, ate pit-cooked pork and poi, and watched the hula dancers. Hawaii was the only R&R location where servicemen were allowed to drive a car, so Junior rented a small Chevy Nova. On their last full day, the two headed northeast out of Honolulu and soon found themselves on Pali Highway. The city quickly disappeared as they drove through tall banyan trees and dense tropical forest. The tranquil, natural beauty of Hawaii began to emerge, and it was gorgeous.

Pali means "cliff" in Hawaiian, and the lookout is perched over one thousand feet above the coastline amid mountain peaks shrouded by clouds. It overlooks Kaneohe and Kailua, Chinaman's Hat, and Coconut Island. The honeymooners gazed across the panorama before them and the blue Pacific beyond. In the distance, they heard the strings of soft Hawaiian music, and everything was perfect.

Emilio and Rosemary continued through the Nu'uanu Pali Tunnels to Windward Oahu, turned left through Kaneohe, and drove through the pineapple fields. Following the lush coastline to Haleiwa and Waimea Bay on Oahu's famed North Shore, the road trip was one they would always remember.

On the morning of his departure, Emilio put on his C uniform, said his goodbyes to Rosemary, and took a taxi from the hotel back to the R&R center. Rosemary did not have to check out of the hotel until 11:00 a.m., and her flight did not leave until 1:00 p.m. The hotel had an airport shuttle that would deliver her to the Continental ticket counter after she checked out. Neither of them had slept much. They wanted to savor every moment they had together.

If Emilio missed his flight, he would be considered AWOL, so he had left early. That was a world of shit he did not need or want to deal with. From the R&R center, he was bused back to Fort DeRussy to be outprocessed and then boarded his commercial charter back to Vietnam. At Ton San Nhut, his jungle fatigues were returned to him; he changed clothes and was transported back to the 2/1 Marines base camp.

Part 4

De La Garza (front row center) and members of his squad

On April 10, the day following his return, De La Garza was thrown back into the regular routine with his squad: day patrols and night ambushes in the paddies and sand dunes south of Đà Nẵng. It was good to see his buddies, and he was happy to see all of them were still there and still healthy. They demanded to be filled in on every detail of his trip and could not conceal their envy. With almost nine months in-country, he was by far the most senior member of his squad, with the exception of Cpl. Peterson, the squad leader. Pete Peterson was on his second tour and had gone to Bangkok the year before. The other guys, including Huff and Abbate, his closest friends, had all been in Nam less than three months. Jimmy Huff was from Goliad, Texas, near where Emilio's father was born, and Antonio Abbate, his ammo carrier, was from Chicago. They were his compadres and always had his back. Emilio was considering extending his tour six months, so he could remain with them until their tours were completed.

Just south of Đà Nẵng's wide bay was the 1st Marine Aircraft Wing's facility. From there, military installations sprawled westward about four miles to the hill mass of Division Ridge. To the immediate south and southwest of Đà Nẵng, rice paddies dominated the landscape, broken only by intermittent hills with thick tree lines and patches of brush. The entire area was dotted with hamlets and small villages. Thousands of grave mounds furnished the enemy cover and concealment, and numerous low hills provided the VC with sites for outposts and defensive positions. Innumerable streams and waterways intersected the coastal lowlands. They included Maj. rivers which flowed out of the mountains to the west and into the South China Sea. The Cu Đê River emptied into the Bay of Đà Nẵng north of the city. The Cầu Do River and the Hàn River encircled the city on the south and east and separated it from the Tien Sha Peninsula (called Danang East by Marines) and the helicopter base at Marble Mountain. The chopper base was actually located on the flat seashore north of the rocky outcroppings that gave the "mountain" its name.

De La Garza on patrol, 1970

On April 11, De La Garza was on a night patrol with his rifle squad near Marble Mountain. The Marines were 4 miles south of Đà Nẵng on their way back to base when they took hit and run gunfire from a group of Việt Cộng. The sun had just risen blood-red out of the South China Sea ("Red sky in the morning; sailor take warning!"). After the attack, the VC melted away into the scrub brush and morning mist. Pursuing the enemy, the Marine unit split up and spread out to search the dunes and tall grass where the enemy troops might be hiding.

De La Garza was accompanied by Tony Abbate, his ammo man, and Peterson, the squad leader. They were pursuing two men they had seen running toward a nearby pond. De La Garza thought he had spotted movement there, so they slowed their advance. The deep reservoir had a growth of thick grass and reeds around the edge and large masses of Vietnamese lotus floating on top of the water, with their delicate pink blossoms gracing the landscape. A thin layer of fog was suspended over the watery milieu, and Emilio could hear frogs croaking as he approached the pond. Handing his M60 to Abbate, the young Marine removed his Ka-Bar knife from its sheath and with knife in hand, he slipped into the murky water. He was sure he had seen someone or something stirring among the tall reeds and rushes at the water's edge.

Moving quietly, De La Garza eased his way around the side of the pond. Feeling his combat boots squish in the soft sticky mud on the bottom of the pool, he barely rippled the water as he moved. Then, without warning, he lunged into the reeds, disarming a young Vietnamese dressed in black, and taking him prisoner. As the VC was being brought to shore, he began to struggle and resist. Abbate and Peterson put down their weapons and waded into the pond to assist hauling the enemy soldier out of the water. Nearing the shore, the VC pulled out a hidden grenade and removed the firing pin. Only De La Garza saw him. Yelling "Grenade!" he threw himself on top of the enemy soldier and grabbed hold of the arm with the grenade, forcing both the soldier and the grenade back under the deeper water. There was a horrendous blast, knocking down Abbate and Peterson, and filling the pond with a turbulent mixture of mud, blood, and gore. Birds in the surrounding trees screamed in protest, and members of the rifle squad came running in response. Jimmy Huff and the squad "doc," Navy corpsman HM3 Sam Lyles were the first to reach the scene.

Huff, Lyles, and two other squad members quickly dragged Abbate, Peterson, and De La Garza out of the water. Abbate and Peterson were stunned from the blast but were basically uninjured. De La Garza's swift action had saved them from the grenade's blast and shrapnel. De La Garza was still breathing but had massive injuries to the back of his head. He was unconscious and bleeding profusely. Doc Lyles tried every trick he knew in his efforts to save the young Marine, but the wounds were too extensive and the trauma too great. Even if Lyles had time to get his patient to a hospital, survival was unlikely. Emilio died within minutes. It had been two days since he returned from Hawaii and his honeymoon with Rosemary.

HM3 Sammy "Doc" Lyles

On the evening of April 12, 1970, a military-green automobile with USMC insignia parked in front of the neatly kept house at 3608 Fir Street in East Chicago. Two Marine NCOs got out and walked to the door.

There was an enclosed porch on the front of the house and nine-year-old Lupito was there playing with his toy soldiers and GI Joes. The boy had heard the car engine stop and had peeked out through the Venetian blinds. He saw the dark green car, the Marines getting out, and walking toward the house, and his heart soared—

maybe it was Junior! But as the Marines neared the house, he realized both men were gringos.

"Mami," he called out, "*aye vienen alugunos* Marines!" (Mom, here come some Marines!)

Answering the door, Lupito stood staring at the tall sergeants in their dress blue uniforms. One of the Marines asked to speak to Mr. or Mrs. De La Garza, and Lupe's world would never be the same.

Only Carmen, Lupe, and a close family friend, Blanca Estella, were at the house when the Marines came. Papi had gone to a banquet and was not expected home until late. When Carmen saw the Marines, she screamed and began to wail before the men could speak to her.

"Mom knew," Lupe said. "She rarely watched the morning news. It was filled with news of the war, and she didn't want to see it, but that morning, she had turned it on. The newscaster had reported 'only one American casualty that day, a Marine,' and she had felt a sharp stab in her chest. She knew, and she began to weep and pray. She had spent most of the day in bed. The Marines coming to the house had confirmed what she already knew in her heart. She knew Junior was dead. Mom and Dad had gotten a letter from him only the day before." Junior had written the letter before meeting Rosemary in Hawaii.

Blanca Estella had gone to school with Junior and frequently helped Carmen with cleaning and laundry. Blanca knew Carmen had not felt well that day, and she was finishing the ironing in a back room when she heard Carmen scream. Running into the living room, she saw the two Marines, and Carmen was still wailing and moaning. Lupito was crying and trying to understand what had happened. Blanca helped Carmen to the couch and sat down with her, holding her in her arms. Lupito, still bewildered, sat next to his mother and clutched her arm as one of the Marine sergeants began to speak. And the news he brought was horrific beyond words.

Marine NCOs also arrived at the Rejón residence. Rosemary had only been back from Hawaii for forty-eight hours. She was still living with her parents. Baby Renee remained unwell and Abuela Rejón was helping to care for her. A suitcase remained on the floor next to the bed in Rosemary's room and had not been unpacked. The orchid lei Junior had given her was still in the refrigerator in a plastic bag. When the Marines told the family what had happened, Rosemary screamed and fainted. As she slowly regained consciousness, Papi Rejón helped Rosemary to her room. She was inconsolable and kept repeating, "How can this be? I just left him—I just left him." Abuela Rejón looked after Renee, who was crying, and Papi Rejón called the family priest, asking him to come to their home.

Blanca called a family friend and asked him to go find Papi De La Garza. He needed to come home immediately. Papi arrived a half-hour later. The Marine sergeants were still at the house, along with a few friends and neighbors. Papi went immediately to Carmen who was now standing in the center of the room. Attempting to console her, he tried to place his arm around her shoulders, but she rudely pushed him away. Standing ramrod straight, and glaring at him with tears coursing down her cheeks, she yelled, "*Es tu culpa, Emilio! Es to culpa que mijo murio!* [This is your fault, Emilio! It's your fault my son is dead!]" And with a final strangled scream, she added, "*¡Usted causó esto!*" (You caused this!) Then, with a glare of pure hatred, Carmen stopped, white faced and rigid. For a long moment, the house was deathly silent. Then she began to weave back and forth and fainted, falling to the floor.

All present, including the two Marines, were transfixed by the scene they had just witnessed. Papi and Blanca rushed to Carmen's aid and lifted her onto the couch. Then Papi backed away with a stunned look on his face. Ashen faced, the man was devastated. He was embarrassed, he was humiliated, he was hurt beyond measure, and he was grieving the death of his oldest son.

With tears in his eyes, Papi placed an arm around Lupito, moved across the room, and slumped down in an upholstered chair. Pulling the youngster onto his lap, he picked up the phone and called Dr. Nicosia, their family doctor. He explained what had happened and asked him to come as quickly as possible.

Papi suddenly felt very old. Kissing away the tears from Lupe's face, he hugged the boy in his grief and quietly rocked him in his arms.

A short time later, the sergeants made ready to leave. Always the gentleman, Papi De La Garza rose to see them to the door, and thanked them for coming. Then he went back to the phone, called his mother, Emilia, in Laredo, Texas, and told her about her grandson. That being done, he began calling extended family members in East Chicago with the terrible news.

Carmen had regained consciousness and Blanca helped her to the bedroom as they awaited the doctor's arrival. "Mom just kept moaning and praying," Lupe said. "She would yell out, '*Porque, porque te llevastes a mijo?*' [Why? Why did you take my son?] Then she would moan and pray again. It just went on and on. What a terrible, terrible night for all of us. The doctor finally arrived and gave Mom something to help her rest."

"I will always remember my big brother," Lupe continued. "I will never forget his last words to me at the airport when he left. He crouched down, tousled my hair, and looked me straight in the eyes. 'Lupe,' he said, 'you're the man of the house now. Take care of Mom and Dad.' Then I saw him walk on to the plane and wave at me from inside the plane. I never once thought I would never see him alive again. Man, I miss him so much."

A funeral mass was held at 9:30 a.m. on April 18, 1970, for Emilio De La Garza Jr. at Our Lady of Guadalupe Church on Deodar St. in East Chicago. The Reverend Father Peter Miller, SJC, officiated, and it appeared as if the entire city of East Chicago turned out for the service. The De La Garza family was well known and well respected for their charity work, and Emilio Sr. had become active politically.

Lupe said, "When I saw my brother in the coffin in his Dress Blues, he looked like he was sleeping. In my nine-year-old mind, I had to keep repeating to myself, '*Esta muerto. Esta muerto.*' [He's dead.] And my mother just kept crying and wailing. It was so horrible."

Burial followed at Saint John Saint Joseph Catholic Cemetery in Hammond, Indiana. Junior De La Garza was twenty years old.

PART 5

On September 9, 1971, Rosemary De La Garza, accompanied by Carmen, Lupe, and Emilio De La Garza Sr. were invited to the White House in Washington, DC. In a simple, dignified ceremony, VP Spiro Agnew presented Rosemary and Renee with Emilio's Medal of Honor. Carmen and Emilio Sr. were also presented with a Medal of Honor at the same ceremony.

VP Agnew, Rosemary Rejón De La Garza, Mr. and Mrs. Emilio De La Garza, Sr., 1971

For conspicuous gallantry and intrepidity at the risk of his life above and beyond the call of duty while serving as a machine gunner with Company E, 2nd Battalion, 1st Marine Division, in the Republic of Vietnam on April 11, 1970. Returning with his squad from a night ambush operation, Lance Cpl. De La Garza joined his Platoon commander and another Marine in searching for two enemy soldiers who had been observed fleeing for cover toward a pond. Moments later, he located one of the enemy soldiers hiding among the reeds. As the three Marines attempted to remove the resist-

ing soldier from the pond, Lance Cpl. De La Garza observed him pull the pin on a grenade. Shouting a warning, Lance Cpl. De La Garza placed himself between the other two Marines and the ensuing blast from the grenade, thereby saving the lives of his comrades at the sacrifice of his own. By his prompt and decisive action, and his great personal valor in the face of almost certain death, Lance Cpl. De La Garza upheld and further enhanced the finest traditions of the Marine Corps and the United States Naval Service.

Lance Cpl. De La Garza's additional awards included the Bronze Star Medal, the Purple Heart, the Combat Action Ribbon, the National Defense Service Medal, the Vietnam Service Medal with two bronze stars, and the Republic of Vietnam Campaign Medal w/1960 device.

Additional honors are as follows:

- Ten years after Emilio De La Garza's death, the School City of East Chicago dedicated a new building in honor of the hometown hero and product of the school system.
- Ivy Tech Community College at 410 E. Columbus Drive honored the memory and valor of De La Garza in 1994 by naming their campus "Lance Cpl. Emilio De La Garza Jr. Campus." A bronze bust of De La Garza graces the conference room at Ivy Tech.
- In 1995, to mark the twenty-fifth anniversary of Emilio's death, the City of East Chicago, Indiana, declared Sunday, April 22, 1995, as "Emilio De La Garza Jr. Day."
- In May 2011, a memorial plaque was dedicated to De La Garza and installed at the Edward P. Robinson Community Veterans Memorial in East Chicago.
- December 2011, De La Garza's name was enshrined on the South Shore Wall of Legends at the Indiana Welcome Center in Hammond, Indiana.

- East Chicago American Legion Post 508 was renamed in honor of Emilio A. De La Garza Jr.
- In 2013, the State of Indiana proclaimed June 23 as Emilio De La Garza Day.

EPILOGUE

ADIÓS, MI HERMANO. ADIÓS!

When Guadalupe Lee De La Garza, Emilio's younger brother, was old enough, he enlisted in the Marine Corps. "My brother told me never to enlist in the Army or the Marine Corps," Lee De La Garza says, "but the Air Force and Navy wouldn't take me. I was seriously overweight.

"One day in April 1978, I got a call from Sgt. Lopez, the USMC recruiter in East Chicago. I was a senior in high school, and he managed to get me to come into the office. My dad took me. My mom didn't know. She would never let me enlist in the Marines if she had her way. I wanted to join their Delayed Enlistment Program for pay purposes, as well as preparation for boot camp. I was only seventeen, so my parents had to sign for me. My mom refused, but I told her if she did not sign, I would enlist anyway as soon as I turned eighteen. I worked for the Lake County DOT that summer patching roads and hoped I would lose some weight. I was really fat. The last advice the recruiter told me was to never let the drill instructors know my brother had been awarded the MOH because it would make it harder for me.

"Fast forward—boot camp at MCRD San Diego was a nightmare. I was a fat body. Remember *Full Metal Jacket*? Well, that movie brought back bitter memories and tears. I was Pyle. That's how I was treated. I will never forget Drill Instructor Sgt. Marley. I literally wanted to put a bullet through his head. He was the most inhumane person I have ever met. I had no idea about his background, but I'm sure he did a tour or two in Vietnam.

"Somehow, Marley found out about my brother. I never knew how he found out, but he brought down a world of shit on me, both mental and physical. Marley never let up on me. He actually spit in my face each time he got 'up close and personal,' which was constantly. He was always shoving his fist into my chest during IT and frequently walked on my back in his combat boots when I was attempting push-ups. I didn't think I'd survive. Marley just punished the shit out of me. It went on and on, but I was determined he wasn't going to break me, and I survived.

"With God's angels looking over me—and maybe my brother too—I graduated from boot camp on December 6, 1978, and I became a Marine. Of the seven fat guys in Platoon 2077, only two of us made it through. My parents flew to San Diego for the ceremony, and they did not recognize me. I had lost thirty-five pounds, and the fat had been replaced with hard muscle.

"Before graduation, Marley had told us, 'When you introduce me to your parents and loved ones, you will address me as Drill Instructor Sgt. Marley. Is that understood? Not sarge or sergeant—*only* Drill Instructor Sgt. Marley. *Do you understand?*'

"Sir, yes, sir, Drill Instructor Sgt. Marley, *sir!*" we had all replied in perfect unison.

"My dad wanted to meet my drill instructors, so I introduced him to DI Marley. I walked him over to Marley, who was standing there with this shit-eatin' grin on his face. Marley stuck out his hand to my dad and said, 'Pleasure to meet you sir.' I said, 'Dad this is Sgt. Marley. He was one of my DIs. Then I looked Marley straight in the face and said, 'Well Sarge, have a good life. See ya! C'mon Dad, it's time to go home,' and I turned my back on that son-of-a-bitch.

"I didn't look back. I'm sure Marley shit his pants. I pictured him turning white in the face, and then red. I'd seen that ugly hate-filled mug in my face so many times. He was a real POS."

"That was boot camp," Lee continued, "I expected to be a 0311 grunt, but I did better than expected on my tests. My first duty station was at Camp Lejeune, North Carolina, and then I was sent to Twenty-nine Palms, California, for the Communication Center Main Course. After graduation, my unit was deployed on a NATO operation to Turkey. Then I was working communications on the USS *Iwo Jima* during the Iranian hostage crisis in November 1979.

Nineteen-year-old Lee De La Garza, 1979

"I worked comms on various ships: the USS *Barnstable County* in the Mediterranean, and the USS *Mt. Whitney*. I was meritoriously promoted to corporal and sent to Okinawa. I then moved to MCAS Yuma. I was meritoriously promoted to sergeant, sent back to Twenty-nine Palms for the Communication Center Chief Course, and trained to work in crypto. During my second enlistment, I returned to MCRD San Diego for recruiter's school and was sent to Minneapolis as a recruiter. That is where I received my honorable discharge. I served seven years in the Corps before I made the decision to return to civilian life. During the ensuing years, I worked as a 911 dispatcher, state police dispatcher, and for an Oregon sheriff's office. I retired after twenty-seven years in law enforcement and now work as an armed security officer for my church in Arizona.

"My mother, Carmen, passed away peacefully early in the evening of April 10, 2004. That would have been early in the morning of April 11, in Vietnam, the same day and approximately the same time my brother was killed thirty-four years before. She was eighty-one years old. She mourned my brother's death every minute of every day for thirty-four years. She and my father visited his grave every day, rain or shine, blizzard or heat wave—they were there. You may say it's just a coincidence she died at the same time as my brother, but I believe it was God's way of showing my mother He recognized the pain and suffering she had gone through by bringing her home on the same day He brought my brother home in 1970.

"Remembering past events and helping to write Junior's story has brought me a sense of peace I have not known since his death. After all these years, I still miss my big brother every day and I think of him every day. *Adiós, mi hermano, adiós.*"

Now the hacienda's dark, the town is sleeping;
Now the time has come to part, the time for weeping,
Vaya con Dios my darling,
May God be with you my love.

"Vaya con Dios"
Larry Russell/Inez James/Buddy Pepper

CHAPTER 3

SHARON ANN LANE

Y tá Thánh

1ˢᵗ Lt. Sharon Lane

Sharon Ann Lane was born on July 7, 1943, in Zanesville, Ohio. When she was two years old, her family moved to North Industry, a suburb of Canton, Ohio, when her father, John, took a job as a bull-dozer operator for a Canton construction company. Sharon attended North Industry Grade School along with her older sister, Judy, and younger brother, Gary.

"Growing up, Sharon was always caring for someone or something," her mother Kay said. "She always had a cat or dog or some animal she was caring for."

Sharon graduated from Canton South High School in June 1961, and it came as no surprise to anyone when she entered Aultman Hospital School of Nursing in September. After graduating in April 1965, Sharon went to work at the hospital and remained on staff there for two years.

In May 1967, Sharon was feeling restless and decided to join the business world. She enrolled at the Canton Business College but soon realized she had already found her true calling. She left after three quarters and joined the US Army Nurse Corps Reserve on April 18, 1968.

Sharon began basic training for Army nursing in May 1968 at Brooke Army Medical Center, Fort Sam Houston in San Antonio, Texas. She graduated on June 14, 1968, with the rank of second lieutenant. Three days later, she reported to Fitzsimons Army Hospital in Aurora, Colorado, where she began work in three outlying tuberculosis wards. While there, she was promoted to first lieutenant and sent to work in the cardiac division's intensive care unit and recovery room.

On April 24, 1969, Lane reported to Travis Air Force Base, California, with orders to proceed to Vietnam. She arrived at the 312th Evacuation Hospital at Chu Lai on April 29, 1969. The medical facility consisted of a series of large Quonset huts with a helipad, an emergency room, an X-ray unit, a prep ward, an operating room, a recovery room, and a quasi-intensive care unit. The complex also had separate wards for Vietnamese civilians, those with tropical diseases, and POWs. The hospital had between fifteen and twenty doctors, some forty nurses, and dozens of Army medics and Navy corpsmen who assisted with the patients. There were also additional support personnel working in supply, security, kitchen, pharmacy, and all departments required to operate a hospital. The Quonset huts were connected by a series of ramps, and there was no air-conditioning—only floor fans to stir the steamy air and provide a miniscule amount of relief.

312th Evac Hospital—Chu Lai

Constantly assaulted by the noise of US fighter aircraft flying in and out of a nearby airstrip, Lane and the other nurses routinely endured twelve-hour shifts, six days a week. They worked extremely hard in conditions that were physically and mentally taxing, and it was a grueling schedule under the best of circumstances. If there was a large influx of wounded GIs, they might work around the clock until the crisis was over.

Each of the nurses had a room in newly built quarters. Their uniforms consisted of lightweight, cotton poplin fatigues, cut in the most flattering style in an ever-popular shade of olive drab. The outfit was topped off by the decidedly unpopular Army baseball cap, combat boots and dog tags.

US servicemen who were wounded in Vietnam and were cared for by these Army nurses at in-country evacuation hospitals like the 312th in Chu Lai, or by Navy nurses on the USS *Sanctuary*, or USS *Repose* hospital ships, know how hard the nurses worked. They can also bear witness to the caring dedication the nurses gave to their patients.

Army and Marine Corps grunts had spent days, weeks, even months out on patrols, or search and destroy missions in jungle covered mountains in I Corps, or the Central Highlands, or slogging through rice paddies and jungle in the Mekong Delta. They had marched, eaten, and slept in mud up to their asses caused by days of monsoon rain. They had come face to face with the enemy and fought for their lives and the lives of their buddies. They had been wounded and evacuated to hospitals like the 312th.

For them, waking and seeing the faces of those nurses, hearing the tenderness in their voices and hearing their encouraging words, was like seeing and hearing angels. And there was also the luxurious feel and smell of clean sheets.

The nurses not only eased the pain of their injuries and began the care necessary for successful recovery; they also brought back a bit of home—a taste of the world the men had left behind before they entered the violence and mayhem that had become their daily way of life.

"We didn't just take care of their physical wounds," one nurse said. "We were their emotional support—their mother, their sister, their wife, their girlfriend. We listened a lot and did a lot of hand-holding, but that was comforting for both the patients and for us. We wanted and needed to be there for those guys. They had given so much."

The medical skill of the nurses and their dedication to the wounded was instrumental in making it possible for higher rates of the wounded in Vietnam to survive the often devastating injuries they were subjected to. Nurses like Lt. Lane and her coworkers were, in every sense of the word, angels to those who needed them the most.

US Army Nurses, Vietnam

When she first arrived, Lane worked in the intensive care ward with wounded US troops for a few days. Then, like most new personnel, she was given the unpopular assignment of working in Ward Four, the Vietnamese ward. Many of the Vietnamese civilians had diseases that compounded any war wounds they might have suffered. Adding to the unpleasant duty of working there was the fact that the ward was not on the sewer system, and many of the Vietnamese did not know how to use the "honey buckets" provided for human waste. The ward always reeked of urine and excrement. After a few weeks, Lane was scheduled to be transferred from Ward Four to a ward treating American soldiers, but she chose to remain where she was.

Lane's commander at Chu Lai said Sharon was a very gentle person, a very quiet person. A couple Viet Cong prisoners were being treated in the Vietnamese ward and that was a difficult experience for us because we were surrounded by our own young men who had been severely wounded by their high velocity weapons. The VC POWs were under guard and strapped to their beds, but sometimes they would kick, or spit, and try to bite the nurses. Most of the nurses didn't want to care for them, but Lt. Lane took their abuse with her usual compassion and good humor. She'd say, "It's a bad situation for them too."

Sharon's primary reason for remaining in Ward Four was caring for the sick and wounded Vietnamese children. Many of the children were Catholic, and so was she. The children watched Nurse Lane as she moved among them with her radiant smile and gentle manner, and unable to pronounce the name "Lane," they began to reverently regard her as "Y tá Thánh" (pronounced Yeeta-Thane: nurse saint or holy nurse). She loved the children, and they adored her.

"It made Sharon so sad to see the wounded children," Kay Lane said. "There was an eight-year-old boy who had been shot in the stomach, and a five-year-old girl who had almost bled to death because there were too many critical patients ahead of her waiting for surgery." Sharon could not bear to leave them as long as they needed her care.

"Y tá Thánh"

Lane usually worked her regular twelve-hour shifts for five days in Ward Four; and then, on the sixth day, volunteered to help care for the most severely wounded GIs in the post-surgical intensive care unit. Sometimes she took the seventh day off—sometimes, if needed, she worked.

She was called in to help care for the men wounded in the Battle of Hamburger Hill from May 10 to 20, 1969. The controversial battle resulted in American losses of seventy-two killed and 372 wounded, and it was "all hands on deck," twenty-four hours a day for two weeks. Nurses and doctors grabbed a couple hours of sleep whenever they could, but they never left the hospital. Sharon Lane spent the entire period working in intensive care.

Two weeks later, on June 4, 1969, Sharon wrote a letter home. She told her mother and dad, "Our unit has reached a milestone by treating its ten-thousandth patient since arriving in Vietnam last September. It's hard work, but we are proud of what we have accomplished."

"I start nights tomorrow," she wrote, "so I don't have to get up early in the morning. That's a nice thought. It will be great to sleep in past 5:00 a.m."

She continued, "It's still very quiet around here. We haven't gotten mortared for a couple of weeks now," and she ended her letter with her customary, cheery comment: "See you sooner!"

PART 2

On the following Sunday morning, June 8, 1969, everything changed. Lillian Gardner, one of Lane's fellow nurses lived a half-mile from the hospital with her husband, Maj. Curtis Gardner, who was an Army doctor. Lill was suddenly jolted awake by a powerful explosion that rattled the windows and sat her straight up in bed. Glancing at the alarm clock on her bedside table, Lill saw the time was 5:55 a.m. She quickly rose from the bed, ran to the door, and walked out onto the front porch of the apartment where they lived. The sun was breaking through the trees on the horizon, and the morning air was already warm and heavy. She saw many of her neighbors appear outside in their pajamas, looking up and down the street. In a few moments, Maj. Gardner sped up the narrow road in his jeep. He slid to a halt in a spray of gravel and red dirt and jumped out. He had been working a night shift at the hospital and informed her that a VC rocket had hit the hospital causing major damage and injuries. He told her to get dressed and they would go back to do whatever they could to help. Lill ran inside, dressed quickly, grabbed a pint bottle of orange juice from the fridge, hopped into the Jeep, and they headed for the hospital complex.

Army Sgt. Wesley Johns of the 23rd Military Police Company was the desk sergeant on duty at MP HQ-Chu Lai on the morning of June 8. "It had been a quiet night," Sgt. Johns said. "We'd had a brief shower during the night; there were patches of ground fog, and it was muggy as hell. I was due to finish my shift at 0700—then everything went to shit. The Cong fired a half-dozen rockets into Chu Lai from the mountains several miles away. I hit the siren, which was sounded whenever the camp was receiving incoming fire of any kind. The area around the hospital was sometimes pelted by VC rockets or mortars, so it wasn't that unusual, but they rarely ever hit anything. It was mostly just harassment. We've learned one of the rockets hit the hospital, and there're lots of injuries, including one of our MPs. He was on duty guarding POWs in the Vietnamese ward. There are both American and Vietnamese casualties. There's gonna be a shitstorm around here for the next few hours."

Soviet-built 122 mm rockets in Vietnam

Marine sergeant Jimmy Mack from Florence, South Carolina, was patrolling the Chu Lai perimeter with a platoon of his Marines when he heard the explosions. "Holy shit," Mack drawled. "We're used to gettin' pounded by mortars and f***in' artillery, 'n' shit, but this was right outa the blue, man. It had been quiet in the AO for weeks, and then those f***in' Cong rockets came out'a nowhere just as it was gettin' daylight. We hit the dirt, and then saw the fire and smoke at the hospital. There were sirens goin' off and horns blaring. We resumed our patrol and then heard later on the radio that one of the Army nurses had been killed. Man that is tough shit."

The big Marine grew silent and stared down at the ground. His mind seemed to wander for a moment and then gently touching the small gold cross around his neck, he whispered in a husky voice, "Those ladies work so damned hard to take care of us. It's just a f***in' shame to lose one like this. God bless 'em all!"

Part 3

Earlier that morning, Sharon Lane took a break from here duties. Glancing down at her Bulova "Clara Barton" nurse's watch, she saw the time was 5:40 a.m. Her father had given her the watch when she graduated from basic training at Brooke Army Medical Center. It had a white dial with luminous Arabic numerals, luminous hour and minute hands, and a red sweep seconds hand so she could accurately measure a patient's pulse. Looking at the watch always brought memories of her dad and a smile to her face. She could hear the soft snoring and deep breathing of her patients as she walked from Ward Four-A to the connecting hallway that led to Ward Four-B. The wide hallway contained a wooden desk, staff restroom, small supply room, two chairs, and the indispensible coffee maker.

Lt. Patsy Carlin, a fellow Army nurse from Kentucky, was seated at the desk filing some of the never-ending stream of paperwork the government required. "Sittin' on the Dock of the Bay" was playing softly on the radio from the AFVN FM station 99.9, broadcasting from atop Monkey Mountain. Navy corpsman, HM3 Cameron Simpson was seated in a chair across from the desk drinking a cup of coffee and wanting the final hour of this graveyard shift to end. He had the next day off. Simpson stood up when Sharon walked in. Nodding to her, the young sailor stepped to a window to observe the sunrise, which had just begun to appear through the trees.

Filling a mug with strong black coffee, Sharon spoke to Patsy and Cam and then strolled back into Four-A, sitting down on the edge of a vacant bed near the entrance. Suddenly she heard an explosion, followed by another and another, some distance away. Sharon jumped up, quickly switched on a light and ordered her Vietnamese patients to get under their beds, as was standard procedure in case of an attack. They would put mattresses and pillows over those in traction or unable to be moved. Those who spoke some English translated loudly for the ones who did not.

Then, with a blinding, earth-shattering roar, Sharon Lane's world exploded. Corpsman Simpson, who had headed into the ward to help, was blown back, crashing through the supply room door, unconscious. Lt. Carlin was somewhat protected by the heavy wooden desk. A 122mm Soviet rocket had struck right outside between Wards Four-A and Four-B.

Ward Four-A, 312 Evac Hospital
June 8, 1969

Maj. Brian Lipe was the first doctor on the scene. "I was heading over for a cup of coffee," Dr. Lipe said. "I heard the explosions and the siren. The building was shaking, but I couldn't tell where the rocket had hit. Then I was confronted by a frantic group of Vietnamese screaming and crying. I hurried on and saw Lt. Carlin crouched behind her desk. I took her arm and we tried to make our way into the devastated ward. Part of the roof had collapsed, and the area was filled with smoke from small fires that had sprung up in the area. It was a scene straight out of hell."

Base-wide sirens had sounded with the explosion of the first rocket, and any of the doctors, nurses, and other staff members who could leave had followed procedure, quickly grabbing their flak vests and helmets, and moving to the relative safety of nearby underground bunkers. Most of the rockets had missed the base, but one had found its mark and landed just outside the Vietnamese ward. When the "all clear" was signaled, staff members rushed to the scene and began the search for survivors.

"I responded to the rocket attack on the hospital," recalled PO Sammy Anderson. "I was assigned to the US Navy's Chu Lai Naval Support Activity, and was a fire truck captain (driver-pump operator). We'd had a member of the fire department badly burned during an emergency operation, so my men and I had been inside the hospital numerous times before they transferred our man to Japan for more extensive treatment. The hospital had also called upon us occasionally to wash blood out of the Med Evac helicopters with our fire hoses."

S. Sgt. Greg O'Leary was the supply sergeant at the 312th Evac. "There were a couple of medical personal in my hooch that worked in Ward Four at the hospital," O'Leary said, "so I had met Lt. Lane. The night before the attack, I was sitting with some of my friends in front of our hooch when Sharon walked by on her way to work. We called out to her, wished her a good evening, and she came over. We were drinking beer. I offered her a beer. She said she would take half a glass. That was unusual for a couple of reasons. Number 1, no one in our circle drank beer from a glass, and number 2, absolutely nobody drank half a beer, but Sharon was special, and she was getting ready to start a twelve-hour shift. I gave her the beer, and she sat down for a few minutes to chat with us. I usually took some sort of food up to Ward 4 during the night when my buddies were working the graveyard shift. That night I had a large can of raviolis, and I heated them up and took them to Ward 4. I don't know if Sharon ate any or not, but if she did, I hope she enjoyed it. She was one fine lady. When the attack began, we ran to the bunker out back of our hooch. Someone told us later that one of the rockets had hit Ward 4, so we ran up there. All we could see was a smoky, gaping hole where the hallway had been going into 4-A. It was awful."

"We responded immediately when the hospital was hit," PO Anderson continued. "When we arrived, nurses and doctors were already their helping people and doing all they could under terrible conditions. It was a disaster. We saw the nurses and corpsmen giving the absolute best care anyone could ask for, and some of those working had injuries of their own. It was a scene I'll never forget. We got the fires under control in short order and then began searching for survivors who were buried under the wreckage of what had been Ward 4-A. Most of the injured were Vietnamese civilians. Cam Simpson, the Navy corpsman who had crashed through the door, had a concussion, along with cuts and bruises from glass and shrapnel, but he was in fairly good shape, considering his proximity to the blast. Many of the injured were Vietnamese women and children. Most of their physical injuries were not critical, just cuts and bruises, but they were dazed and in shock from the rocket blast. We located an Army MP sergeant who had been guarding wounded VC POWs in the ward. The man was unconscious with head injuries and a broken arm, but he would survive.

"Then I spotted a nurse's uniform under some of the wreckage. Man, I was praying, but there was so much blood. Next to the body of the nurse was a small Vietnamese girl. Both of them had been struck by a barrage of shrapnel that had burst through the side of the Quonset hut, and both were dead. As my men and I removed the chunks of wreckage, I saw the name tag on the nurse's uniform. It was Lt. Sharon Lane. I had met Lt. Lane during previous visits to the hospital, but I didn't really know her. We had just shared a brief hello and a smile. She was always busy."

"I was nearby, so I went looking for Sharon," Jim Richards, said. "I was a doctor in the Intensive Care Unit, and we had worked closely together back in May during the Hamburger Hill operation. I had seen here earlier that night and knew she was on duty in the Vietnamese Ward. I often dropped by to see her during our nights on duty, and we'd had coffee together several times during our breaks. I fought my way through the mayhem, but I was too late. There was nothing I could do. I couldn't have done anything for her if I had been right beside her when she was hit. The shrapnel had struck her carotid artery and she was gone in seconds. You were a kind and gentle soul, Sharon Ann Lane. I'm so sorry you didn't stay with us in the ICU, but I guess it wasn't meant to be. God bless you, my friend. You were gone way too soon."

"I was on duty that day," Lt. Marge Wilde said, "and I remember the terror we all felt when we learned one of our own had been killed. As ICU nurses, we dealt with death all day every day, but somehow, I guess we all thought we were invulnerable—that it couldn't happen to one of us. Just because it had never happened before, we thought we were safe, but Sharon's death brought all of that false sense of security crashing down on our heads, and damn! It really hurt. Not just because we had lost a wonderful friend and coworker, but in a sense, we had also lost our virginity. We were no longer those sweet, young nurses who had volunteered to save the world. None of us would ever look at our job quite the same again. Sharon was not with the 312th long, but her life and her death impacted all of us dramatically."

Lt. Betsy Dolby, another 312th nurse, said, "Sharon's death brought the war closer to home for us. We were treating wounded GIs all day every day, but we [nurses] hadn't been hurt. When one of our own was killed, we were more understanding of how the GIs felt, who were losing buddies every day."

> *Just before 6:00 a.m. on the morning of 8 June 1969, an hour before the end of 1Lt. Sharon Ann Lane's twelve-hour shift, the enemy launched four to six rounds of 122mm Soviet rockets at the sprawling Chu Lai facility. Although most of the rockets went wide, one landed just outside the Vietnamese ward. Shrapnel injured twenty-seven patients and staff, and killed a twelve-year-old Vietnamese girl. Lt. Lane was trying to move patients to safer areas when a jagged piece of shrapnel from a rocket ripped through a Quonset hut wall and hit her in the throat, killing her almost instantly. Nurse Lane died less than a month before her twenty-sixth birthday; she had been in-country only forty-five days.*

A memorial service for Lt. Lane was held in the Chu Lai post chapel on June 10, 1969, with all hospital personnel attending who could possibly be available. On the following day, June 11, a Catholic requiem mass was held in her honor, which allowed many others to pay their respects.

Sharon Lane's funeral services in Canton, Ohio, were held on June 14, 1969. The funeral was followed by burial with full military honors at Sunset Hills Burial Park in North Canton, Ohio. Sgt. Sean Hampton said, "When I returned from Nam, I was selected to serve as a member of a team that traveled around the US performing military funerals for soldiers who had died in combat. Lt. Sharon Lane's funeral was one of the services I was called on to perform. My life has never been the same since that time. Her funeral was one of the most difficult, poignant, and heartbreaking events I took part in. My team and I were all battle-hardened GIs, who had seen more than our share of death, but it was all we could do to hold it together during that service. We struggled to keep our emotions in check during the entire ceremony and did not dare look at the Lane family.

Lt Lane's awards included the Bronze Star with "V" device for valor, the Purple Heart, the National Defense Service Medal, the Vietnam Service Medal with one bronze campaign star, the Vietnam Military Merit Medal, and the Republic of Vietnam Campaign Medal. She was also awarded the Vietnamese National Order of Vietnam Medal (Knight), the Vietnamese Gallantry Cross with Palm by the Republic of Vietnam (South Vietnam).

PART 4

In the years following Sharon Lane's death, many institutions, groups, and organizations honored her in a variety of ways:

- On November 11, 1969, the Fitzsimons Hospital named its recovery room the "Lane Recovery Suite" and placed a plaque and her photograph on display.
- Daughters of the American Revolution named her "Outstanding Nurse of the Year" 1969.

85

- In 1970, Lane was posthumously presented the Dr. Anita Newcomb McGee Award by the National Society of Daughters of the American Revolution.
- In 1973, a seven-foot bronze statue of First Lt. Lane was dedicated in front of Aultman Hospital in Canton, Ohio. A plaque at the base reads, "Born to honor, ever at peace," and contains the names of 110 local servicemen who died in Vietnam.
- In 1986, Aultman Hospital opened the "Sharon Lane Woman's Center" in its front lobby.
- The Canton Chapter of the Vietnam Veterans of America officially changed its name to the "Sharon Lane Memorial Chapter #199."
- Roads in Denver, Colorado, and at Fort Belvoir, Virginia, were named in her honor.
- VFW Post 11920 in Evans, Georgia, was named the First Lt. Sharon A. Lane Memorial Post.
- In 1995, the volunteer center at Fort Hood, Texas, was named after Sharon Lane
- In 2001, the medical library in Evans Army Community Hospital at Fort Carson, Colorado, was named the Sharon A. Lane Medical Library.
- In 2002, a medical clinic for women and children, built by the Sharon Ann Lane Foundation in Chu Lai (Tam Hiep Commune), Vietnam, was dedicated as the "Sharon Ann Lane Clinic." It was paid for by Vietnam veteran nurses in Sharon's memory.
- In 2003, First Lt. Lane was inducted into the Ohio Military Hall of Fame in Columbus, Ohio and awarded the Ohio Medal of Valor.
- In January 2019, a new exhibit about Lane was put up at the US Army Medical Department Museum at Joint Base San Antonio-Fort Sam Houston.

A total of ten American military nurses (including two male nurses) lost their lives in the Vietnam War, and their names now appear on the Vietnam Veterans Memorial Wall in Washington, DC. Nine were in the Army, and one was in the Air Force.

The nurses died of various causes, including accidents and a stroke, but Sharon Ann Lane is the exception. She will be remembered most because she was the only American military woman killed as a direct result of enemy fire throughout the twenty-year war in Vietnam. First Lt. Lane was also the only US servicewoman to be awarded a Bronze Star with the *V* for valor decoration on the ribbon. You can rest in peace, Sharon Ann Lane. You will not be forgotten.

With scrutiny calm, and with fingers
Patient as swift
They bind up the hurts and the pain-writhen
Bodies uplift,
Untired and defenseless; around them
With shrieks in its breath
Bursts stark from the terrible horizon
Impersonal death;
But they take not their courage from anger
That blinds the hot being;
They take not their pity from weakness;
Tender, yet seeing;
Feeling, yet nerved to the uttermost;
Keen, like steel;
Yet the wounds of the mind they are stricken with,
Who shall heal?
What song shall be worthy to sing of them
Braver than the brave?

"The Healers"
Laurence Binyon

EPILOGUE

HONORING VIETNAM WAR NURSES

The Vietnam Women's Memorial commemorates two hundred sixty-five thousand women who served our country during the war. Many served as nurses—all deserve our respect.

Every nurse that served in Vietnam left a part of themselves there. It never occurred to anyone in the 1960s and 1970s that a nurse could suffer "battle fatigue," when she was nowhere near a battlefield. After all, they were just nurses. But the "battles" they fought every day and night during those interminable twelve-hour shifts were every bit as real as those on the actual battlefield. The nurses were tasked with caring for thousands of horribly wounded and disfigured GIs who were really no more than boys. The average age of the soldiers, sailors, and Marines they treated was nineteen years old. Many of the men had never experienced actually making love or falling in love with someone and might have lost any chance they had at leading a happy and fulfilled life. For those young nurses, whose average age was just over twenty-three, it was heartbreak. The emotional toll was devastating. A 2012 VA study estimated 25 percent of the nurses who served in Vietnam were left with long-term post-traumatic stress disorder (PTSD).

"The wounds we saw were beyond words," one nurse said, "just horrendous. An arm blown off, or a leg blown off, or a face blown off was not something one would see in a civilian hospital, and it wasn't something you could be prepared for. No amount of training could prepare us in advance for what we saw every day."

And after they returned from Vietnam and were discharged, female nurses were completely ignored by the government they had so faithfully served—especially when they sought to apply for veteran's benefits. Legally, women veterans were eligible for the same benefits as male veterans but often found VA hospitals were unable to care for women. The VA contended there were so few female Vietnam veterans; there was no need for special facilities and programs for them. Women accounted for 2 percent of the total veteran population, so there were thousands of women not receiving the services they needed and deserved. Numerous VA studies were conducted on the needs of Vietnam veterans; however, none of the studies included women.

The US government was not the only entity that ignored the plight of women veterans. Organized veteran support groups ignored them too. The VFW (Veterans of Foreign Wars) did not allow women to become full members until 1978 (decades after some had served), and it took the Vietnam Veterans of America (VVA) several years after that. Mental health research now indicates combat nurses were still experiencing PTSD symptoms such as severe depression and multiple physical problems even thirty years after their time in Vietnam. There were probably several reasons why they continued to suffer, the primary one being they were ignored for the first ten to twenty years after the war when they could have had psychological therapy. Secondly, many of the nurses still harbored feelings of guilt about the men they had failed to save and wondered what they could have done better to change the outcome. They had the same "survivor's guilt" as combat veterans who returned from a battle alive when their buddies did not. And finally, there were feelings of shame associated with such an unpopular war. Most were not comfortable telling people they had served in Vietnam, fearing retribution or condemnation for their service, even from family members. The combat nurses wanted and needed recognition and gratefulness from their country. They needed to know that their selfless and dedicated service to their nation was honored and appreciated in order for them to put those experiences behind them, and it took far too long for them to receive it.

CHAPTER 4

PAUL WAYNE ANTHONY

Carolina Boy

Paul Anthony

The aunts and cousins loved to see Paul Wayne come to South Carolina in the summertime. His visit was always the high point of their summer.

"He was cute as a button," his Aunt Maggie said. "He was such a delightful child and had such nice manners."

"He visited our home many times when he was a young boy," Cousin Elizabeth, said. "We all remember that blond-haired, blue-eyed little boy that had such a gentle, kind nature. He had such a sweet spirit about him."

Paul Wayne loved those summers—warm, carefree days spent playing under the moss-draped live oaks; sipping cold glasses of tart lemonade and sweet tea; taking weekend trips to the sandy beaches where he and his brother, Buddy, bedeviled their sisters, Martha, Mary Elizabeth, and Patty, along with their cousins. The boys would drag out whatever gross things they could find among the driftwood and chase the girls through the dunes. The children spent hours looking for fossil sharks teeth in the surf and chasing hermit crabs. Those were good days, creating memories for a lifetime, and the children thought they would never end, but of course they did. "We all grew up," Elizabeth said wistfully.

Paul Anthony was born and raised in Charlotte, North Carolina, and his mother, Willie Mae, made sure he knew how to behave in public. Good manners could be the key to success for him, especially in the South, and she wanted to give him every advantage. Paul's father, John, had died of a heart attack when Paul was six years old. His older brother, John Jr., known as Buddy, was fifteen.

Highly intelligent, Paul performed well in high school with little effort, and after graduation, he enrolled at the University of North Carolina-Charlotte. Upon completion of his freshman year, Paul was unsure what he wanted to do with his life. He was bored with school but knew if he dropped out he would be drafted. He was certain he did not want that. Several of his friends had received draft notices, and Paul was feeling pressured to act. After careful consideration, he elected not to return to college in the fall of 1968 and enlisted in the US Air Force.

During basic training at Lackland AFB in San Antonio, Texas, Anthony was subjected to an intensive battery of tests. He had no idea what he was being tested for, but every few days, he was pulled out of whatever activity his flight (company) was involved in and sent to take more tests. After completion of basic, he was informed he had been selected for Air Force Security Service. He would never know what it was like to be in the "real" Air Force.

Composed primarily of airmen culled from the cream of the thousands of Air Force enlisted recruits (the top half of the top one percent), USAFSS was a tight-knit, top-secret command which operated under the direct authority of the National Security Agency (NSA). Its members had the highest security clearances issued by the FBI (Top Secret—"Code Word") and were tasked with monitoring, collecting, and interpreting ELINT—the military communications (voice and electronic signals) of "countries of interest." The intelligence which Security Service operatives collected was often analyzed in the field and the results transmitted directly to NSA for further analysis and distribution to other intelligence recipients who had "the need to know."

During his first year in the Air Force, while undergoing training at Sheppard AFB in Wichita Falls, Texas, Paul met a special young lady and they fell in love. Sgt. Carol Sanderson outranked her fiancé by one stripe, but rank was not as significant in Security Service as in regular branches of the military. Officers and NCOs worked side by side with their enlisted coworkers and frequently socialized together when off duty or were involved together in on-base sports and clubs. It did not take long for each to realize they had found someone special. Paul took Carol Ann home to meet his family in Charlotte and traveled to northern Ohio to meet her parents. The two were wed on Saturday, January 10, 1970.

After a year of intelligence analysis schools and other training, the time arrived for Anthony to deploy to his foreign assignment. He was assigned to the "Tigers" of the 6924th Security Squadron (USAFSS) at Danang Air Base, Vietnam. He hated leaving Carol Ann, but they had known from the beginning he would go overseas. There was only one Security Service base in the US, Goodfellow AFB in San Angelo, Texas, and it was primarily a training base for teaching technical foreign language to voice-intercept operators. If you were in Security Service, you worked in a foreign country, intercepting and analyzing intelligence for NSA.

Arriving at the 6924th on April 4, 1970, Paul had a couple of days to get settled in and meet the men he would be working with. The barracks were broken up into cubicles, with open air circulation at the floor and ceiling, and two or three men in each "cube." Paul was assigned a recently vacated bunk by the door and unpacked his bags. This would be his home for the next long year.

Eddie Brower was one of the airmen who lived in Paul's barracks. "The first week of April 1970, I was about half-way through my one year assignment," Brower said. "We saw men rotate in and out of our unit on a regular basis. Upon an airman's arrival, he would be shown around and introduced to members of the squadron. I'll never forget Paul Anthony's big smile, his extended handshake, and his outgoing personality when he came into my cubicle. He was just a great guy. We were both from the Carolinas and we'd both gotten married immediately prior to coming into the unit. He was four days younger than me. Both of us were twenty years old on that hot day in Southeast Asia, and we were fifteen thousand miles from home."

Anthony outside his barracks Danang Air Base, South Vietnam

Paul was introduced to "Da" and "Mou," the "mama-sans" who polished the airmen's boots and washed their clothes. The two Vietnamese ladies spoke little English, but each airman knew if they called him "number 1," it meant they liked him; however, if they called him "number 10," he was in big trouble. It was always beneficial to be in their good graces. They would cook awful-smelling lunches, usually consisting of fish-head soup, over an open fire outside at midday. The airmen all tried to stay downwind or far away at lunch time.

There was a beer hut right outside the barracks. At night, the off-duty men would pop fresh popcorn, sit outside drinking warm beer, and watch the Air Force gunships work Việt Cộng and NVA positions around Đà Nẵng. It was like some sort of surrealistic movie and difficult for Paul Wayne to believe he was actually watching real warfare.

Anthony received his share of kidding about being the new guy. One of the typical pranks was for an "old" guy to climb up the telephone pole, which was outside the door where Paul's bunk was located. At the top, the veteran airman would attach a telephone receiver to the line. He would then pretend he was talking to his wife or mom at home. There would be about four or five more men at the bottom yelling, "Time's up! It's our turn!" When the new guy showed up and asked what they were doing, the old-timers would "be nice" and let him go to the head of the line to be the next lucky one to shinny up the pole and call home. When the "nug" reached the top and tried to talk, one could hear the laughter and good-natured ribbing from a block away.

As usual, Paul Wayne took everything in stride with his bright smile and good humor. No one knew him well, but it was impossible not to like him, so they were pretty easy on him. Ironically, most of those doing the teasing had only been in-country two or three months. The real "old-timers" who had been there six or eight months were more sympathetic. Paul asked Ron Crews, one of his bunk mates, to take his photograph by the bunker outside their barracks. He wanted a photo to send to Carol Ann and his family. He knew they were worried about him.

The "newbie" was taken into the top-secret communications center where he would be working and shown around the area. His work site would be the "delivery window" on the "mids" (midnight) shift to start, and he was warned about the meal he would be served in the early hours of the morning: "On the night shift, we get two choices of entrees—bologna with stale bread or olive loaf with stale bread."

"I've always loved olive loaf," he drawled in his soft Carolina accent. His blue eyes twinkled, and he broke into a wide grin. Anthony was going to be a great addition to Team Tiger.

Anthony reported for duty at midnight on April 7, and was still being introduced to those he had not met. With the twenty-four-hour operation and rotating days-off, it would take time for him to meet everyone. He was introduced to Ken "Wiz" Wizinski who worked in the room next to his, and they joked about his time in-country and "enjoying his tour of duty."

About 2:15 a.m., Paul was talking to Sgt. Ralph Joseph. "I came on for the midnight shift," Joseph said. "It was a slow night, and we were shooting the breeze—getting to know each other. We heard a big explosion. The first round hit down the road from us. The second round hit, and I was on my way to the floor. The third round exploded about twelve feet from us." Then everything went black.

The third rocket, a Soviet-made 140mm BM-14 with a high-explosive fragmentation warhead blew in the side of the communications center office. The building was fortified with rows of sandbags and barrels filled with rock, but the rocket blast was so powerful, it penetrated the defenses, filling the main office with flames and a blast of deadly shrapnel, rock fragments, sand, and building debris.

Fortunately, most of the personnel on duty had hit the deck at the sound of the first explosion, but the scene within the smoke-filled room was total chaos. Sirens were screaming, men were yelling, all lights had gone out when the building exploded, and the offices were plunged into complete darkness. The only light came from flickering fires amid the thick, acrid smoke that added to the hellish milieu.

Danang Marine Air Group Navy corpsmen who were based nearby rushed to the scene to assist the blast victims. Air Force Security Service compounds were some of the most secure, top-secret facilities in South Vietnam. The elite Air Police sentries who guarded them were crack shots and had standing orders to shoot anyone who tried to breach their defenses without proper clearance, but the corpsmen ignored the warning signs and climbed over the barbed wire enclosures. They entered the classified area at great risk to themselves, but their assistance was badly needed. The guards knew it and held their fire, allowing the medics inside.

Fighting their way through the wreckage, the corpsmen helped the dazed and battered airmen out of the building and worked their way toward the epicenter of the blast. Moving aside the shattered remains of wiring, insulation, broken tables, chairs, file cabinets, top-secret radio intercept equipment, and highly classified material, the corpsmen reached the last few victims.

Wiz Wizinski had been working in an adjoining room and was found unconscious under his toppled worktable. Ralph Joseph had been with Anthony and was severely injured. He was bleeding extensively from shrapnel wounds, had serious burns, and was unconscious. Paul Anthony had suffered massive chest injuries and was dead. He had been in Đà Nẵng three days.

"I was in the room right next to Paul when the rocket hit," Wizinski said later. "We were all totally shocked when we heard he was killed. A couple of days later, a memorial service was held for Paul in the base chapel. It was a very somber and moving event. We had lost one of our own, and it was his first day on the job. So young, so many years lost. I'll never forget the tremendous sorrow we felt that day."

Ron Crews, who had taken Paul's photograph, said, "I don't think any of us will ever forget the night Paul was killed or the following few days. The war touched us all that night. Each of us will carry those feelings for the rest of our lives."

Patrick Sutton had returned to the 6924th for his second tour and sat next to Paul on the flight to Vietnam. "I felt like a big brother," he said. "We lost a fine young man that night."

Ralph Joseph was rushed to a nearby naval hospital and later medevaced to the States. His injuries were so extensive he was medically retired after months of surgeries and rehabilitation.

For Paul's wife, Carol Ann, the news of his death was beyond comprehension. They were still newlyweds. They had known he was heading into a combat zone, but their mutual agreement had been that he would come home to her. Carol was scheduled to be transferred to Hawaii in August, and the two had planned to meet there for a second honeymoon. The idea that he would die three days into his Vietnam tour was not part of the deal. "No!" she screamed. "No, no, no, no, no, no…"

Paul's entire family was devastated by his death. It was as if a light in their lives had suddenly been extinguished, and only darkness prevailed.

"Paul loved life and lived life to the fullest each day of his short twenty years," his sister Martha recalls. "You will always be my little brother."

Leoramae Sanderson, Paul's mother-in-law said, "Paul had been married to our daughter for eighty-eight days when he was killed on his first night of duty in Danang. Our family and his family in Charlotte were just shattered by this tragic loss. He was such a wonderful young man."

Funeral services for Amn 1st Class Paul Wayne Anthony were held on April 14, 1970, at McEwen Funeral Chapel in Charlotte. The service was conducted by an Air Force chaplain, assisted by Dr. Henry Pressly, minister of Tabernacle Associate Reformed Presbyterian Church. Those attending were Paul's wife, Sgt. Carol Ann Sanderson Anthony, Offutt AFB, Nebraska, Carol Ann's parents, Kirk and Leoramae Sanderson, Broadview Heights, Ohio, Paul's mother and stepfather, Mr. and Mrs. James A. Lipe, Fort Mill, South Carolina, sisters, Mary Elizabeth, Martha Jane, and Patricia Irene, and brother, Joseph "Buddy" Anthony, along with a large number of additional family members and friends. The funeral was followed by a graveside service with full military honors at Evergreen Cemetery in Charlotte. Paul was buried next to his father, Joseph D. Anthony Sr., who was a veteran of WWI.

"Paul was gone before we really got to know him," fellow Carolinian Eddie Brower said. "I'll always remember the sights and sounds of that attack. Years later I visited his mother who was abiding in an assisted living facility in Gastonia, North Carolina. When I met her, I told her about that terrible night and about the memorial service that was held for Paul in the chapel. Finally, I asked her if I could hug her neck. With a slight smile, she said softly, 'Yes, of course.'

While hugging her, I just lost it. I broke down completely. Tears filled my eyes and I cried for Paul and all the other guys I had known who had died over there so needlessly. I had held all that emotion deep inside of me for years. With tears in her eyes, Willie Mae patted me on the back while hugging me and said, 'Don't cry, son. Don't cry. I'm just so thankful you are here and so grateful you have come to see me.' I still get tears in my eyes recalling her kindness. Other members of Paul's family told me my coming there was the closest thing to Paul coming home they could have wished for or experienced. They were so thankful I had made the trip."

Down on the Lumbee River
Where the eddies ripple cool
Your boat, I know, glides stealthily
About some shady pool.
You will not, will you, soon forget,
When I was one of you,
Nor love me less that time has borne
My craft to currents new.
Nor shall I ever cease to share
Your hardships and your joys,
Robust, gentle-hearted
Sunburnt boys.

"Sunburnt Boys"
~John Charles McNeill

Members of the 6924th Security Squadron Association established The Paul Wayne Anthony AFROTC Scholarship at the University of North Carolina-Charlotte. "Paul will never be forgotten by the Tigers of the 6924th Security Squadron, USAF Security Service He was the only member of our unit to die due to enemy fire during the Vietnam War."

Paul Anthony's awards included the Purple Heart Medal, Vietnam Service Medal, Republic of Vietnam Campaign Service Medal, and the National Defense Service Medal.

99

CHAPTER 5

HENRY NICHOLAS HEIDE II

The Shadow of His Smile

Henry Heide

On November 28, 1969, a "Project Left Bank" Huey helicopter with the callsign *Jaguar Yellow* was shot down by ground fire near LZ Buttons in Phước Long Province, South Vietnam. All four American crewmen on board were killed. The crew was assigned to the 1st Cavalry Division, and its mission was ARDF (Airborne Radio Direction Finding). The Army Security Agency team was attempting to locate the transmitters of enemy units threatening the 1st Cavalry's area of operations. *Jaguar Yellow* was the first Army Security Agency flight crew to die in Vietnam.

Among the dead in that destroyed helicopter was a young man named Henry Nicholas Heide II. Henry was one of those bright lights who might appear only once in a lifetime—one of those young men who is remembered decades later by even the most casual acquaintances for his kindness, his intelligence, the immediate rapport they felt with him, his striking appearance, and especially his smile, which would light up any room he walked into. For those who really knew him, Henry's death was a life-altering event of tragic proportions.

Henry Heide was born in Hollywood, Florida, on December 23, 1948. He was the perfect Christmas gift and the firstborn son of Walter and Evelyn Moore Heide. He joined a two-year-old sister, Carole Marie, and a younger brother, Carl Frederick, would come along in 1950.

Henry attended Catholic parochial schools in Hollywood, including Chaminade High School, an all-male college prep school through his sophomore year. His parents then enrolled him in South Broward High School for his junior and senior years. Highly intelligent, he made decent grades in high school with little effort. He was president of his junior class, vice president of his senior class, and vice president of the Future Business Leaders of America Club his senior year. His steady girlfriend was Susan Wilson, and they enjoyed an active social life. Everyone at South Broward knew Henry and Susan. After graduating in 1967, Henry enrolled in Broward County Junior College. He was not that interested, but the college was nearby, and it was the "expected" thing for him to do. He was soon bored; however, and dropped out of college after one semester.

Henry yearned for something different, a path that would challenge him and stimulate his interests more than the traditional academic route. Knowing he would soon be drafted without a college deferment, he talked to an Army recruiter and took a series of aptitude tests. Henry scored high marks on the exams and the recruiter suggested there might be a course of action for him not available to most of those who enlisted.

In a "hush-hush" voice, the sergeant explained, "There is a top-secret Army group affiliated with one of the most secretive government organizations." He made the group sound "mysterious" and on the forefront of "emerging technologies."

"This unit only accepts the cream of the crop," the recruiter continued. "Only the top 10 percent are considered. Those who qualify sign a four-year contract, but the best news is once these men are trained, they are so valuable to the government. They're never sent to Vietnam."

Needless to say, Henry was sold. He drove home and discussed what the recruiter had told him with his parents and Susan. Henry's parents were not enthusiastic about him enlisting. They were both WWII Army veterans. Walt had served from 1940 to 1945, being discharged as an artillery sergeant, and Evelyn had served as a WAC, but the Vietnam War had become so controversial. They were concerned about Henry's involvement. Both, however, agreed—enlistment was better than waiting around to be drafted. He might have some choice about his training and where he served. Henry enlisted in March with their reluctant blessing and, a few weeks later, left for basic training at Fort Jackson, South Carolina.

Within his basic training company, there were a dozen soldiers destined for assignment to the Army Security Agency. Always a capable athlete and quick-learner, Heide was named "Outstanding Soldier" in his training company. After eight weeks, he and his fellow ASA prospects were shipped to Fort Devens, Massachusetts, to learn their special skills at the ASA Training Center. Henry's MOS was 05H20, EW/SIGINT Morse Interceptor (Electronic Warfare/ Signal Intelligence Morse Interceptor). Known as "Ditty Boppers," Henry and his classmates would be trained to intercept and transcribe enemy Morse code communications. The nine-month course was the biggest challenge Henry Heide had ever tackled.

"We started learning Morse code," Henry said, "and it was tough. We put the headsets on, and for eight hours a day, five days a week, all we listened to was dash, dash, dot, dot. After a few days of that, we dreamed Morse code at night. There were many that washed out. They couldn't handle the Morse. We also had several who failed the FBI security clearance investigation. Some of those who washed out stayed in ASA if they had received their security clearances, but they served as MPs or cooks. One of several things the recruiters neglected to tell us was that the four-year obligation to the Army was still in place, even if we flunked out. And the never-sent-to-Vietnam thing? Well, that wasn't exactly true either."

Heide finished the 05H basic course at Devens near the top of his class in mid-March 1968 and was named "Soldier of the Month." After Fort Devens, Henry and his classmates boarded a military flight at Logan Airport in Boston, and flew to Travis AFB, north of San Francisco, California. At Travis, the group was transported by Army bus to Two Rock Ranch Station, just a few miles from Petaluma, California.

313th ASA Battalion, Two Rock Ranch Station, California.

Two Rock Ranch Station had been established during WWII by the Army's Signal Intelligence Service to serve as an intelligence gathering station during the war in the Pacific. Along with Vint Hill Farms, its sister station on the East Coast, TRSS played a pivotal role in eavesdropping on enemy communications during the war years.

After the war ended, the two sites became field stations of the Army Security Agency, a subordinate of NSA. ASA conducted signals intelligence operations there and trained radio-intercept operators, cryptanalysts, and radio-repair technicians. Henry Heide and his fellow 05H trainees received four weeks of radio intercept training at Two Rock Station before being deployed to their overseas assignments.

Completing his intercept training in April, Henry caught a military transport to San Francisco International Airport. From there, he would fly TWA to Chicago O'Hare and Eastern Air Lines nonstop Chicago to Miami. He had thirty days leave before deploying to Vietnam.

Military uniforms were not recommended for travel. The anti-war protestors and left-wing media had been at full hue and cry since the Tet Offensive the year before, and the commander at Two Rock advised all of those going on leave to wear "civvies."

"It was cool in San Francisco with a chilly breeze," Henry said, "but I knew it would be warm in South Florida, so I dressed accordingly. The bus driver allowed us to change into our civilian clothing on board the bus so we could avoid being harassed in the terminal. San Fran and LA were two of the worst places in the country when it came to protestors attacking GIs. There were five of us. We all had civilian-looking baggage, which we checked out front with the skycaps, and then we split up. There was less chance of being ID'd as military if we were alone."

Henry was wearing a pair of plaid Ralph Lauren slacks, a pale blue cotton shirt with a narrow brown tie and a tan linen jacket. Tassel loafers completed his civilian costume. He had also allowed his hair to grow a bit longer than usual, so he appeared to be a student from one of California's exclusive private schools.

"I strolled along like I owned the world, and no one bothered me," Henry said. "I had a leather portfolio with my paperwork in it. Of course it was early. My departure time was 6:00 a.m., and we were there at 4:45. It was too early for the hippies to be out. Most were sleeping off their weed and wine from the night before. They might make it up to protest by midafternoon."

Henry checked in at the TWA counter and found his boarding gate. He then picked up a cup of dark-roast coffee and a croissant from Tartine's pastry counter and proceeded to the gate.

Arriving early at Miami International Airport, Evelyn Heide parked her car and strolled into the terminal. She walked up to the Eastern Air Lines ticket counter, searched for Henry's flight number, and noted the gate where it would be arriving. EAL Flight 73 was ahead of schedule and expected to arrive at 10:20 a.m.—in about forty-five minutes. Mrs. Heide presented her ID card and was escorted into the Ionosphere Club, Eastern's VIP lounge. She happily accepted a white porcelain demitasse cup of hot Café Cubano, which a hostess brought by on a silver tray. It was already eighty degrees outside, but the small cup of strong, sweet Cuban espresso always brought a smile to her face. Evelyn was enjoying the cool quiet atmosphere and soft Latin music emanating from somewhere inside the club. Opening her leather clutch, she removed a pack of Marlboros and a small lighter. Lighting a cigarette, she turned the silver lighter over in her hand and looked at the engraving on the side of it: LOVE HENRY—1968. Henry had sent it to her for her birthday in August. She could see the gate area through the tall tinted windows and would wait there in comfort for the arrival of her son's plane. Evelyn flew frequently on business. She was purchasing manager for one of the nation's leading manufacturers of equipment for pleasure boats and yachts, so she traveled to major boat shows from coast to coast and beyond.

As Henry's flight taxied in toward the gate, he was increasingly excited. He had not seen his family in over a year. It was Friday, so his father should be home for the weekend. Walter also traveled but had promised Henry he would see him at dinner tonight. Henry knew his mother would be waiting for him in the terminal. His brother, Fred was a senior at South Broward, his sister Carole was a senior at Florida State, and Susan was away at Marymount College in Boca Raton. He had just received a letter from her suggesting plans for the weekend.

Henry was the first person off the Eastern plane and walked into the terminal searching eagerly for his mother. Waving to get his attention, Evelyn moved through the throng of people meeting the flight and embraced her son.

"Henry," Evelyn said laughing, "I do believe you have grown." Admiring the way he was dressed, she said, "You look wonderful."

Unable to speak, Henry looked back at his mother with tears in his eyes, and then broke into a dazzling smile. Holding his arms, Evelyn moved her son out at arm's length to take a better look—then shaking her head, she said, "Wow!"

Henry Heide II

Henry enjoyed his time at home. Susan and most of his other friends were away at college, but his parents had made plans to take vacation days and spend as much time with him as possible. He played tennis with his mother and met his dad for golf at Orangebrook Golf and Country Club near their home. Henry had always been a good athlete, and he came by it naturally. On the weekends, he had a chance to hang out with Fred and Carole by their pool. Susan also came home on weekends; they saw movies (*Goodbye, Columbus* with Ali MacGraw and *Mackenna's Gold* with Gregory Peck) and spent time on Hollywood Beach. It was good to be home and relax with his family.

As the time drew nearer for Henry to leave, he became more introspective. Susan and Carole were away during the week and Fred was in school during the day. He began to spend time alone in his room. He gave away some of his most prized possessions to friends and relatives. He even took his pair of Florida kingsnakes to the Berman Wetland Preserve, a few miles from the house, and set them free. He'd had the snakes for years, and they were nearly five feet long.

He confided to a cousin he'd had a dream in which he died in Vietnam, and his parents were never able to find out the true story of what had happened to him. Walter and Evelyn were simply informed by the government their son was missing and would not be coming home. The dream weighed heavily on him. He could not get it out of his mind and could not tell his mother.

Evelyn was not sorry to see the kingsnakes go, but she was increasingly concerned about Henry's state of mind. It was not normal for him to be quiet and morose. She missed his smile and his sunny disposition. After dinner one evening, Henry and his mother were alone on the patio by the pool. Evelyn had brought out flutes of pinot gris, and they sat quietly drinking the cold, clear wine. Evelyn broke the silence and asked her son the question that had been on her mind for days: "Henry, if I arrange for you to move to Canada for a while, will you go?"

Henry took a sip of his wine, then turned and looked at his mother with a slight smile on his face. One look told him she was deadly serious. He knew her well enough to know she had the resources, the contacts, and the means to make it happen. He had only to say the word.

There was what seemed to be an interminable period of complete silence before Henry spoke, and he said, "Mom, you have no idea how much I love you, and I'd do about anything you might ask me to do, but I cannot do this. I chose the path I'm on. I need to see it through."

As Henry finished speaking, Evelyn nodded and smiled. He said, "Thank you, Mom," rose to kiss her on the cheek, and then broke into a spectacular smile. With that small bit of conversation, Henry's entire mood seemed to lift, and his usual bright personality returned. "Besides," he said, "I can't leave. I've asked Susan to marry me, and she said yes!"

On Sunday, May 25, 1969, the Heide family, including Susan, attended early mass at Nativity Catholic Church, and then went for breakfast at Jack's Hollywood Diner. This had been a favorite family breakfast spot for many years. Henry ordered his favorite banana and pecan pancakes, with extra bacon and a sunny-side-up egg, and was all smiles. Susan sat very near holding his hand and sporting a beautiful diamond solitaire engagement ring. They would marry when he returned from Vietnam in June 1970.

Henry was scheduled to fly out of Miami International Airport on Eastern flight 236 at 2:55 p.m. He would change planes in Louisville and fly direct from there to Seattle-Tacoma. His United charter would leave from McChord AFB at midnight, en route to Tan Son Nhut AB, Saigon. The family had him checked in at the airport by 2:00 p.m. Their last glimpse of Henry was a bright smile and a wave from the window as the aircraft pulled away from the terminal.

PART 2

Henry moaned audibly and said, "The training in Devens and Two Rock didn't prepare me for my arrival in Vietnam. I disembarked from the United Airlines charter at Tan Son Nhut about 6:00 a.m.

on May 29, and I was immediately assailed by two physical elements: the humid heat and the stench of the place. Give me a break. I'm from South Florida—our heat and humidity are legendary, but this is unlike anything I've ever experienced. And the stink of the place is staggering. It is overwhelming to the point of being almost palpable. I guess I had a somewhat pampered childhood in Hollywood, but I can't believe people are actually breathing this stuff.

"Our instructors at Devens and Two Rock tried to prepare us for what we would face in Vietnam. They talked about it on a daily basis, but they missed the boat on the actual physical collision of me and this country called Vietnam. And the result isn't pretty. This place's a cesspool. Phew!"

Henry reported in at the 90th Replacement Battalion and was called out of formation. His orders stated he was to be assigned to the 371st Radio Research Company, 1st Air Cavalry. The 1st Cavalry had been moved from the Central Highlands to Phước Vĩnh in the southwest part of the country.

Henry and several infantry troops were loaded onto an aircraft, and it was nearly noon when the C-130 landed at Camp Gorvad. It was an unnerving way to begin his tour in Vietnam. As the plane taxied to a stop, the crew chief told those on board to hit the ground running. "There's intermittent sniper fire in the area," he said. "So it's best to be a moving target."

Henry discovered that running with a duffel bag and a B-4 bag was impossible, but walking brought on a harsh shout-out by the military police directing the operation to "Double-time it!"

Henry soon realized the old guys or "short-timers" were wearing fatigues faded by the sun and the frequent scrubbing they endured. The new guys, or "nugs," were wearing dark green fatigues that were obviously newly issued. The old guys could spot them a mile away and always hazed the nugs, so he had that to look forward to for a few weeks.

"I signed in at the orderly room," Heide said, "and then I was sent to supply. I was issued a flak jacket, helmet, M16, and three loaded 5.56mm magazines. The supply sergeant told me I was to have those items on or near at hand at all times. My billet was a large tent where all the ASA personnel were housed. I found an empty cot with mosquito netting and no pillow. The Boca Raton Waldorf Astoria, it was not. That night, I showered in what had to be the coldest water I have ever subjected myself to in my life. My goose bumps had goose bumps. My teeth were chattering. It was dark as hell, but by flashlight, I washed my fatigues with a big bar of GI soap. I hoped I could remove some of the dark-green dye. We were to use that soap to wash everything, including ourselves.

"Man, we're in the Army now," Henry mumbled as he scrubbed away, "This is something else that f***in' recruiter forgot to tell me while he was assuring me I wouldn't go to Vietnam."

"Later, I was lying on my cot wondering if there was anything I could do to be more comfortable inside the mosquito netting. It kept the mosquitoes at bay, but it also trapped the heat inside. If there was any air moving, I couldn't feel it. I was told to sleep with my pants and socks on and to either keep my boots on or have them nearby. I thought it was more hazing until I saw the old guys doing it, so I followed suit."

Henry was bathed in sweat and totally miserable, but he was also exhausted. He managed to drift off to sleep, and then he was jolted awake by the loud clatter of machine gun fire and the sound of explosions somewhere on the perimeter of the base.

"I sat straight up on my cot and could see dim flashes of light above the sandbags stacked around the tent," Henry said. "Stray tracers were visible in the darkness. They were neon green. I was told the color indicated the machine gun fire was from Charlie. Our tracers were red."

The gun fire soon died away as Henry tried to relax and go back to sleep. Morning would arrive all too soon, along with a day full of unknowns. "Welcome to Vietnam," Henry whispered to himself. "Welcome to f***in' hell."

Ten days after Henry's improbable start at the 371st; James R. Smith arrived at Phước Vĩnh. "Smitty" was a twenty-year-old Morse-intercept op from Oklahoma, newly married to his high school sweetheart (Kathy). He piled his gear on a cot next to Heide in the 371st RRC tent.

James "Smitty" Smith

PART 3

Project Left Bank was a highly-classified joint effort between the 1st Cavalry and ASA. The 1st Cavalry provided three UH-1D "Huey" helicopters (named The Good, The Bad, and The Ugly) and the pilots to fly them. The 371st RRC provided intercept operators and intelligence-gathering equipment (intercept radios and antennas). Heide and Smith would become the newest members of the flight crews that were so essential to the project's success, but they would begin their journey in the 371st operations center, intercepting North Vietnamese manual Morse communications. Like most of the 05Hs on the flight crews, they would have to wait their turn.

Capt. Carlos Collat was the Left Bank Platoon leader with the 1st Cavalry in early 1969. One of Collat's fellow pilots was a warrant officer by the name of Jack Knepp. For a period of time, Capt. Collat and Mr. Knepp were the only pilots assigned to the Left Bank Platoon, so one or the other (or both) was on call most of the time.

Capt. *Carlos Collat, 371st Platoon Commander*

What made Left Bank so successful was the combining of the ASA direction-finding platform with the firepower and mobility of airborne warfare. If the Left Bank team located a "fix" in the jungle, the pilot hovered over the area at canopy level looking for evidence of troop movement or enemy installations.

If enemy personnel were spotted, the pilot called in Arc Light missions (B-52 bombers), 1st Cavalry gunships or infantry. During January 1969, Left Bank was responsible for six B-52 strikes, multiple artillery rounds fired, and troop insertions resulting in over three hundred enemy killed.

In early 1969, Collat and Knepp developed the "drop down" procedure and hardwired the Morse operator's intercept equipment (in the back of the helicopter) to an indicator instrument right in front of the pilot's cyclic (the pitch-control stick between his legs). With that indicator, the pilot could visually track the signal and know which way to turn the aircraft at the same time the Morse operators in the back knew. The advantage was that the pilots up front could relate the signal tracking with the terrain in front of them and get a better insight as to where the signal was emanating from (the tree line, rice paddies, caves, etc.). The pilot could then communicate directly with the accompanying "Pink Team" (1st Cavalry scouts and gunships) as to the more precise location of the enemy transmitter. There was a standing rule within the platoon, however, that pilots would never use low level procedure two days in a row against the same target.

"We knew the odds were against us," Collat said. "We normally flew the missions between 1,000 and 1,500 feet altitude. Only by exception would we drop to tree top level. If we did, we had a pretty good history of the target. This drop down to tree-top level maneuver, along with that extra indicator instrument up front gave us the opportunity to get the precision data for the scouts and guns to do their thing, but we knew it could be a deadly procedure."

Pink teams were a combination of red teams and white teams. The mission of the white team Loaches (LOH) or "scouts" was to fly as low as possible searching out the enemy. Those crews were a different breed. Each time they flew out on a mission, they knew they could be shot down, and many were. If they were only shot at, they called in the red team for support. Red team AH-1 Cobras were armed with rocket pods on their sides and mini-machine guns. If the white bird was shot down, the blue reconnaissance teams were called in to secure the site and aid in the extraction of the team and helicopter. In the worst-case scenario, the blues were called in to recover the remains of the lost team or teams.

1st Cavalry Hunter—Killer Team

Part 4

In southern Vietnam, the wet season lasts from May to November. The months of June, July, and August receive the highest rainfall of the year. When Henry and Smitty arrived at Phước Vĩnh at the end of May and the beginning of June, the "wet season" was in full gear with downpours nearly every day. The storms usually came midafternoon and seemed to crop up out of nowhere. One moment the sun was shining; the next one was inundated by a wall of water.

Monsoon!

In September, Henry Heide and James "Smitty" Smith were selected to begin OJT for Left Bank. Both soldiers were adept at the job they had been trained for at Devens and Two Rock and had honed their skills during the three months they had worked positions in the 371st; however, performing their job within the confines of a comparatively quiet and secure compound and doing the job on board a helicopter hovering two thousand feet above the trackless jungle was an entirely different matter. Several weeks of training and flying under the supervision of senior personnel were required before the men would be ready to handle missions on their own.

"I love flying in the choppers," Heide said. "It's great to feel like we are going to actually make a visible contribution to the war effort. I know the intelligence we gather on the ground contributes to the overall effort, but we never know what we've got. Everything is in code. We have no idea what results come from the data we've collected. However, with Left Bank, the ops spot the bad guys, call in the Cavalry [literally] and watch them destroy the enemy based on the job we have done. That's pretty awesome, and I know it will be a real feeling of accomplishment when we start flying missions on our own. Of course Left Bank is highly classified, so we won't be able brag about it, but we will know—we will know. I can't wait to get started."

Spc.4 Heide (far right) converses with a mechanic
Note "elephant brander" antenna on front of Huey

Also in September, a new and somewhat unusual member of the ASA team arrived. David Hewitt was a 98G, a Vietnamese linguist (North Vietnamese dialect) from Kenosha, Wisconsin, and the unit was not quite sure what to do with him.

"I came straggling into the ASA company tent dragging all my gear," Hewitt said. "It was pouring rain. Everyone inside just sat there and stared at me like I was from outer space. Then a tall soldier stood up, walked over to me with an amazing smile, and held out his hand. He said, 'Hi, I'm Henry Heide. Welcome aboard,' and that was the beginning of our friendship."

"I was the only 98G2LVN the 1st Cavalry had seen," Hewitt said, "I'm not sure how or why I ended up there. No one in the 1st Cavalry or the 371st knew either. The commander had no idea what to do with me—the operations center wasn't equipped for voice intercept, so I volunteered to fly Left Bank. That's where the men in my unit were working, so that's where I wanted to be."

The unit did not have a crew member slot open, but since Hewitt was not an actual member of the Left Bank crew, he was permitted to begin going on the missions without the normal required weeks of OJT. He rode on the jump seat in the Huey with a battery-powered transistorized radio on his lap and searched for voice communications. The radio was small and folded up in a metal case about the size of a textbook.

"There was a lot of pot in Vietnam," Dave Hewitt mused, "and it was tolerated to a point, at least where we were. It was tolerated, with the understanding that one had to be able to perform at 100 percent peak function within a few seconds of an alert. I had never enjoyed tobacco, so I'd had very little smoking experience—limited to partially smoked butts my buddies picked up on the side of the road when we were kids. Despite numerous opportunities to try pot during my college years in 1966 and 1967, the first time I tried it was in the spring of 1969, toward the end of my time in language school (DLIWC) in Monterey, California. I knew I was going to Vietnam and decided I'd better try it in case I never got another opportunity. I was not impressed. I couldn't understand what the buzz was all about. The second time I tried pot, I was in Vietnam.

Dave Hewitt, 1969

"One sunny morning, Henry invited me to go for a walk with him," Hewitt continued. "We walked down the road toward the rubber plantation in our company area. It was a beautiful morning, and we had the day off. Henry said he was going to have a smoke, but said nothing about what he really had in mind. I only discovered the true purpose of the mission when we stopped walking, and he pulled out a package of reefers [marijuana cigarettes]. Henry was capable of being serious and happy and smiling, all at the same moment, so it wasn't always easy to ascertain what he was thinking. He took a cigarette out of the pack and offered me one. I put it in my mouth, Henry lit it, and I kinda puffed at it. Henry laughed at me, in his friendly Southern way, and said something like 'Here you are, in the Army, in Nam, twenty-one years old, and you don't know how to smoke. You need to inhale, like this…' So Henry coached me until I got the hang of it. There I was, on a sunny day, standing among the regularly spaced trees, on a red dirt road through a rubber plantation, fifteen thousand miles from home, and I was talking with my new friend from Florida, Henry Heide. Henry was basically a happy human, which enabled me to feel like a happy human again for the first time in a long time, so my second experience was a good one. I can't recall if I ever smoked weed with Henry again, but I certainly did smoke with other people after that first time in the war, and it became like a visit with an old friend."

Hewitt continued, "I remember one day when we were cruising around at our usual altitude and somebody on the other side of the ship from me saw tracers go by. That was sobering. Another member of the 371st crew named Mike Likens, an O5H, took a .51 cal round in his thigh. The round came up through the bottom of the aircraft, shattered his femur and hit his arm. For some reason, I still was not as scared as I should have been."

Mike Likens—Ditty Bopper

"The first time I was on board one of the choppers, and we dropped down to the deck to drop smoke on our fix, I was really uneasy," Hewitt said. "I put away my radio, picked up my M16, and made sure it was locked and loaded with the switch on full-auto—not that it would do any good. We didn't have door guns, and nobody else was in a position to return fire, so I figured I might be able to discourage somebody, if they conveniently happened to be on my side of the ship. We were flying through a clearing along a riverbed. I was looking up at the treetops, and we were moving at 120 knots. We survived that one without incident. I was on at least one more of those; and after we landed at Phước Vĩnh, our ground crew chief, Ted Hurth, pulled me aside. In a low voice, he said, 'This is nuts, somebody is going to die.'"

Henry Heide and Ted Hurth

Hewitt paused for a moment and then said, "Oddly, I hadn't really thought it through. Intellectually, I understood the risks we were taking, but in my gut, I wasn't really afraid enough. That was probably because we'd gotten away with the drop-down maneuver several times, but Sgt. Hurth, with his words, by his tone and manner, had figuratively grabbed me by the scruff of the neck and shook sense into me. He'd gotten through to me. The more I thought about it, the more I realized this maneuver was sheer folly, sheer macho bravado. I went to my CO and said I wanted to do something else. He said 'OK,' just like that. I don't remember if I voiced my concerns. I suspect they had weighed the risks—the testimony of an E-4 linguist wouldn't have swayed them one iota. My last flight on board Left Bank was on the sixth anniversary of the day John F. Kennedy died. That would have been November 22. I then moved to LZ Thomas on top of a mountain named Núi Bà Rá and was provided with a bunker and my own intercept equipment.

On the morning of November 29, Richard Schlies, along with Wayne Boyce, were scheduled to fly Left Bank. Richard and Wayne were both Morse intercept ops and had been at Phước Vĩnh since April. "We flew at least five or six days a week," Schlies said, "and we weren't really too concerned about the danger involved.

WO1 Dennis D. Bogle

"We usually knew who was going where and when and with whom, but the morning of the twenty-ninth, everything seemed to be up in the air," Schlies continued. "Mr. Rohman was scheduled to fly that morning, but Mr. Knepp asked if he could take the mission. He wanted to fly the new guy, Mr. Bogle, on his first mission. On top of that, Heide and Smitty Smith had been OJTing for two months. They had been flying missions with a senior op in charge. Now they wanted to make their first solo run together. Let's be honest here. They were begging to go—on their own, and Jack Knepp was hands-down the best, the safest, the most reliable pilot we had. Jack was the old guy, twenty-nine years old, a former Marine, and a great pilot. He was the logical choice to take all these nugs up on their cherry missions. The mission call sign was *Jaguar Yellow.*

CW2 Jack D. Knepp—Hands-down the best!

The rumor later was that the enemy was tired of being pounded whenever this chopper with the funny-looking antenna on the front arrived on the scene, so they set a trap. The *Jaguar Yellow* crew flew low and was caught in the crossfire of .51 cal machine guns and rockets. An RPG round blasted through the chin bubble and brought them down. It is not likely anyone could have survived the RPG explosion within the helicopter cabin and the ensuing fiery crash, but that was followed by the additional explosion of white phosphorous grenades on board the ship. Referred to as "Willie Pete," they were carried to destroy the aircraft and its top-secret ASA intercept equipment in the event the helicopter went down. WP grenades would burn for sixty seconds at temperatures exceeding four thousand degrees F.

Two Loaches and a Cobra, which were covering *Jaguar Yellow*, were also caught in the hail of gun and rocket fire and were downed. Fast movers were scrambled and napalmed the area to keep the classified materials out of enemy hands. Later, blues of the 1/9th Cav were inserted, secured what was left of the wreckage, and initiated recovery of bodies from the various aircraft.

"I was working on the twenty-ninth when I got a call from my second lieutenant at Buttons on my trusty 'prick-25' [PRC-25 field radio]," Dave Hewitt said. "He told me we had lost a ship and all aboard were killed. I'm not sure if he told me who was flying that day. I knew they were friends of mine, regardless of who it was. I went into shock. I remember an odd numbness set in, and I could barely function for two or three days. In retrospect, I was dealing with all kinds of guilt and emotions. The fact that I was not officially assigned as part of the flight crew had allowed me to depart on a moment's notice, while our ditty boppers, like Henry and Smitty, were stuck in a suicide mission. I really had no business going on those missions, but that did not relieve the survivor's guilt I felt for still being alive and healthy."

Richard Schlies said, "When we heard the other ship had gone down, it was a gut-blow for us. These were our friends and teammates. When we got back to camp that afternoon, and I walked through the gate into the 371st base area, one of the supply guys came running up and said, 'Man, I thought you were dead! The whole thing was so surreal.'

"That evening at the mess hall, Capt. Kucera, our commander, told us he wanted to meet with all the 371st crew members after chow, so we gathered at his office. All of us just sat there. We were stunned, still in shock. No one could think of anything to say. We stared at the floor or stared off into space. Kucera came in and told everyone to keep their seats. The captain sat back against the edge of his desk and began to speak to us in an informal and intimate way. He spoke somberly but very clearly and very concisely. He praised us for the job we had been doing and thanked us for what we had accomplished. He expressed his sorrow for what had happened that day to Henry and Smitty, Jack and Mr. Bogle—then he said: 'Tomorrow morning, we're going out, and we're going to find those guys. We've determined it was the NVA 141st Battalion. We'll find them—and we will destroy them.' There was complete silence in the room. I could almost feel the grit and determination of the men around me. We had the skills and the resolve to locate the enemy unit that had destroyed *Jaguar Yellow*, and nothing was going to stop us from doing it."

After a moment of silence, the captain stood up and said quietly, "You are dismissed." A sergeant yelled, "Attent-HUT!" The soldiers jumped to attention as the commander left the room.

Early the following morning, two crews of pilots and Morse intercept ops were transported to the flight line. None of the men had slept much. Sgt. Hurth and his maintenance team had been on duty for hours assuring the two remaining ships were in first-class operating condition.

Richard Schlies and Wayne Boyce were on board one of the ships. There was a feeling of excitement and anticipation as the choppers lifted off and headed toward Sông Bé.

"There was heavy ground fog," Schlies said, "but the sun would burn it away quickly. We knew what we had to do, and we knew exactly how to do it. This was a large enemy force we were dealing with, and it wasn't going to disappear overnight. The area we were heading for was about twenty miles due north of Phước Vĩnh."

"As we drew near to the Bé River area, we picked up a signal," Schlies said, "and immediately began to take heavy ground fire. We dove down to tree-top level to avoid the fire, and the adrenalin was really pumping. We knew this had to be the guys we were looking for, the NVA 141st. We flew along the river below treetop level and then began climbing and searching for the signal again, trying to pinpoint the exact location of the enemy transmitter. The pilots had a null meter up front, so they were tracking the signal too. We started taking ground fire again, and we dove back down into the protection of the trees. By that time, we had a location fix of the NVA camp, and we called in the Arc Lights."

Three B-52 Stratofortress bombers from U-Tapao Royal Thai Navy Airfield in Thailand had been summoned in advance and were in the area awaiting a successful mission by the 371st RRC. Each B-52D carried 108 500-lb. bombs, or a mixed load of sixty-four 500-lb. bombs in the bomb bay and twenty-four 750-lb. bombs on underwing pylons.

"We pulled out a safe distance away and watched," Richard Schlies said. "It was a beautiful day with some high thin clouds overhead and a few patches of light fog still visible along the river. The bombers were too high to be seen or heard, but suddenly, the jungle before us began to convulse in a series of massive explosives, and it seemed to go on and on. I felt like cheering, but I just watched and thought about Jack and Smitty and Henry and Bogle with a kind of grim satisfaction. We had done what we had come to do, and now the Arc Lights were finishing the job. As Boyce and I watched the conflagration we had brought about, there was this eerie feeling that our four friends were there watching with us."

PART 5

Early Wednesday morning, December 3, 1969, a dark blue van with "Western Union" stenciled on the doors drove along a palm-lined boulevard in the Hollywood Hills area of Hollywood, Florida. The uniformed driver turned into a long, curved driveway leading to a spacious Florida-style home at 806 N. Highland Dr. He parked, walked to the door, and rang the doorbell.

The Heide home

Walt Heide was just finishing his second cup of coffee when the doorbell rang. Evelyn was in the master bedroom finishing her makeup. Peering out through a side window, Walt saw the vehicle and was more curious than concerned. Opening the door, he was handed a clipboard to sign his name, and then a telegram.

Closing the door, Walter sat looking at the telegram and was hesitant to open it. "Oh my God, oh my God," he said to himself, and then he called for Eve to come into the living room. She came in with an inquisitive look, and Walter waved the telegram in the air.

"This was just delivered, Eve," he said, and he slowly tore open the envelope. The telegram was official notice from the Department of Defense that their son, Pvt. 1st Class Henry Nicholas Heide II had been missing in action since November 29, 1969. And so the nightmare began.

The first telegram was followed by a series of telegrams telling the family Henry had been a passenger "aboard a US Army gunship" shot down in enemy territory in South Vietnam, and reaffirming their son was still MIA. One of the telegrams stated bone fragments had been found in the wreckage of the gunship but had not been identified. Henry remained MIA another month.

Walt emerged from their master suite through French doors that opened onto the pool area one evening. Evelyn was relaxing by the pool after dinner with a glass of wine and trying to clear her mind. She'd had a stressful day at work. "Eve," he said, "I know Henry. I think he is somewhere in the jungle, and he's going to come walking out with one of his buddies on his back! That's Henry."

"After a while, we began to believe that," Evelyn said. "We wanted to believe it so desperately. We just refused to accept the idea that our beautiful boy was dead—not our Henry."

Walter grew increasingly bitter through the month of December as he feuded with what he perceived as Army ineptitude and indifference. "It was like the regular Army had no clue who, what, or where the Army Security Agency soldiers were or that they even existed. It was so damned frustrating. "It's like these assholes don't have a clue the ASA guys are even there!" Walt groused. "Fortunately Henry had sent me a copy of the special order promoting him to Spc.4. The Army insisted he was a private first class. I told them he was a radioman on a combat mission, but they insisted he was just a passenger on a goddamned gunship. Henry was ordered on that mission. Why in hell would a gunship be hauling passengers? You tell me. My God in heaven! What planet do these sons-o-bitches live on?"

Christmas morning dawned cool and overcast in South Florida. It was fifty-five degrees when Evelyn slipped on her housecoat and moved to the kitchen to turn on the coffee pot. There were few signs of the holiday season apparent around the house. The past few weeks had seemed like a continual bad dream. Carole and Fred had done their best to cheer their mother and support her—she had helped them put up a Christmas tree, but her heart was not in it. The family had attended midnight mass the night before. Susan was home from Marymount on Christmas break and had accompanied them along with her parents, but nothing felt right. The mystery of Henry's disappearance overshadowed everything, especially Christmas.

Evelyn had gone back to work within a few days of their first notification. She could not bear to sit at home, but it was difficult for her to concentrate on anything but Henry. She was ready to know something, anything. It was the waiting that was killing her and destroying Walt. He was so angry no one could stand to be around him. They needed answers and not just the continual stream of Army drivel masquerading as information.

Finally, on January 8, 1970, Walt and Eve received a telegram stating that, although their son's body had not been identified, none of the four crewmen aboard the downed helicopter were believed to have survived. "At least it was somewhat definitive," Evelyn said, "compared to what we had been getting. And we began to hope we would finally get to bury our son."

On Sunday, January 25, one month after Christmas and almost two months after *Jaguar Yellow* was shot down; the Heides were notified by the DOD that their son had been officially declared dead by an Army investigating board. "The Army doesn't care that they are letting people live in a nightmare," Walt Heide said. "They just don't care."

The first public notice of Spc.4 Henry Heide's death was published in the *Miami News* on January 27, 1970. The Department of Defense press release still listed him as a private first class. "I say if these boys are going to die for this country, the Army could at least give them their proper status," Walter said. "This says to me the Army couldn't care less. They just send some new ones—some better ones, but there was no one better than my boy. I tell people we've lost forty thousand men and my son over there already. It's time for it to stop."

"I urged Henry to go to Canada," Evelyn said, "but he refused. This entire experience has been bungled and chaotic. No US citizen should have to risk their life in war if the US Congress doesn't declare war. A man should have a right to that."

The family was notified some of the bone fragments found within the wreckage of the Huey had been identified through DNA as Henry's. The fragments were comingled with those of Dennis Bogle, and the two would be buried at Arlington National Cemetery on February 10, 1970.

The weather was cool and clear as the Heide family watched the horse-drawn caisson carrying the flag-draped coffin up the narrow road at Arlington. They were standing with Robert and Kathleen Bogle, Dennis Bogle's parents, along with Henry's fiancé, Susan

Wilson, her parents, and other family members who had flown in for the funeral. It had been comforting to meet and talk with the Bogles. Knowing they had gone through the same torment and suffered the same terrible loss somehow helped to mitigate their own personal feelings of loss.

In September 1970, Walter and Evelyn Heide were invited to a special ceremony at Homestead Air Force Base, south of Miami. During the outdoor event, as US flags whipped in the ocean breeze, an unclassified version of Henry's combat mission was read, "While flying at low altitude, Heide continually exposed himself to intense enemy ground fire as he endeavored to mark enemy positions for the 1st Cavalry Division. In the accomplishment of the mission, his aircraft received unexpectedly heavy automatic weapons fire, which set the aircraft ablaze and resulted in his death."

Henry's parents were then presented with his Distinguished Flying Cross (for valor in action on November 29, 1969), the Air Medal with "V" device and Oak Leaf Cluster (for valorous action from September 1 through October 31, 1969, during which time he located and identified enemy elements and equipment as he flew low level at reduced speed with only his personal weapon for protection), the Bronze Star (by direction of the President for meritorious service in ground operations in Vietnam from May 1969 until November 1969), and the Purple Heart.

> As goes the Sun god in his chariot glorious,
> When all his golden banners are unfurled,
> So goes the soldier, fallen but victorious,
> And leaves behind a twilight in the world.
>
> And those who come this way, in days hereafter,
> Will know that here a boy (for freedom) fell,
> Who looked at danger with the eyes of laughter,
> And on the charge his days were ended well.

"The Fallen Subaltern"
Lt. Herbert Dixon Asquith

EPILOGUE

ANOTHER LOST JAGUAR

On March 1, 1971, fifteen months after the downing of *Jaguar Yellow*, a second Left Bank Huey, call-sign *Jaguar Yellow Bird*, was lost over Kampong Cham Province, Cambodia. It is believed the ship was brought down by a 37mm antiaircraft gun. NVA gunners had developed considerable expertise with antiaircraft weaponry, and along the border region of Vietnam and Cambodia, the 37mm gun had proven effective against piston-driven aircraft and helicopters.

Left Bank Huey with elephant-brander antenna

The 1st Cavalry was flying in support of Operation LAM SON 719, a limited-objective offensive campaign against NVA forces conducted in the southeastern portion of the Kingdom of Laos. Their AO included the region along Highway 75, a major conduit at the southern tip of the Ho Chi Minh Trail. At noon, the pilot of one of the 1st Cavalry Cobras, serving as the command and control aircraft, decided to land in a clearing. As a second Cobra was providing air cover, one of its crewmen, Sgt. 1st Class Richard Herron, saw the Left Bank Huey pass by and fly approximately two miles south. The Huey had begun a tight turn when it suddenly tipped nose down and then straight down. As the Cobra crew watched, the pilot radioed, "Downed bird!"

Sgt. Herron said, "The main rotor blades came off intact with the main rotor head. They separated, and the aircraft just fell straight down from approximately 2,200 feet." Just before impact, the aircraft began to spin. "The tail rotor and the nose of the aircraft hit at exactly the same place, and it looked like a knife stuck in the ground. When it impacted the ground there was an explosion. It looked like a petrol explosion. Black smoke came boiling out both sides."

Capt. Rodolfo Gutierrez, one of the Loach pilots, said, "We were flying at about 2,500 feet when I noticed the H-model north of our area of operations…I warned the birds in the area that there might have been ground-to-air fire. As I began making my large circle, the H-model passed underneath and was climbing. As I was headed to the south, I looked out the left door and saw the H-model start to fall. The aircraft was at about 2,200 feet."

Gutierrez continued, "As soon as I saw the aircraft fall, I looked at the head. There were no rotor blades… There was a mast. I looked up and searched for the rotor blades. I did see the blades and grips. They were intact and going up, from about 1,600 to 1,800 feet. The aircraft descended vertically to the ground, exploding in a fireball upon impact. About ten to fifteen seconds later, the blades hit the ground a little to the southwest of the aircraft. I believe they were intact when they hit… Upon impacting the ground, the aircraft exploded and was engulfed in a fireball. There was an explosion inside the aircraft," Gutierrez concluded. The internal explosion may have been from ordinance designed to destroy the intercept equipment installed within the passenger area.

The location of the crash was approximately twenty-seven miles east of Kampong Cham, Cambodia. It was nineteen miles northwest of the nearest point on the South Vietnamese border. On March 2, an ARVN unit reached the crash site and recovered "fragmented" remains that were transported to a US military mortuary for identification. Those remains were later identified as WO1 Robert D. Uhl, the co-pilot, Spc.5 Gary C. David, and Spc.4 Frank A. Sablan, the ASA Morse intercept operators. The remains of WO1 Paul V. Black, the aircraft commander, were not located at that time. The formal search for Black was concluded on March 16, 1971, and he was listed as MIA. Some years later, after considering the testimony of those who witnessed the crash, that designation was changed to KIA/BNR.

WO1 Paul V. Black

In the fall of 1995, a team from the Joint Task Force for Full Accounting (JTF-FA) traveled from Hawaii to Kampong Cham, Cambodia, to investigate the crash site. They found a local resident who knew the point of impact, surveyed the area, and began to excavate the site. Their initial test dig resulted in bone fragments and an upper-jaw piece containing two teeth. The site was thoroughly excavated recovering thousands of small helicopter parts, personal items from the crew, and nearly a thousand bone fragments. The team also recovered twenty teeth or portions of teeth, some of which contained dental fillings and other identifying markers. The fragments were sent to a laboratory in Hawaii for DNA testing and comparison with samples from Paul Black's family. At that time, no matches were found, and none of the teeth matched his dental records.

For thirty-two years, Jim and Jane Black waited, not knowing if Paul had died in the crash or been taken prisoner. Finally, in April 2003, they received an unexpected call. JTF-FA had found a match. Using new techniques that tested mitochondrial DNA, they had retested materials from the crash and positively identified some of the remains as belonging to their son. Paul was coming home.

On November 6, 2003, Black was buried at Arlington National Cemetery along with his three comrades: Robert Uhl, Gary David, and Frank Sablan. In the presence of some seventy-five family members and friends, the remains of the four young soldiers, 1st Cavalry and ASA together, were borne on a horse-drawn caisson to their joint gravesite through a cold November drizzle.

The four young soldiers, 1ˢᵗ Cavalry and ASA, together forever

During the funeral service, Chaplain Douglas Fenton told mourners he hoped Arlington would serve as "a place of profound peace" after so many years of uncertainty.

Paul Black's parents, both in their eighties, attended the service. The families of the four soldiers heard the volleys of rifle fire, the bugler playing "Taps," and they prayed for closure. As the service concluded, Jane Black said, "Let this be the end."

Based on Chapter 28—*Unlikely Warriors: The Army Security Agency's Secret War in Vietnam 1961–1973* by Lonnie M. Long and Gary B. Blackburn

CHAPTER 6

HILLIARD ALMOND WILBANKS

Willy

Hilliard Wilbanks

Cornelia, Georgia, was a quiet town in the 1930s with a population of 1,500 citizens. Located in the southern foothills of the Blue Ridge Mountains in northeastern Georgia, Cornelia had been one of the last Confederate strongholds in the waning days of the Civil War. Known as the "Breadbasket of the Confederacy," Cornelia had provided thousands of bushels of corn and wheat for Southern forces long after other communities had been overrun and placed under control of the Union Army. Continuing his Southern Campaign after the fall of Atlanta, Gen. William Tecumseh Sherman sent a detachment of his cavalry to raid Cornelia and the surrounding area in search of food and supplies. Receiving word that "the Yanks 'er comin'!" the Confederate Home Guard, which was made up of men too old for military service, left the mountain on which Cornelia resides and met the Yankee raiders at a narrow pass some four miles east of the town. By making considerable noise, stirring up clouds of smoke, and making it appear the unit was a much greater force than it actually was, the Guard scared off the enemy and saved Cornelia from complete devastation. That skirmish was later remembered by the somewhat grandiose name of The Battle of the Narrows.

Born on a hot July day in Cornelia in 1933, Hilliard Almond Wilbanks was eight years old when the Japanese attacked Pearl Harbor on December 7, 1941, and he spent his most formative years watching and reading about the war.

On Saturday morning, Willy, along with his brothers, Eddie and Norm, would run to the Grand Theater on Main St. The boys were excited at the prospect of seeing the latest Gene Autry and Smiley Burnette epic *Heart of the Rio Grande*; however, unlike the other children, Willy was even more excited to see the weekly newsreel of the Flying Tigers shooting down Japanese Zeros over China. Willy could watch Gene shoot bad guys in Texas any old time, but watching the P-40 Warhawks painted with menacing shark mouths as they raced across the screen was a heck of a lot more fun. Flying planes was all Willy thought about—all he dreamed of—and all he would work toward in high school. Willy wanted to be a fighter pilot.

After graduating from Cornelia High School in 1950, Wilbanks enlisted in the US Air Force. He was seventeen years old. One could not become a pilot in the Air Force without college, so after basic training, Will was trained as an air policeman (AP). He spent almost four years in the Strategic Air Command and took college courses in his spare time. In 1954, Wilbanks qualified for the Aviation Cadet Program. Candidates had to be between the ages of nineteen and twenty-five, athletic, honest, and have an excellent record. Two years of college or three years of a scientific or technical education was also required. Cadets were supposed to be unmarried and pledge not to marry during training.

Wilbanks went through the cadet training program at Laredo AFB, Texas. He made his first solo flight in a Piper Cub on July 19, 1954.

Will said, "Man, all I can say is wow! I've dreamed of this day all my life. It is impossible to put into words how I feel. I've worked toward this for so long. Now it's on to jets!"

Wilbanks received his commission, the gold bars of a second lieutenant, and the silver wings of an Air Force pilot at graduation in June 1955. He was also named a "distinguished graduate" from class 55-P.

After graduation, Will's first duty station as an officer was Greenville AFB, Mississippi. He was assigned to the 3506th Pilot Training Squadron as a T-33 instructor pilot, so Lt. Wilbanks, who had been an outstanding student, now became an excellent teacher. During his stay in Greenville, Will Wilbanks met and later married Rosemary Arnold of Glen Allan, Miss. in 1956. He was promoted to first lieutenant on December 15, 1956.

In February of 1959, Wilbanks was reassigned to the mainte-nance officer school at Chanute AFB in Rantoul, Illinois. After com-pleting that schooling, he was stationed at Eielson AFB, Alaska. The base was located about twenty-six miles southeast of Fairbanks and 110 miles below the Arctic Circle. Will and Rosemary loved Alaska.

"This was some of the most beautiful country we had ever seen," Wilbanks said. "It was definitely a long way from Georgia and Mississippi, but there was so much to do, and we did not have to deal with the heat and humidity. In the summer, there was hiking, fish-ing, camping, and canoeing. In the winter, we loved cross-country skiing, snowmobiling, and some of the most spectacular Northern Lights in the world. We didn't want to leave."

While stationed there, Wilbanks qualified on F-86 Sabre Jets (of Korean War fame) as a test pilot. He was assigned as an aircraft maintenance officer and was promoted to captain in 1961.

In May of 1962, Will received orders transferring him to Nellis AFB in southern Nevada. He and Rosemary were not ready to leave

Alaska; however, the new assignment was going to move him nearer to his dream. He would be a flight-line maintenance officer on F-105D fighter-bombers. A fast mover designed to carry a nuclear weapon, the F-105D became the Vietnam War's most important conventional fighter-bomber. Named the "Thunder Chief" and called the "Thud," pilots loved the plane, and it had few detractors. Aviators, as well as ground crews and maintenance technicians graced the airplane with the kind of loyalty that is rarely seen.

"I loved it from the moment I saw it," Wilbanks said, I couldn't wait to get my hands on it. I had never seen anything so beautiful. The jet was sixty-four feet long and had a thirty-five-foot wingspan. Powered by a Pratt and Whitney J-75 engine that developed over twenty-six thousand pounds of thrust, it was fast. An F-105B, an early test model, had set a world speed record in December 1959: 1,216 mph over a sixty-two mile circuit that required the pilot to maintain a precise course while pulling a steady 3.5 Gs for three minutes. The aircraft had been planned as a nuclear weapons carrier, designed to streak in low and lob a small nuclear bomb toward its target. She was all lethal beauty and grace.

F-105D Thunderchief

"The system the plane used for delivery of an atomic weapon was called an over-the-shoulder bomb toss," Wilbanks continued. "The jet would gain as much speed as it could in a dive, then pull up in a climb to near vertical and release the bomb at the apex of the climb. The jet would then continue with an 'immelman' to maneuver away from the target and hit the afterburners. Theoretically, the aircraft was so fast, it would be miles into its escape by the time the bomb hit its target, and hopefully outrun the blast radius which would travel outward at slightly more than the speed of sound [under ideal conditions, 761 mph].

"All the instrumentation was controlled through a central air-data computer and the main computer was in a cavity reached from a panel on the belly of the aircraft. My worst nightmare was my technicians having to pull the instrument panel out on the flight line in the middle of the afternoon. Working on the aircraft in the Nevada sun, coupled with no breeze, was akin to being in a Georgia cornfield in August. There was absolutely no air to breathe, and anyone who tells you 'Oh, it's dry heat, you won't feel it' is full'a shit. The gyro controlling the aircraft's attitude was in an area behind the cockpit. Of course there was air to breathe there, but it was too hot to enjoy it—I mean we're talkin' 120 to 130 degrees in the shade!"

Wilbanks loved the nearly four years he spent maintaining F-105Ds. "The Thuds were such a special aircraft," he said. Then, on March 30, 1966, he was scheduled to leave for his next assignment, Southeast Asia.

Will and Rosemary had started their family with two children, Tommy and Paula, who were born during his first two duty assignments, and now Rosemary was expecting again. A few days before Will departed, Rosemary's doctor told them their soon-to-arrive next "child" was actually going to be twins. They were born two weeks after he deployed. The fraternal twins, a boy and a girl, were named John and Debbie.

Before deploying to Southeast Asia, Capt. Willbanks was sent to Hurlburt Field at Eglin AFB, Florida. There he was trained to be a Forward Air Controller (FAC) in a Cessna O-1 Bird Dog. The O-1E aircraft (Cessna 305C) Wilbanks would be flying was a lightweight, high-wing, tail-wheel landing, single-engine, two-seat aircraft. The engine was a Continental 0-470-11, 213 hp flat (opposed) six cylinder machine with a maximum speed of 150 mph. Normal cruising speed was 104 mph. The plane's range was 530 miles. The F-105D, this was not.

With no armament or ordnance, the Bird Dog carried four 2.75 inch white phosphorous smoke rockets for marking ground targets. Pilots usually flew alone, and although issued flak vests, many of the pilots opted to place the vests on their seats and sit on them, literally saving their asses. Flying low and slow, small arms fire could easily penetrate the underside of the aircraft, and it was nice to know one's prime assets (so to speak) had some protection.

PART 2

Upon his arrival in the Republic of Vietnam, Wilbanks was stationed at Nha Trang AB and assigned to the 21st Tactical Air Support Squadron. The squadron reported to Air Force Lt. Col. Norman Mueller, air liaison officer for the Central Highlands. Mueller was also an FAC, and his group was attached to the US Army advisory team with the ARVN 23rd Division based in Ban Mê Thuột. This group of FACs covered the southern half of II Corps.

This was the largest military region in South Vietnam, an area covering approximately ten thousand square miles. Of the thirty FACs assigned, only twelve were on station in February of 1967. Additional help was badly needed, but open slots were slow to be filled.

Willy Wilbanks (as the other FACs referred to him) had spent most of his time stationed at Bảo Lộc, one hundred miles north of Saigon. During the eleventh month of his twelve-month tour, an opening developed at Đà Lạt, higher in the mountains, and he was transferred there.

"I reassigned Willy there in recognition of his hard work," Lt. Col. Mueller said. "He had already received the Distinguished Flying Cross, along with seventeen Air Medals, and had flown over 480 combat missions. He was scheduled to finish his tour and leave Vietnam on March 18 and had orders for Laughlin AFB, Texas. He was going to be an instructor pilot in the T-37 flight training program.

"Đà Lạt was everyone's dream assignment," Mueller continued, "so when I had an opening there, I sent Willy to finish out his tour. Đà Lạt was considerably cooler and less humid than the coastal plain, and South Vietnam's military academy was located there."

"I wasn't keen on movin' just a month before I was due to DEROS back to the States, but I had to go where I was assigned," Wilbanks said. "I've been countin' the days until I can see Rosemary and the kids. I've never seen my twins, and I'm plannin' on gettin' back in time to celebrate their first birthdays. It's gonna be a great day," he said, laughing.

The weather in the Đà Lạt region was ideal for farming and growing tea. It was a beautiful area and had been a popular vacation spot before the war. Surrounded by pine-forested hills, lakes, and waterfalls, it was known as the City of Eternal Spring for its temperate climate. The French had built luxury resorts and spas there during the colonial days. Now; however, its location made it a dangerous place to be. Đà Lạt was an infiltration point for the Ho Chi Minh Trail coming in from Laos. The Việt Cộng routinely attacked railway and road traffic in the area.

On February 22, 1967, an NVA battalion (some 560 troops) joined forces with local VC near Di Linh, approximately fifteen miles from Bảo Lộc. The following day they captured a large tea plantation and forced the owners and laborers to build ambush sites on the surrounding hills overlooking the road from Saigon to Đà Lạt. On February 24, an ARVN company (180 men) based at Di Linh started its morning patrol of the area, and walked straight into the ambush. All of the officers and NCOs were killed, and the remaining survivors taken prisoner. No radio transmission had been made to alert their base. The NVA then cleared the area of all signs of the fight, thus setting the stage for another ambush. By midday, having received no communication from the unit, two ARVN Ranger companies and their US Army advisors from Bảo Lộc proceeded toward the same area searching for the missing company.

Capt. Darrell Westby, who had replaced Wilbanks at Bảo Lộc, flew three reconnaissance sorties during the afternoon to assist in the search, but by late in the afternoon, he had seen no sign of the missing unit or of enemy forces in the area. In support of the search mission, Lt. Col. Mueller and Army Maj. Robert Snell flew from Ban Mê Thuột in Mueller's FAC plane. They met Capt. Westby over Bảo Lộc and took over the search mission, giving Westby time to rest.

When Mueller and Snell flew over Di Linh they saw the Rangers and their advisors approaching the tea plantation, but no sign of the enemy.

There were two flights of F-4 Phantom jets in an orbiting pattern overhead awaiting instructions, but they were low on fuel and needed to return to Cam Ranh Bay. Before leaving the area Mueller instructed them to expend their ordnance into a wooded section of the plantation that seemed like a possible hiding place for the enemy. Two flights of fighters were en route to replace the departing Phantoms. Capt. Wilbanks (call sign Walt 51) was flying in the area of Đà Lạt when Mueller radioed him to request assistance in the search mission.

"I knew Willy had flown over four hundred missions in that area," Mueller said. "He was extremely familiar with the trails, streams, villages, plantations, the daily activities and travel routes. There was no one better."

Wilbanks joined the search and flew ahead of the Rangers. He stayed in constant radio contact with Army Capt. R. J. Wooten, who was the senior American advisor.

O-1 Bird Dog

When he arrived in the area, Wilbanks immediately recognized changes in the landscape. The camouflaged emplacements among the tea bushes were the most noticeable.

"Man, all that fake crap stood out like a sore thumb," Wilbanks said. "I spotted it a mile away. I saw the Ranger companies were walking into an ambush, so I radioed Capt. Wooten and advised him there was danger ahead."

Realizing Wilbanks had spotted them, the NVA commanders sprung the trap, opening fire. The two Ranger companies were pinned down and the forward positions took heavy casualties from a barrage of 60mm mortars, Czech 12.7mm machine guns, .30-cal. CHICOM machine guns, and countless small weapons. Lt. Col. Mueller had been circling above Wilbanks, observing the ground movements. Within a few seconds his plane became a target for enemy .50-cal. guns, and with tracers streaming past, he made evasive maneuvers flying out of the danger zone. Wilbanks brought in three helicopter gunships to respond to Mueller's call for help, and then flying into the center of the NVA concentration, he fired one white phosphorous rocket to mark the location of the enemy forces for the Rangers and the gunships. As the gunships approached the area, the enemy opened fire from the surrounding hillsides. One chopper was hit and lost its hydraulic system, but the pilot regained control and withdrew.

Wilbanks allowed the two remaining gunships to escort the disabled helicopter back to their base. When the NVA realized the gunships had left the area, they renewed their attack on the Rangers, who were now alone in the fight. There was no airpower to cover them or attack enemy positions, and the situation quickly became critical. Vastly outnumbered, the Ranger companies were in dire need of help.

Help now presented itself in a most unlikely form. Capt. Hilliard Wilbanks, flying in his O-1 Bird Dog, was fully aware of the situation. He knew the lead elements of the Ranger company were heavily outnumbered and in danger of being overrun. Wilbanks flew directly toward the enemy force and fired his remaining three white phosphorous smoke rockets into their positions. Seeing this, Lt. Col.

Mueller radioed him and informed him of heavy ground fire in the area. Wilbanks acknowledged the warning but continued to press his attack. The NVA immediately responded, concentrating their fire on the small, pesky aircraft. As it buzzed overhead, the commanders ordered their gunners to squash it like the "con muỗi" (mosquito) it resembled.

The only weapon on Wilbanks' plane was the M16 rifle he carried for protection in the event he was shot down. With the rifle in one hand and the O-1's controls in the other, Wilbanks made three low passes over the NVA positions, firing the assault rifle on full automatic from the side window. This act of bravura slowed the enemy advance as many of their troops ran for cover, and it allowed the Rangers time to regroup and move to a more secure position.

The Rangers could hear the enemy bullets impacting the small plane as it passed overhead. After his third "gun run" on the enemy positions, Wilbanks seemed to lose control of his aircraft. He was flying erratically, and as the American advisors watched, the O-1 crash-landed in the open area between them and the enemy positions. The propeller was still spinning, and as if in slow motion, the light plane gracefully flipped onto its back. US Army captains Gary Vote and Joseph Mucelli, and Sgt. 1st Class Clifton Tanksley quickly made their way to the crash site and pulled the unconscious Wilbanks from the smoldering wreckage as it burst into flames.

Now, however, the three Rangers, along with Wilbanks, were pinned down by a barrage of NVA gunfire. During the time Wilbanks was attacking the NVA positions, Mueller recalled the departing gunships, and they returned, along with a "dustoff" medevac chopper. The continuing heavy enemy ground fire prevented them from immediately rescuing Wilbanks and the Rangers, but Mueller was able to fly his O-1 close to the area and draw the enemy's attention for a brief time. That, along with attacks by the two gunships, allowed the medevac to successfully land and pick up the three Rangers and Wilbanks. Just as the gunships were running out of ammunition, US fighter aircraft arrived on the scene and attacked the NVA force with a devastating barrage of cannon fire and napalm.

Wilbanks died while en route to the medical station at Bảo Lộc. His actions that day saved the lives of over 130 American and Vietnamese Rangers. Without his courageous effort, most or all of the Ranger Company would have died.

PART 3

Wilbanks was returned home to his family and funeral services were held on Friday, March 3, 1967, at Glen Allan Methodist Church in Glen Allan, Mississippi. Interment with full military honors took place at the Fayette Methodist Cemetery, Fayette, Mississippi. Willy Wilbanks was thirty-three years old. He never saw his twins.

On January 24, 1968, the Medal of Honor was posthumously awarded to Capt. Hilliard Wilbanks, US Air Force, for his actions and sacrifice in the service of his country. The presentation took place at the Pentagon in Washington, DC. Rosemary Wilbanks received the Medal of Honor and its citation from Secretary of the Air Force Harold Brown and Air Force Chief of Staff, Gen. G. P. McConnell. Rosemary was accompanied by Tommy and Paula, their two oldest children, and Hilliard's mother and father. Also attending were his two brothers, his sister, and their spouses. Also in the audience were Lt. Col. Norman Mueller and several of Capt. Wilbanks's comrades.

The final sentence of the Medal of Honor Citation reads: "His unparalleled concern for his fellowman and his extraordinary heroism were in the highest traditions of the military service, and has reflected great credit upon himself and the United States Air Force."

In addition to the Medal of Honor, Willy Wilbanks was awarded the Distinguished Flying Cross, the Air Medal with nineteen Oak Leaf Clusters, the Air Force Commendation Medal, and the Purple Heart. He also received the Republic of Vietnam Gallantry Cross with Silver Star, along with nine additional medals and unit citations.

Once you have tasted flight
You will walk the earth
With your eyes turned skyward,
For there you have been,

And there you would return.

"Once you have tasted flight"
John H. Secondari

EPILOGUE

HONORING HILLIARD ALMOND WILBANKS

- 1984—A reproduction of his Medal of Honor portrait that is displayed in the Pentagon was presented to the Town of Cornelia, Georgia, by the US Air Force.
- American Legion Post 201 is the home of the North Georgia Chapter 576, Military Order of the Purple Heart-Hilliard A. Wilbanks Chapter
- 2000—The FAC Memorial at Hurlburt Field, Florida, was dedicated in memory of the two hundred nineteen Forward Air Controllers who perished while fighting for the cause of freedom during the war in Southeast Asia to salute the courage and sacrifice of those special aviators from the US, Australia, and New Zealand who served together. Wilbanks was recognized by a bronze plaque on a pedestal near the O-1 Bird Dog display.
- 2001—The seventeenth Air Support Operations Squadron Building at Fort Benning, Georgia, was dedicated in his honor. His widow was presented with the Vietnamese Ranger Badge on behalf of the US Ranger advisors.
- 2001—Wilbanks was inducted into the Georgia Aviation Hall of Fame, Warner Robins, Georgia, Lt. Col. Mueller was present and spoke at the banquet, sharing Wilbanks' story.
- 2001—Habersham County Georgia Community erected a six-foot-tall, two-sided, black granite memorial marker on the grounds of the Cornelia Community House honoring the county's only Medal of Honor recipient.

- 2003—USAF Pilot Training Class 55-P (Wilbank's class) sponsored a granite bench with his name at the National Museum of the US Air Force, Dayton, Ohio.
- 2008—Joseph Habersham Chapter, Sons of the American Revolution, started an annual remembrance for Capt. Wilbanks.
- 2011—The Hilliard A. Wilbanks Foundation was established to honor his life, to perpetuate his legacy of courage, sacrifice, and patriotism, and to promote the advancement of higher education through scholarships.
- 2011—To honor the memory and actions of Hilliard A. Wilbanks, the Habersham County Board of Education voted unanimously to name their new school in Demorest, Georgia, for him. The dedication took place on August 13, 2011. Keynote speaker for the dedication was another Georgia native, Medal of Honor recipient, Col. Joe M. Jackson, USAF retired.

Willy Wilbanks

The Hilliard A. Wilbanks Foundation is a 501(c)3 public charity established to honor the life and the legacy of Capt. Wilbanks. The foundation promotes the advancement of higher education through scholarships.

CHAPTER 7

JOHN ANDREW BARNES, III

Jackie

Jackie Barnes

Carson Barnes Fleming laughed, crinkling up her nose. Tossing her head back to clear the hair from her eyes, she continued speaking in a soft Boston accent: "I honestly thought my mother was crazy. I was a freshman at Hood College in Frederick, Maryland, and had come home for the weekend. We were seated in the kitchen drinking coffee on a gorgeous Saturday morning in October 1947. It was one of those rare Indian-summer days in New England, when the air is crystal-clear. The sunshine was brilliant, streaming in through the kitchen windows, and everything seemed so perfect. It was my first visit home since the semester had started in September, and I was telling her about my classes, showing her my red "dink" hat [for freshmen], and talking about how much I loved Frederick. There was not even a hint my world was about to be turned upside down—and then, out of the blue, Mother said, 'Carson, how would you like to have a baby brother?'"

Slowly shaking her head, Carson continued, "I don't really remember—I think I kind of zoned out, but I must have spit coffee clear across the room. When I finally regained some measure of composure, I asked her what she was talking about. She explained very quietly and calmly, as only my mother could, that she and Daddy were considering adopting a child."

"I had been out of the house barely a month. Apparently 'empty nest syndrome' had hit my mother like an atom bomb, and there was not enough excitement in her social circle [bridge does have its limitations]. Her solution was to replace me with another child. Needless to say, I was not too receptive to the idea. My parents were forty years old. Why in the world would they want to start over with a baby? I had not heard Daddy's side of the story, but I knew he could not stand up to my mother for long. Whatever Katie wanted, Katie eventually got. I was devastated."

During the course of the next few weeks, there was little additional discussion about the impending adoption. When Carson tried to talk to her father, he had little to say, other than reassuring her that she would always be loved and she had nothing to worry about regarding her standing in the family. She had given up trying to talk to her mother.

Carson came home on Christmas break in mid-December. Her mother met her at the front door and said, "Carson, darling, there's someone I want you to meet." Katherine took her daughter's hand and the two walked down the hallway to what had been a guest room. It had been redecorated in pale blues and yellows, and was dimly lit by an antique Tiffany lamp. Carson heard a Brahms symphony playing softly somewhere in the house. There was a beautiful rocking horse, a baseball, and bat—stuffed bears and toy soldiers were evident in the dim recesses of the room. Walking over to an exquisite antique crib, Carson looked down and saw the curly head of the most beautiful little boy she had ever seen, and she was in love. This sleeping child was her little brother, John Andrew Barnes, III, the son her father had always wanted.

The small boy, soon referred to as Jackie, was two years old when John and Katherine adopted him. They had assumed they would adopt a baby, and their attorney had put them in touch with a Catholic orphanage in Boston. They had visited the facility and met with the staff. There was a waiting list for babies, and it could take a year or more for that to happen, Katherine was distressed at the thought of waiting. She and John were not getting any younger. After their meeting, the director, Father Galligan, showed them around the facility and suggested they meet some of the children residing there. When they met the small toddler whom the nuns called Johnny, they stopped looking. All thoughts of waiting for a baby disappeared. This tiny bundle of energy was the son they were looking for—the son they were meant to have.

Carson had done no Christmas shopping before arriving home from college. She was out the next day, shopping for her mother and dad, and hitting every toy store in town. It was going to be a very special Christmas.

PART 2

Carson left Hood College after her freshman year and enrolled at Kathleen Dell, an exclusive women's business school in Brookline, Massachusetts She met James Fleming during her time there and fell in love. Brookline was a wealthy suburb on the south side of Boston and James was a junior at Harvard. He had come home for a weekend, and they met at a party. Tall and handsome with a bright future, he was every '50s girl's dream catch. She brought James home to meet her parents and Jackie spent the weekend playing "hide and seek" with him. The boy was a bit shy around strangers, but he and

James hit it off immediately. He was five years old and obviously very intelligent.

Carson Ellen Barnes

Carson and James were engaged in June 1952 after he had graduated from Harvard. Congress had passed the Universal Military Training and Service Act in 1951 requiring males between eighteen and twenty-six to register for the draft. James was exempt as long as he was in school, but after graduation, he expected to be immediately drafted into the Army. Major battles were taking place in Korea and demand for additional troops was high. Making the decision to enlist, James joined the Marine Corps and applied for Officer Candidate School at Marine Corps Base Quantico, south of Washington, DC. OCS consisted of two six-week sessions, after which James was commissioned a second lieutenant in the US Marines.

After graduation, Lt. Fleming remained at Quantico for several weeks of additional combat training. He and Carson were married on the Saturday after Thanksgiving. Per Carson and James's wishes, Katherine had planned a small elegant wedding at St. Bartholomew's, and Jackie was their ring bearer (The boy had turned seven in April.) Ed and Mary Fleming, James's parents, hosted a dinner for the wedding party at Joe Tecce's Ristorante (one of the most popular and exclusive restaurants in Boston) on the night before the wedding.

Lt. James Fleming was deployed to Korea on December 15, 1952. Throughout December and January there was a lull in fighting on the Korean peninsula. Francis Cardinal Spellman, Archbishop of New York and Vicar for Catholic Chaplains of the Armed Forces, conducted a Christmas mass for the Marines at the division command post. On December 31, His Eminence visited Pohang, where he delivered an address to about a thousand Marines. He shook hands with nearly all of them and later heard confessions from many. No major action had taken place in December, although Marine patrols, on a half dozen occasions, had engaged as many as fifty Chinese troops for brief clashes. That activity continued into spring. There was a tremendous increase in fighting in March and April as the weather improved, and truce negotiations resumed at Panmunjom. The Chinese and North Korean leadership wanted to capture as much territory as possible before the conflict came to an end, and Chinese forces attacked en masse.

James Fleming was wounded in combat on April 19, 1953. Jackie had just turned eight years old three days before and was distressed James had been hurt. He wanted to join the Army and go help him. The Korean Armistice was signed in July 1953. James finished his enlistment and was discharged from the Marine Corps as a first lieutenant in 1956.

During Jackie's sophomore year in high school, Katherine and John moved from Belmont, Massachusetts, to Dedham, Massachusetts, a distance of about twenty miles. Dedham was a very historic community dating back to the early 1600s, and Jackie was enthralled with the history of the area.

He liked Dedham High School and was diligent with his studies but still tended to be quiet and shy. He was slow to make friends. Hearing about the Civil Air Patrol, he joined the local unit and drilled at South Weymouth Naval Air Station. He made friends with the CAP members and felt like he belonged there. Jackie turned eighteen in April of his junior year and decided he was going to quit school and become a Marine Corps aviator. It took every bit of effort Katherine, John, Carson, and especially, James, could muster to convince him to stay in school and graduate. He was determined to make his mark in the military and was impatient to get started.

Graduating in June 1964, Jackie immediately enlisted in the Army and left for basic training at Fort Pickett near Blackstone, Virginia. He was nineteen years old.

"I was surprised he left so quickly," Carson said. "He hardly gave us an opportunity to tell him goodbye! He graduated and boom! He was gone. I would have loved to throw him a going-away party, but that was not Jackie's style."

After boot camp, the young private left for airborne training at Fort Benning, Georgia, and additional training as a combat engineer. Upon graduation, he was awarded his jump wings and became a proud member of the 82nd Airborne Division. He was stationed at Fort Bragg, North Carolina.

On April 24, 1965, a long-simmering political crisis in the Dominican Republic exploded into civil war. By 3:00 p.m., Santo Domingo's streets were filled with looting and lawlessness as the Soviet-oriented Dominican Revolutionary Party and the Castroite Fourteenth of June Revolutionary Party armed their members. Bands of teenagers, called Los Tigres, swarmed through Santo Domingo shooting any policemen they could find. The pro-government forces, called Loyalists, were outgunned and outmanned. Both sides were heavily armed, and civilians were caught in the crossfire. Dominican security forces were quickly overwhelmed by the pro-communist forces, and on April 28, armed rebels took over a police station and executed all the officers. The US ambassador was in regular communication with President Johnson and told him they were dealing with "collective madness." He declared, "There is foreign involvement [Russia and Cuba]. If the president doesn't want another Cuba in the Western Hemisphere, he needs to intervene."

The last thing the US government wanted to deal with in the mid-1960s was another Cuba on America's doorstep, so Johnson ordered American forces to restore order. Over three thousand US citizens were assembled in the Hotel Embajador and US diplomats were attempting to evacuate them as the crisis escalated. Washington began preparations for the evacuation of its citizens and other foreign nationals who might wish to leave the Dominican Republic.

Stating the need to protect American lives and property, Johnson sent in the Ei82ndAirborne, the US Marines and a fleet of forty-one vessels to blockade the island. The Seventh Special Forces Group, Psychological Operations units, and various logistical support elements also participated. Of the roughly twenty-three thousand US troops involved in the intervention, nearly all but the Marines came from Fort Bragg. More specifically, they came from various units of the 82nd Airborne Division. On April 29, 1965, the 34d Brigade, 82nd AD landed at San Isidro AB under the command of Lt. Gen. Bruce Palmer. That was Jackie Barnes's unit.

"We saw little resistance," Barnes said. "We expected to see some action, maybe snipers or some sign of the rebels, but they kept their heads down. We didn't have much advanced notice we were shipping out, but once they told us, we were eager to get to the action."

During the next few hours, two brigade combat teams and heavy equipment were dispatched, and at sunrise, units of the 508th Infantry Regiment moved up the San Isidro Highway, securing a position east of the Duarte Bridge. US units had close air support from Marine F-4 Phantom jets. The 1st Battalion, 505th Infantry Regiment remained at the airbase and sent out patrols to the perimeter.

A force of seventeen hundred Marines of the Sixth Marine Expeditionary Unit landed and occupied an area containing a number of foreign embassies The area was proclaimed an International Security Zone by the Organization of American States. Earlier in the day, the OAS also issued a resolution calling the combatants to end hostilities. At 4:30 p.m., representatives of the loyalists, the rebels, and the US military signed a ceasefire to take effect at 11:45 p.m.

On May 5, the OAS Peace Committee arrived in Santo Domingo, and a second ceasefire agreement was signed, which ended the main phase of the civil war. Under the Act of Santo Domingo, the OAS was tasked with overseeing the implementation of the peace deal as well as distributing food and medication through the capital. A day later, OAS members established the Inter-American Peace Force (IAPF) with the goal of serving as a peacekeeping formation in the Dominican Republic. The IAPF had seventeen hundred Brazilian,

Paraguayan, Nicaraguan, Costa Rican, Salvadoran, and Honduran troops and was headed by Brazilian Gen. Hugo Panasco Alvim, with Lt. Gen. Palmer serving as his deputy commander.

82ⁿᵈ Airborne in Santo Domingo—May 1965

"We walked in and took about thirty blocks in the first couple days," Barnes said. "We were encountering some resistance, but most of the time, we served as a buffer between the various fighting groups and distributed food, water and medical supplies to both sides. We also passed out milk and rice and set up medical centers for the local people."

On May 5, the Eighty-Second AB distributed twenty tons of rice. On the evening of May 6, despite a cease-fire being in effect, American forces were experiencing sporadic sniper fire. Pro-communist rebels were using small boats on the Ozama River as sniper positions, and US forces returned fire sinking some of the small boats.

There was also a freighter, the SS *Santo Domingo*, which had been abandoned by its crew after returning to its namesake port amid the war. After the crew fled, the freighter was briefly taken over by members of the Dominican national police before again being abandoned. This time, the ship was taken over by rebels, and the boat's new masters used it as a protected site to direct fire at 82nd Airborne troopers who had taken up positions on the other side of the river.

"We were patrolling along the river front," Barnes said. "It was so damned hot I could barely breathe. We were definitely a long way from New England. We ain't in Kansas anymore, Dorothy," he said, laughing, "The sweat was streaming down from under my helmet and soaking into my soggy collar. All I could think about was a big, frosty mug of Piel's Beer. Man, what I would give for that. Suddenly, we began to take incoming fire from the opposite bank. We hit the dirt and returned fire, but we weren't sure what we were shooting at. We soon realized the snipers were firing from this big-assed freighter that was tied up across the river, and our M14s were not making much impact on the sides of the ship. Our lieutenant called up a crew with an M40 recoilless rifle, and they blasted the shit out of the snipers. The 105mm explosive shells stopped the sniping immediately and set the ship on fire. The hulk burned and eventually sank in the river while we watched and cheered. I don't know if the Eighty-Second had ever sunk a ship or not, but we did that day, and I was there to see it."

On May 26, US forces began gradually withdrawing from the island. On June 15, the leftist rebels launched a second and final attempt to expand their stronghold. In the bloodiest battle of the intervention, they attacked US outposts using the greatest firepower yet: tear-gas grenades, .50-caliber machine guns, 20mm guns, mortars, rocket launchers, and tank fire. The first battalions of the 505th and 508th Infantry quickly went on the offensive. Two days of fighting cost the US five KIA and thirty-one WIA. The OAS forces, consisting of a large number of Brazilians, counted five wounded. The rebels claimed sixty-seven dead and 165 injured.

The first postwar elections were held on July 1, 1966, and pit Reformist Party candidate, Joaquín Balaguer, against former president Juan Emilio Bosch Gaviño. Balaguer was victorious.

Jackie Barnes spent a year in the Dominican Republic and returned to Fort Bragg the last week of April 1966. He went home on leave and enjoyed seeing everyone. Carson thought he had actually grown while he was gone. He had definitely gained muscle weight during his time in the Army. He was unsure where he would be deployed next, but Vietnam was a good possibility. The airborne units were being moved around to cover shortfalls in manning. He would find out when he returned to his 82ndAirborne Unit in North Carolina.

PART 3

When President Johnson gave his OK to introduce US combat troops into Vietnam, the 173rd Airborne Brigade was the first to go. The Brigade was ordered to provide security for Bien Hoa AB, twelve miles northeast of Saigon. Based in Okinawa, the 173rd AB was theoretically prepared to respond to any crises in the region. Its maneuver forces were two airborne infantry battalions, the first and second battalions of the 503rd Infantry Regiment, and an armored cavalry unit, Echo Troop, 17th Cavalry Regiment, supported by the 3rd Battalion., 319th Field Artillery Regiment.

A status report prepared for MACV stated the 173rd Airborne Brigade was ready and in "the best possible equipment posture." In reality it was 10 percent understrength—sixty-one officers and twenty-eight hundred enlisted men out of an authorization of more than thirty-three hundred. The bulk of the brigade moved to Bien Hoa AB and established positions facing War Zone D, an area with a heavy concentration of Việt Cộng forces, but the 1st Battalion, 503rd Infantry, was temporarily detached to provide security for the port facilities and airfield at Vũng Tàu, sixty miles southwest of the capital.

The Sky Soldiers of the 173rd were the first to go into War Zone D to destroy enemy base camps and relieve pressure on Saigon. The 173rd was the first to use long range reconnaissance patrols. In November of 1965 the 173rd took part in Operation HUMP, north of Bien Hoa on the outskirts of Saigon. In 1966 they participated in Operation CRIMP to root out enemy forces from the tunnels at Cu Chi.

Jackie Barnes finished his leave and returned to Fort Bragg. He was then quickly deployed to Vietnam as part of the 173rd Airborne

Brigade on May 31, 1966. Barnes had six months left in the Army, but there was a personnel shortage, and experienced soldiers were especially prized.

Arriving at the 1/503rd Infantry Regiment HQ at Bien Hoa AB in early June, Barnes was assigned to Charlie Company as a grenadier. Located in Đồng Nai Province, sixteen miles northeast of Saigon, the sprawling base was near the city of Biên Hòa and many rural villages, all of which were regularly visited by roving bands of Việt Cộng. He soon found himself in the Vietnamese countryside nearly every day on short patrols and in frequent clashes with enemy troops.

The area was about a month into the summer monsoon season and the weather was unlike anything Barnes had experienced in his life. "The rain is constant, all day every day," Jackie said, "and it comes from all directions. It is impossible to get away from it. The drops are huge, and they just simply batter us from every direction at once. On top of that, the red mud is ankle deep muck. God, what a shit-hole this is!"

In late July, Barnes and his squad were on patrol across the Đồng Nai River when they were ambushed by a VC force with a .50-cal. machine gun. It was near dusk, and the unit was en route back to base. The rain, which had plagued them all day, had ceased for the moment and thick fog had begun to settle in along the river. As the troopers moved along the river trail, a concealed .50-cal. suddenly opened up on them from the left front, followed by snipers firing from a tree line to their rear. This was a classic L-shaped ambush favored by the VC and had the troopers backed up against the muddy bank of the river. The Americans had dived behind some rocks and logs along the river, but were pinned down with little room to maneuver and no way to escape.

Cpl. Schmidt, their squad leader, radioed for assistance, but in the meantime, the .50-cal. was chewing its way through their meager defenses, and the snipers were moving in for the kill. As Schmidt and other members of the team concentrated their fire on the snipers to the rear, Barnes moved back, eased himself over the riverbank into the water, and managed to move upstream a short distance undetected. Crawling back up the bank into the cover of brush and scrub palms, he judged his distance to the enemy machine gun to be about 350 yards. Placing his M79 "thumper" to his shoulder, the young grenadier aimed carefully and fired. Quickly breaking the weapon open, he reloaded and fired again. The machine gun position had erupted into a huge ball of flame as the grenades exploded, destroying the weapon and killing those operating it. The massive explosion was followed by almost total silence. Then the paratroopers let out a cheer and resumed their fire into the trees; however, the VC troops had disappeared. Two of the troopers had minor wounds, but otherwise, the squad had survived in good shape, thanks to Barnes.

Cpl. Schmidt submitted his report upon the squad's return that night. The following day, the Charlie Company commander recommended Jackie Barnes for a Bronze Star Medal for Heroic Service with "V" device for Valor. Barnes did not think it was that big a deal and did not mention it in his letter home.

From the 1940s to the 1960s, the heavily forested area stretching northwest of Saigon was a major communist base of operations. What became known as War Zones C, D, and the Iron Triangle served that purpose for the Viet Minh against the Japanese, the Viet Minh against the French, and for the Việt Cộng against the Republic of Vietnam. Until early 1966, this sanctuary complex, which was the known location of the (communist) Central Office-South Vietnam (COSVN) and the main base of the Việt Cộng 9th Division, was virtually inviolable. The 9th Division was comprised of the 271st, 272nd, and 273rd VC Regiments and was one of the most effective and feared enemy forces in South Vietnam. The Ninth had achieved an almost unbroken string of victories throughout II Corps prior to 1966. It was this division which combined two regiments, in December 1964, for the first multiregiment VC attack of the war. The attack was directed against Bình Giã, a district capital, and it was a complete success for the VC, inflicting heavy losses on South Vietnamese forces.

Operation ATTLEBORO was a search-and-destroy operation launched by the US and South Vietnam against enemy forces, base camps, and supply areas located in War Zone C. It began on September 14, 1966, and was part of the continuing effort to destroy the 9th Division and deny them their area of operation. The 196th Light Infantry Brigade was given operational control, and the operation included units of the US 25th Division, III Corps "Mike" Force, and the 503rd Infantry Regiment.

On October 19, a battalion of the 196th was ordered into the area west-northwest of Tây Ninh to search for VC storage areas holding rice and other supplies. Meanwhile, the VC 9th Division was making preparations to launch a winter offensive. The enemy unit had completed resupply of its ammunition by September 30 and was moving south into a base area northwest of the Michelin Plantation. Their mission was to draw the 196th LIB into battle near Dầu Tiếng and defeat it on a field of their choosing. That would serve as a major propaganda victory on the eve of US Congressional elections and expose the entire area to the full force of a Việt Cộng offensive. The enemy forces massing northwest of Michelin were in good position to strike either the Soui Da Special Forces Camp, six miles to the west, or Dầu Tiếng, ten miles to the southeast.

Other VC units were moving into position to coordinate simultaneous attacks during the expected confrontation with the 196th. By October 19, elements of the 272nd VC Regiment began to move into positions south of Dầu Tiếng, in preparation for an attack on November 4. On October 28, the 1st Infantry Division, while conducting Operation SHENANDOAH, encountered the 3rd Battalion of the 273rd VC Regiment five miles east of the Michelin Plantation. This action effectively eliminated the 273rd from the support of other battalions of the Ninth VC Regiment and from the defense of their base areas during the hard fighting that was to come during the ensuing two weeks.

The 101st NVA Regiment was moving south from bases near the Cambodian border to the build-up area where the 1st and 2nd Battalions of the 273rd VC Regiment were deployed. The commanding officer of the 3rd Company, 3rd Battalion, 101st NVA Regiment, was captured on November 8, and revealed during interrogation that his unit had left their base area on November 1 and moved south, along the eastern boundary of Operation ATTLEBORO, toward resupply camps.

By October 30, the 196th Light Infantry Brigade and elements of the US 25th Infantry Division were continuing their sweeping operations near Dầu Tiếng. The units had now penetrated the fringes of the major Việt Cộng build-up area and were threatening to disrupt their offensive plans. The Americans were also threatening to uncover the major VC base and supply area. On October 31, the US 2nd Battalion, 1st Infantry Regiment located a major logistic base of the COSVN Rear Service Department and captured over eight hundred tons of rice. This was a major blow to the VC logistic system in the area.

The stage was set for a major confrontation between the 9th Division and US forces in the jungles of War Zone C. It was a contest that, over the next two weeks, would result in some of the heaviest and bloodiest fighting of the Vietnam War.

The operation that started out as a small search and destroy mission north of Saigon eventually involved twenty-two thousand troops from twenty-one battalions. Captured documents revealed that the 3rd Battalion of the 101st NVA Regiment was so ravaged by the American attacks and firepower that, without withdrawal orders, its troops simply fled the battlefield.

The Operation ATTLEBORO story ended with most elements of the 9th VC Division having either been run out of the battle area or desperately evading the forces they had been sent to destroy. The heroic performance of the US battalions in early November ensured there would be no communist offensive in the Saigon Corridor during 1966.

After serving six months in Vietnam, Jackie Barnes deployed back to the US. His enlistment was complete. He received his discharge and returned home to Massachusetts.

PART 4

Arriving at Logan Airport in Boston just a few days before Christmas 1966, Jackie was met by Carson and James. Their father had been quite ill with a lingering heart ailment since retiring the summer before. Carson had insisted John and Katherine remain home in Dedham. They were both eager to see their son, but subjecting John to pre-Christmas traffic and crowds at Logan Airport was not considered to be in his best interest.

Jackie was delighted to see his beautiful sister, grabbing her around the neck for a big hug and shaking hands with his favorite ex-Marine at the same time. He and Carson were both laughing and crying together. It was wonderful to be home. Katherine and Carson had written to Jackie every week, but they had downplayed his father's illness. They did not want to worry him while he was in Vietnam. John's condition had not shown much improvement since his heart attack a few months earlier. Coronary bypass surgery was still a rather new procedure, but one his doctors were considering.

"Where are my nieces and nephews?" was Jackie's next question. Carson and James were the proud parents of seven children, and Jackie could hardly wait to see them. He knew the kids had really grown since he had left in the spring. "Home with the nanny," Carson replied. "We had to leave before they were all home from school. They will start Christmas vacation, and you will see them tomorrow."

Stepping out into the brisk evening air in Boston, Jackie shivered. He was wearing his wool uniform, but after tropical Vietnam, thirty degrees felt very cold. Snug in a warm red fox coat, Carson placed her arm around her little brother's shoulders and whispered in his ear that they were expecting snow for Christmas. "Wow," he thought, his dark eyes twinkling in the lights. "My first Christmas home, and it's going to snow just for me." And he chuckled softly to himself.

When they arrived at the family home in Dedham, James stopped the car to allow Jackie and Carson to get out at the front walk. He would park the car and bring in Jackie's duffel bag. As they approached the door, Katherine opened it. She had been watching for them. Wrapping her arms around Jackie with tears in her eyes, she said, "My precious boy, thank God you are home safely. Your father is waiting for you in the den."

As Jackie, Katherine, and Carson moved into the den, the young man saw his father seated in a rocker by the fireplace. He had a coverlet across his knees and a broad smile on his face. John struggled to rise, and Jackie ran to him, wrapping his arms around his father. John appeared to have aged twenty years, and his hair had turned white in the months since Jackie had deployed. Jackie was concerned about how pale and fragile the man appeared, but he did not reveal his thoughts. He and his mother would have that conversation later. James came in with Jackie's bag—for now, the family would just enjoy being together. And tomorrow, Carson was taking Jackie Christmas shopping.

Starting on December 23, a low pressure system departed the Gulf of Mexico. Bringing abundant moisture with it, the system began the classic move up the East Coast. In the days preceding the storm's arrival, frigid Arctic air spread down through the central and eastern US. It was so cold thermometers as far south as Virginia struggled to rise above the twenties, and the atmosphere was primed for the upcoming Christmas snowstorm.

Jackie and Carson were out early on Friday and managed to get their shopping finished by early afternoon. A brutally cold wind had sprung up out of the northwest and they were happy to get back to the Barnes residence in Dedham. John had a roaring fire going in the fireplace, and James arrived with the children who were excited to be out of school for Christmas vacation. Katherine soon had steaming mugs of thick, rich "drinking chocolate" ready for the entire crew, along with fresh-baked anise-flavored sugar cookies. Jackie was so happy to be home.

On Christmas Eve, a strong coastal low formed off Cape Hatteras, slamming bands of heavy, wet snow into the Mid-Atlantic States. The nor'easter continued to trek northward and strengthened throughout Christmas Eve afternoon. For most of the Northeastern US, the storm was in full swing by nightfall forcing many religious services to cancel. The intense storm not only blanketed the coast from Virginia all the way to Maine with snow, but also lit up the sky with lightning and thunder. By midnight, the storm was so severe in the Boston area that the family had to cancel their traditional outing to St. Bartholomew's for midnight Christmas mass.

When the Barnes and Fleming families sat down to have dinner on Christmas day, the nor'easter had passed, but it had left over a foot of snow in its wake. It was a "welcome home" Jackie Barnes would never forget—nor would his nieces and nephews. They spent Christmas afternoon building forts and having snowball fights with their favorite uncle.

PART 5

For the first few weeks he was home, Jackie Barnes seemed to be making the adjustment back to civilian life. He spent most of his time with his father. He rarely strayed from the house for long, but gradually depression began to set in. The days were long, dark and gloomy. He had enjoyed his time in the Army and missed the kinship and camaraderie of his buddies. The few high school friends he had made were all married and/or had moved away for work or school. He began to have nightmares about action he had seen in Vietnam and would wake up soaked with sweat. He dreaded bedtime. As the months passed, his condition worsened, and the family grew increasingly concerned. He had started drinking, which only worsened the situation.

John Sr. had bypass surgery in April, and his health improved dramatically. With the return of warmer weather and out of concern for his father, Jackie seemed to take a positive turn, but his gain was short-lived. The dog days of summer brought a return of the malaise and depression that had plagued the young man for most of the past year.

James Fleming was especially concerned. As the only other combat veteran in the family, he understood what Jackie was going through. He knew of friends after Korea who had undergone similar changes, some battling depression and alcoholism for years. Psychologists had struggled to find a name for the condition, referring to it as "shell-shock" or "battle fatigue." James knew his brother-in-law needed help, so he began to counsel him and spend more time with him. By late summer, Jackie had gotten his life back in control and had joined the local VFW in Dedham. He had also made a life-changing decision. He had been in contact with the local Army recruiter, and he was going to reenlist. He had requested to rejoin his old unit: Company C, 1st Battalion, 503rd Infantry, 173rd Airborne, and he wanted to be a machine-gunner.

The day Jackie made that decision, his entire demeanor changed. He stood taller and straighter, his chin held high, and he had a real smile on his face for the first time in months—not a pretend smile to satisfy someone else. Jackie was back. James was unsure how much sense Jackie's decision made, but he understood his reasons and he supported him.

Carson and Katherine were horrified. Both women talked to him at length and Katherine seemed to be in a perpetual state of mourning, but Jackie would not be dissuaded. He was dying at home. The need to be with his fellow soldiers within the structure and support of the Army culture was so strong in Barnes; the lack of it was eating him alive. He was doing what he had to do—what he was driven to do—what he was destined to do.

The entire family took Jackie to Logan Airport in Boston when he shipped out in early October. Katherine and Carson were in tears, of course, but tried to keep their emotions in check. All seven Fleming nieces and nephews were present and excited to see the airplanes. James and John Sr. were both quiet and supportive, clapping Jackie on the back and wishing him well. Jackie was so pleased to see his father well again, bright-eyed, alert, and tanned.

James remained in the terminal with the children as Carson, Katherine, and John walked Jackie out to board the Eastern Air Lines Shuttle to New York-La Guardia Airport. The young soldier was back in uniform, laughing and joking like he was going home. Katherine took some comfort in seeing how happy her son was. He'd had a tough year, and she had felt helpless. Only James had been able to reach him in his desolation, but all that was behind them. She could only trust he had made the right decision for himself and pray for his safety. With one last round of hugs and kisses, Jackie boarded his flight. The three rejoined James in the terminal, watched the blue-and-white DC-9 taxi out, and depart toward a West Coast connection in New York City.

▨ PART 6

"I couldn't believe Jackie Barnes was back in Nam," Sgt. Don Martinez said. "And back in Charlie Company Man he's a glutton for punishment. He's quiet and kinda keeps to himself, but he's one of the bravest mother***ers I've ever known. He ain't afraid a nothin.' I'd only been in-country a couple months when he DEROSed back to the World and got out of the Army. I never expected to see him back in this shit-hole—and on top'a that, he's volunteered to be in a line company and be a goddamned machine-gunner. Ain't no logic there, man. He's just f***in' nuts! Whatever reason, he's back. He's my platoon gunner. I'm happy I got him. He's a class guy."

"I arrived at Bien Hoa in the middle of October and was just getting settled in when we were ordered to move up into the Central Highlands," Barnes said. "It's beautiful up there, but it's some rough country to move around in. We choppered in near a Special Forces camp at Dak To. It's surrounded by waves of ridges that rise into towering peaks—then they stretch west and southwest toward where South Vietnam, Laos, and Cambodia meet. The area is covered with triple-canopy rainforest, and the only open areas are filled with bamboo groves that are eighty to a hundred feet tall. LZs large enough for choppers are few and far between—that means most troop movements are carried out on foot—we have to hump it. Temps up there can reach 95°F in the daytime and drop to 55°F at night. Shit, we'd be wringing wet with sweat one minute and freezing to death in our soggy BDUs the next. It is one badass place, man, for a lotta reasons."

Barnes's ammo carrier was a young soldier from Virginia named Charlie Lee Jones. Jones was a country boy who had grown up on a farm along the Dan River in Pittsylvania County. He had a wonderful sense of Southern humor, unlike anything Jackie had encountered before, and he loved talking to Charlie Lee.

"Son, this is one ugly place," Charlie Lee drawled. "Every tree is bound up with vines. Every vine is full a f***in' thorns. There's every kind a leech known to man. They even fall out a the trees on us; and at least half the world's population a mosquitoes is live'n right here on our blood. And I don't even wanta think about the f***in' snakes.

Ain't no wonder nobody lives here. Can y'all 'splain to me why we are gettin' ready to fight for this piece-a-shit place?"

The NVA was pouring thousands of troops into the Central Highlands. They were seeking to destroy the Special Forces camps at Ben Het, five miles east of the Cambodian border, and Đắk Tô, ten miles east of Ben Het. The US camps were a major roadblock at the southern end of the Ho Chi Minh Trail The North Vietnamese leadership determined the camps must be eliminated.

The Americans reacted to the NVA buildup by launching Operation MACARTHUR, with the 4th Infantry Division assuming operational control over the 173rd Airborne Brigade. The 4th Infantry Division's 1st Brigade included the 1st, 2nd, and 3rd Battalions of the 8th Infantry Regiment; 1st and 3rd Battalion of the 12th Infantry Regiment; and the attached 2nd Squadron, 1st Cavalry Regiment.

The 173rd Airborne Brigade fielded the 1st, 2nd, and 4th Battalions of the 503rd Infantry Regiment, and supporting units such as the 335th Aviation Company. Some fifteen Army artillery batteries along with tactical air support provided backup firepower.

The 1st Cavalry Division units included 1st Battalion, 12th Cavalry Regiment and 2nd Battalion, 8th Cavalry, and the 23rd and 26th Mike Force companies (indigenous units led by Green Berets) were engaged as well. Also in the mix were six ARVN battalions.

The first fighting of the new operation erupted on November 3 when companies of the 4th Infantry came across NVA defensive positions. The next day the same thing occurred to elements of the 173rd AB. The 173rd companies applied a methodical approach to combat in the highlands. They combed the hills on foot, ran into fixed enemy hill-top defensive positions, applied massive firepower, and then launched ground attacks to force the NVA out. In all instances, the NVA troops fought stubbornly. They inflicted casualties on the Americans and then withdrew, melting into the thick jungle surrounding their positions.

"The fighting was brutal," Jackie Barnes said. "Charlie Lee and I were in the thick of it. He got nicked by a grenade frag. It didn't amount to much, but it bled a lot. We had on flak vests. It was so damned hot—we had on tee shirts and had the vests open in front. Sweat was pouring off of us, and we could hardly breathe. The doc patched Charlie Lee up, and we kept pushing and firing. Finally the NVA cleared out, and we could stop and rest for a bit. The front of Charlie Lee's tee shirt was covered in dried blood. He said he looked like he'd been killin' chickens. I'm not completely clear on what that means, but I'm sure Charlie Lee will explain it later."

1ˢᵗ Battalion 173rd Airborne Setting up positions on Hill 823

The following morning on November 11, the 1/503rd was divided into two small task forces: Task Force Black consisting of Company C, supported by two platoons of Company D, and Task Force Blue, which was composed of Alpha Company and the remaining platoon of Company D. Task Force Black left Hill 823 to find the NVA unit that had attacked the 4/503rd on the day before.

At 8:30 a.m., after leaving their overnight camp and following an NVA communications wire, the American force was ambushed by units of the 66th NVA Regiment and had to fight for its life. Task Force Blue and Company C, 4/503rd was sent to relieve the beleaguered Task Force Black. Blue encountered fire from all sides during its relief attempt, but finally fought its way through, reaching the trapped men at 3:30 p.m.

"It was one hell of a day," Barnes said. "The NVA just came out of nowhere, and they were everywhere. We were caught in crossfire, and a lot of our guys went down before we knew what had hit us. It was so early in the day, man; it was still dark in that goddamned jungle. Charlie Lee kept feeding me ammo, and we were shooting at muzzle flashes. By the time we could see, the situation had settled into a stalemate. We were sure glad to see the guys from Alpha show up in the afternoon. We were in bad need of some relief, not to mention food, water, and rest."

US losses for the day were placed at twenty killed, 154 wounded, and two missing. The commanding officer of Task Force Black, Capt. Thomas McElwain, reported an NVA body count of 175 killed.

One newspaper reported:

VIETNAM FIGHTING GROWS IN HIGHLANDS

SAIGON, South Vietnam, November 11, 1967-Fighting in the Central Highlands exploded with new fury today as American paratroopers of the 173rd Airborne Brigade and foot soldiers of the United States 4th Infantry Division fought two battles near the Cambodian border southwest of Dak To.

The paratroopers, with two companies totaling about 300 men, lost more than half their number killed and wounded in fighting that broke out at 8:30 a.m. and ended at 4:30 p.m. Intelligence estimates place enemy strength in the Dak To area at about two regiments of perhaps 5,000 men.

PART 7

Jackie Barnes jolted awake early on November 12, 1967. He and Charlie Lee Jones were hunkered down in a foxhole along the perimeter of the Charlie Company base camp on Hill 823. He could hear other troopers in the vicinity who were still sleeping and snoring loudly. They had been getting three or four hours sleep a night, if they were lucky, followed by hours of horrendous combat, so all were exhausted. Barnes had suffered another of his nightmares—he woke up bathed in sweat and troubled. The fighting he and his buddies had seen the past few days was the most violent and bloody he had ever been involved in. Each day was worse than the day before, and he felt a sudden urgency to write to his mother. He needed to let her know one last time how much he loved her, how important it was to him for her to know that, and how much he appreciated her and his father taking him home with them all those years before. Jackie had always been shy and had found it difficult to communicate his most intimate feelings, but he wanted to be sure his parents understood. The past year had been difficult on everyone in the family. They had to know that regardless of what happened in the next few hours or days, he felt only love for them and the family, and none of the past year's difficulties had been their fault.

Reaching into a backpack, Jackie retrieved a small flashlight Carson had given him for Christmas; then, he located a small sundry pack containing paper and a pencil and began to write. It was just a brief note, but it said the things foremost in his heart, and he felt better after he had finished it. Most of the jungle vegetation had been blasted away from the hilltop where Charlie Company was encamped, and looking up, Jackie was able to see stars overhead. The night air was cold and thick fog had settled into the valley below them. He was sure enemy troops were down there busily preparing for the day's fight. He had come to the conclusion they never slept; they just spent their time getting ready for the next battle.

The early morning breeze freshened, and the young soldier shuddered as the wind ruffled his dark hair. His tee shirt was still damp with perspiration. He placed his helmet on his head and closed the opening on his flak vest. Charlie Lee had been on watch for the past hour and turned to look at Jackie. "You doin' okay, son?" he asked. "You look like you been rode hard and put up wet. You need to get some more shuteye."

Barnes was afraid to close he eyes again. He could not face another nightmare. It would not be long before daylight. He'd just break out some c-rats and wait. "I'm not going back to sleep, Charlie Lee," he said. "You get some rest if you want. I will keep watch."

A couple of hours later, Sgt. Martinez came by to make sure everyone in Charlie Company was awake. The day had dawned dark and ominous. As the "Sky Soldiers" moved out, the men glanced at each other nervously, then ducked their heads. Without saying a word, their eyes spoke volumes about their forebodings of the day's events. Every man wondered the same thing: "How many would still be there later—how many would be alive and well at the end of the day."

As the unit moved out on its search and destroy mission in the valley below, it encountered resistance from NVA snipers in the trees. Within an hour, the soldiers found themselves surrounded and fighting for their lives. Capt. McElwain called for reinforcements and airstrikes against the entrenched enemy troops. There was a continuous roar of gunfire and explosions from hand grenades, mortars, and rockets coming from both sides in the conflict. Purple and green smoke began to rise above the tops of jungle trees as the troopers attempted to mark their positions for the coming air strikes. F-100s roared in and dropped fragmentation bombs around the perimeter of the beleaguered soldiers' positions. Helicopter gunships arrived, flying above the tall bamboo with door gunners blazing. The scene was total chaos as the battle continued.

Among those caught in the middle of the Charlie Company chaos were Jackie Barnes and Charlie Lee Jones. Both soldiers had been wounded by the blast of a Chicom B-40 rocket and were unconscious. Medics had hauled them, along with other wounded, to a semiprotected area along the banks of a small stream in the valley. The firestorm of the battle continued to explode all around the men and over them. As Barnes regained consciousness, he was aware he could not hear what was happening. He could see the action, but heard only a dull roar. Turning his head, he saw Charlie Lee, bruised and bloody, lying on a stretcher beside him. He put his fingers to his right ear and was relieved to feel his ear was still there, but when he looked at his fingers, they were covered in blood. He was bleeding from both ears and his nose. He attempted to raise his head from the stretcher, but it was as if all hell came crashing down on him. Everything swirled around him, and he was hit with an overwhelming wave of nausea. Quickly closing his eyes, Barnes shook his head to clear away the fog in his brain and settled back onto the stretcher. He was unsure where he was or what had happened to him, but he recognized Charlie Lee was his friend, and he was concerned about him. *Holy shit*, he thought. *What has happened to us?*

Drifting in and out of consciousness, Barnes gradually regained his senses. Charlie Lee had also regained consciousness, and the two had managed some limited communication, although their hearing was still impaired. Barnes managed to raise himself up to a sitting position and check himself for physical injuries. His arms and legs seemed to be sound, although he was suffering from abdominal pain and a splitting headache. He was aware the action around the area was rapidly intensifying, and the medics were attempting to move the wounded nearer to the embankment where they would be better protected from gunfire.

Operation MacArthur—November 1967

169

Suddenly, there was a massive explosion directly above where Jackie and Charlie Lee were located. Large quantities of red mud and sod rained down on the men below, along with clouds of thick, choking smoke and the acrid smell of rotten eggs, scorched earth, and death. An RPG had hit a sandbagged M60 machine gun emplacement located on the bank above them, killing the three US soldiers manning it.

As the attack continued to intensify, it was apparent the location of the Charlie Company wounded was in danger of being overrun. Rising from his stretcher, Barnes stumbled across the shallow stream, with bullets flying all around him. Upon reaching the embankment, Barnes peered up over the edge and could see the gun, along with the bodies of the dead soldiers. Pulling himself up over the bank, Barnes crawled the three yards into the destroyed bunker and determined the weapon was still operational. Moving in behind it, he began to fire. There were three or four NVA soldiers breaking through the bamboo thicket and charging toward the stream, but Barnes quickly cut them down. Seconds later, another enemy soldier jumped out with a rocket launcher, but Barnes killed him before he could fire the weapon. During the ensuing twenty to thirty minutes, the young soldier managed to keep the NVA force at bay, killing another half dozen of them as they tried to charge his position. Then he ran out of ammo.

Sliding back down over the embankment, Barnes's only thought was the need for more M60 ammunition. He had no other weapon with which to hold off the enemy troops attempting to overrun their position. He was still struggling with his sense of balance, and as he staggered back across the shallow stream, he saw a Chicom hand grenade land among the wounded, just to the right of his buddy, Charlie Lee. Many of the men were too injured to move. Without hesitation, Barnes ran the last ten feet and threw himself on top of the grenade. There was a loud but muffled explosion as the soldier took the full force of the blast with his body. None of those already wounded men in the area received further injury.

The nearest medics came running, along with a rifle squad that quickly fought off the attacking enemy soldiers. Barnes was still breathing when the docs got to him. A medic turned him onto his back to examine his extensive wounds and saw he was trying to speak. "Don't try to talk," the medic said. "Save your strength."

Staring up into the doc's face with tears in his eyes, Jackie Barnes whispered, "Tell my mom I love her," and then he died.

PART 8

On the morning of November 13, 1967, a US Army vehicle parked in front of the large, white split-level home at 246 Colwell Dr. in Dedham, Massachusetts. Two uniformed men, an Army sergeant major and an Army chaplain, got out and walked slowly to the front door. Katherine Barnes answered the door, called for her husband, John, and then collapsed. The soldiers helped John get Katherine into the den and then explained why they had come. John called Carson, Katherine's doctor, and the family priest.

Ten days later, a funeral mass was conducted for John Andrew Barnes III at St. Bartholomew's Catholic Church in Needham, Massachusetts. Burial with full military honors followed on Veteran's Hill at Brookdale Cemetery in Dedham, Massachusetts.

On the same day, five miles across the same valley where Jackie Barnes died, the 2nd and 4th Battalions of the 173rd AB fought an even bigger battle for Hill 875. Over a hundred paratroopers died, and some 250 more were wounded in the five-day battle. While the fighting raged, Gen. William Westmoreland, Commander of US Forces in Vietnam, was in Washington, DC, telling the National Press Club how well the war in Vietnam was going.

173rd Paratroops on Hill 875—Thanksgiving Day 1967

Hill 875 was taken by the 173rd paratroops only to be abandoned days later as the entire unit was pulled from the area. The only positive thing to come from those battles was that most of the NVA's 1st Infantry Division would have to sit out the Tet Offensive (two months later) due to their severe losses. By the end of November, the NVA withdrew back into Cambodia and Laos. They had failed to wipe out a major American unit, but the US Army had paid a high price for their valor—376 US troops had been killed or were missing and another 441 were wounded.

One of the wounded soldiers at Dak To was an Army lieutenant who had observed Jackie Barnes's takeover of the M60 machine gun, which protected the wounded from the encroaching NVA troops. He had already made a note to recommend Barnes for a Bronze Star for that action before his final heroic act. A few days after Jackie Barnes's death, Capt. McElwain, the Charlie Company commander, recommended Barnes for the Medal of Honor, one of three that would be awarded to members of the 173rd Airborne Brigade for their actions during the battle.

In November 1969, John and Katherine Barnes, along with Carson and James Fleming and their four oldest children, flew to Washington, DC, where they accepted Jackie's Medal of Honor at a White House ceremony. "It was such an honor," Carson Fleming said years later. "It's still impossible to believe my brother is gone. He was such a special young man, but he died doing what he wanted to do. I'll always believe his death brought about the early deaths of my parents. Neither ever recovered from Jackie's death. My father died of a broken heart in 1973. My mother followed in 1977."

Within hours of learning Barnes was to be awarded the Medal of Honor, a Blue Ribbon Commission was established by the Town of Dedham to make plans for a John A. Barnes, III Memorial Day.

On April 19, 1970, The Town of Dedham rededicated Memorial Field as John A Barnes III Memorial Park. At the ceremony, local dignitaries, members from the Dedham VFW where Barnes was a member after his first enlistment, members from dozens of VFWs from surrounding towns, and local marching bands marched through Dedham to the park where a marble monument was unveiled in Barnes's honor.

Each year on Memorial Day weekend, the town of Dedham conducts the annual John A. Barnes, III Vigil. It starts at 7:00 a.m. on Sunday and runs to 7:00 p.m. Members of the elite New England Chapter# 9, John A. Barnes, III Chapter of the 173rd Airborne Brigade Association stands a silent twelve-hour vigil at the John Barnes Monument in Dedham.

Barnes additional military honors include the Bronze Star Medal w/OLC, the Purple Heart w/OLC, Combat Infantryman Badge, Marksmanship Badge, Parachutist Badge, National Defense Service Medal, Vietnam Campaign Medal, Vietnam Service Medal, and the Vietnamese Gallantry Cross.

By beauty lavishly outpoured
And blessings carelessly received,
By all the days that I have lived
 Make me a soldier, Lord.
By all of man's hopes and fears,
And all the wonders poets sing,
The laughter of unclouded years,
And every sad and lovely thing;
 Make me a man, O Lord.
 I, that on my familiar hill
Saw with uncomprehending eyes
A hundred of Thy sunsets spill
Their fresh and sanguine sacrifice,
Ere the sun swings his noonday sword
 Must say goodbye to all of this;
By all delights that I shall miss,
 Help me to die, O Lord.

"Before Action"
Lt. William Noel Hodgson

CHAPTER 8

JOHN PAUL BOBO

Great Heart

John Bobo

Born on Valentine's Day 1943, no one had more heart than John Paul Bobo. "There was a farmer had a dog, and Bobo was his name-o," the children would chant, but it was all in good fun. At Our Lady of Lebanon Parochial Grammar School in Niagara Falls, New York, little Johnny Bobo, might not be the biggest boy, or the fastest runner, or the best hitter on the baseball team, but he was always the first one picked when teams were chosen because he was a winner. No one had more heart, more grit, or was more determined to win. That was what set him apart from other children his age. If Johnny was on your team, he took charge and usually found a way to win. John's younger brother, Bill, loved to tell the story of how heartbroken the boy was when a JV football coach who did not know Johnny rejected the youngster for their team because of his small stature. Subsequently, John began weight training. He promised that would never happen again, and it did not. He joined the YMCA and became active in the Bar Bell Club, a weightlifting group comprised of Y members.

As John progressed through high school at Bishop Duffy, an all-male Catholic high school in Niagara Falls, he earned a reputation not only as a winner playing intramural sports and running track, but as one friend remembered, for being a "class guy" when it was not necessarily the popular or expected thing to do. John Bobo was always special.

After graduating from Bishop Duffy in 1961, Bobo enrolled at Niagara University, where he majored in history. He was a member of the varsity track team; he was an intramural wrestling champion and played on intramural football and basketball teams. He joined the US Marine Corps Reserve in Buffalo in May 1965, received his BA degree in June 1965, and was commissioned a second lieutenant in the Marine Corps Reserve on December 17, 1965. He completed the Officer Candidate Course, The Basic School, Quantico, Virginia, in May 1966, and a month later, 2nd Lt. Bobo was ordered to Vietnam where he was assigned duty as the Weapons Platoon commander, India Company, 3rd Battalion, 9th Marine Regiment, 3rd Marine Division.

Any military veteran will tell you that second lieutenants get more than their share of disrespect. Referred to as *nuggets, butterbars, shavetails,* and various other derogatory nicknames, they have to earn the respect of their men and fellow officers. It is not automatically bestowed upon them. Especially in time of war, new lieutenants just out of school were often asked to assume command of combat-hardened Marines. The learning curve was steep, and it was not easy to gain the trust of those men, but Bobo the youngster who had never stood out as a scholar or athlete now rose to the occasion and fulfilled the role he was destined for. He quickly earned a reputation for being a quiet, competent, and decisive leader who cared deeply about his men. He would never put their lives at risk if there was any way to avoid it. His Marines soon realized that fact, and in a short period of time, they were ready to follow him anywhere.

John Bobo—December 1966

The 3/9th Marines had been relieved of SLF (Special Landing Force) duty in early March 1967 and airlifted by helicopters into Đông Hà. They were then relocated by truck to Camp Carroll to provide perimeter security for a brief time—then began search and destroy operations north of Cam Lộ.

The town of Cam Lộ was located nine miles west of Đông Hà and twelve miles northwest of Quảng Trị between Highway 9 and the Cam Lộ River. It was only five miles south of the DMZ. Bobo had been in South Vietnam for ten months and had seen a lot of hard fighting against seasoned NVA and VC troops. He was a month past his twenty-fourth birthday and had three more months to go on his first tour.

2nd Lt. John Bobo—Mỹ Lộc

On March 27, Bobo and India Company, numbering 220 Marines, embarked on Operation PRAIRIE III. The company was tasked with finding and engaging two North Vietnamese Army battalions and elements of the Việt Cộng that were known to be operating four miles north-northwest of Cam Lộ.

On March 30, the India Company commander, Capt. Mike Getlin, sent his three platoons out to set up ambush sites in the area of Hill 70, west of Con Thien. Then he, along with, the rest of the India Company command group, and a security element comprised of two squads of Marines from 2nd Platoon and Lt. Bobo (who was XO and Weapons Platoon commander) with his Weapons Platoon, slowly moved through waist-high brush, small trees and elephant grass up Hill 70. Capt. Getlin was planning to establish an additional night ambush site and hoped to snare one of the NVA patrols as they moved through the area.

About 6:00 p.m., as the Marines began to settle into their defensive positions on the hill, they saw two NVA soldiers strolling across an open area. One of the Marines opened fire, and the Americans were hit with a barrage of 60mm mortars and heavy .30-cal. machine gun fire. That was followed by a full frontal attack from a North Vietnamese Army battalion. Some seven hundred to eight hundred well-trained enemy soldiers suddenly appeared out of nowhere.

The NVA had used the thick ground cover to maneuver in close to the company command post before launching their attack and the Marines took a number of casualties before recovering from the surprise onslaught. What would be known as the Battle of Getlin's Corner had begun.

Organizing a counterattack by his Weapons Platoon, Bobo drove back the enemy force, but there was no doubt the Marines were outmanned and outgunned by the huge NVA force. The command post consisted of less than forty Marines. The lieutenant moved forward to support his rocket teams who were engaging the enemy in close-quarters combat. Firing his Remington 870 shotgun, the young officer almost singlehandedly prevented the unit from being overrun.

Under tremendous pressure from the enemy force, and with mortar shells exploding all around them, Bobo recovered a 3.5-inch rocket launcher from a dead Marine and organized a new launcher team, directing their rocket fire on the NVA .30 cal machine gun positions that had his unit pinned down.

The Weapons Platoon Marines fought like they had never fought before. Inspired by their commander's grit and determination, they forced the enemy soldiers back up the hill and into a densely wooded area near the top. The Weapons Platoon Marines, two squads of 2nd Platoon Marines, and the NVA troops would continue the ebb and flow of the battle for several hours.

Cpl. Jack Loweranitis, who had already received the Silver Star for heroism during the previous September, had taken over a 60mm mortar position, and was delivering devastating mortar fire into the attacking enemy force. When the corporal ran out of mortar ammunition, he started pulling wounded Marines to whatever positions he could find that provided some cover, while continuing to fire on the advancing NVA troops. Although suffering from multiple shrapnel and gunshot wounds, Loweranitis continued to refuse evacuation. The Marine stood his ground until he was finally overrun and killed. When his body was recovered on March 31, the recovery team discovered there was not a single round left in his weapon.

Cpl. Jack Loweranitis

Capt. Getlin, despite multiple gunshot and shrapnel wounds, refused medical attention and remained on the exposed forward slope of the hill. From his position, he calmly called in artillery fire and directed helicopter strikes on the advancing enemy troops. Getlin also used a shotgun and fired it so fiercely the barrel split open from the heat. The commander remained with his Marines, fighting heroically until he was mortally wounded by automatic weapons fire and an NVA hand grenade.

Capt. Mike Getlin

Additional NVA troops arrived in the area and blocked the rifle squads that had been on ambush duty as they attempted to reach and reinforce their embattled command post. About three hours into the attack, a mortar round exploded near Lt. Bobo. He was thrown through the air with violent force and crashed to the ground deep in a patch of the tall elephant grass. He lay there stunned and unmoving. Slowly his head began to clear. He was lying face down in the red dirt and could taste the metallic flavor of blood in his mouth. He was dazed, unsure where he was or what had happened to him. He saw flashes of colored lights; scenes of his mother, dad, and siblings flashed through his mind, and he yearned for home. He could hear nothing but a slight roar. It felt as if hot ice picks had been rammed into each ear, and then everything faded to black. He tried to move, but nothing seemed to work.

PO Ken Braun, a nineteen-year-old Navy corpsman, had seen the lieutenant get hit by the exploding shell and struggled to reach him amid the chaos of the attack. The Marine counterattack had brought about a renewal of the mortar and machine gun fire. That would precede another full frontal attack by the NVA. The Marines were outnumbered four to one.

Navy corpsman Ken Braun

By the time the corpsman reached Bobo, he was sitting up shaking his head and trying to clear his vision. The explosion had hit him like a Mack truck. His uniform was soaked with blood from hundreds of shrapnel wounds, and he felt as if his skin was on fire. Braun assessed his injuries and saw immediately that the man's right foot and ankle had been severed by the explosion. He was going to bleed out quickly without help. Removing his web belt, the corpsman wrapped it around Bobo's leg below the knee and pulled it tight, using it as a tourniquet to help staunch the blood flow. Administering a shot of morphine, Braun began to drag the officer toward the rear, but the lieutenant had regained his senses and ordered him to stop.

"I'm not leaving," Bobo said emphatically. "Help me to that tree. Prop me up. Get my shotgun and ammo!" Not daring to defy the clear-eyed second lieutenant, Doc Braun did as he was ordered.

Cpl. Jack Riley, one of the squad leaders, had crawled in to assist. He and the corpsman dragged the lieutenant to a nearby tree that had some elevation to it. The corpsman handed Bobo his weapon and the men watched as he jammed the stump of his wounded leg into the dirt to help stop the bleeding and steadied himself against the trunk of the small tree. Bobo had always been decisive. Knowing his injury would slow his company's withdrawal, he ordered the men to retreat while he stayed behind to cover them.

Turning to the squad leader, he said, "Get these Marines out of here, Riley. Pull them back."

"But, Lieutenant, we can't—" the corporal began to argue.

"I said pull back, Cpl. Riley!" Bobo said cutting him off. "That's an order, goddamnit!"

The NVA were now attacking full-force down the hill. Automatic weapons fire was increasing. The enemy commanders were intent on overrunning the Marine positions regardless of the cost, but as Bobo rapid-fired his Remington into the main point of the enemy attack, those leading the charge began to turn back. Charging into a hail of buckshot was like fighting a hornet's nest. The enemy advance slowed and then ground to a halt. Meanwhile, the Marine squad leaders were quickly moving their men down the hill to a better protected position and reestablishing their defensive line.

Braun the Navy corpsman had remained with Bobo, and the squad leader called for him to move back with the company. As he started to leave, a North Vietnamese soldier who had crawled through the grass stood up with an AK-47 and fired, seriously wounding the medic and killing Bobo. Hearing the automatic weapons fire, Cpl. Riley rose from his position and killed the enemy soldier. He then ran to assist the corpsman. Realizing the lieutenant was dead, Riley half-carried the sailor, and the two men moved down the hill to rejoin the company of Marines.

From its new position, India Company was able to repulse the renewed NVA attack. With heavy loss of life and the onset of total darkness, the North Vietnamese forces melted away into the jungle. The time Bobo had bought his men by his selfless action was sufficient to allow them to reorganize and win the day against overwhelming odds. They had held off the enemy force and dealt them a devastating blow. "There were enemy dead everywhere," one Marine stated.

The Marine toll was sixteen killed on that fateful evening. That number included the company commander, Capt. M. P. Getlin and Second Lt. Bobo. In Addition, India Company suffered fifty-two wounded, but John Bobo's actions undoubtedly saved the lives of many Marines. NVA dead numbered at least 150.

"The Lieutenant never hesitated," Jack Riley said later. "He was decisive. He made up his mind and that was it. He had great heart. He saved our lives."

"I saw him kill at least five attacking North Vietnamese soldiers after he was wounded," 1st Sgt. Ray Rogers said. "He also killed the North Vietnamese soldier who had wounded me in the leg and was standing over me [ready to finish the job]," Rogers concluded.

During the entire Vietnam War, no battle of such brief duration would result in as many of the nation's highest decorations for valor being awarded to a Marine Corps unit. There were numerous other awards and many acts of heroism that doubtless went unrecorded, but in six hours, the Marines of India Company were honored with four Navy Crosses, six Silver Stars, three bronze stars with "V" device for Valor, and one Medal of Honor—to 2nd Lt. John P. Bobo of Niagara Falls, New York. As another lieutenant commented, "A lot of Marines did a lot of good things on a very bad day in Quảng Trị Province.

Back in the States, John Bobo's story barely made a ripple. Thanks to the US media, the tide of public opinion was already turning against the war effort and against the men who were being tasked with fighting the war; the story of a Marine lieutenant's heroism did not fit their agenda. Bobo's death was noted in the local Niagara Falls newspapers, but the true story of his self-sacrificial effort to save his Marines would not come to light until many years later.

A funeral mass was celebrated for John Bobo at Our Lady of Lebanon Catholic Church in Niagara Falls in April 1967. The funeral service was followed by burial with full military honors at Gate of Heaven Cemetery in Lewistown, New York.

PART 2

Secretary of the Navy Paul Ignatius presented Lt. Bobo's Medal of Honor to his parents, Paul and Jane Bobo on August 27, 1967, in Washington, DC. It was a bitter-sweet day for the Bobo family as they proudly accepted the nation's highest honor and listened to a recounting of their son's courageous sacrifice. The other Bobo children included 2nd Lt. Willliam M. "Bill" Bobo, USAR, 2nd Lt. Timothy J. Bobo, USAR, J. Patrick Bobo, and sister, Mary J. Bobo.

John Bobo's other decorations included the Purple Heart with gold star, the Combat Action Ribbon, the National Defense Service Medal, the Vietnam Service Medal with bronze star, the Republic of Vietnam Campaign Medal, and the Vietnamese National Order of Vietnam Fifth Class, Knight, with Gallantry Cross with Palm.

- The USMC Officer Candidate School Mess at Quantico, Virginia, is named "Bobo Hall."
- John Bobo's name is memorialized on the Medal of Honor monument in Niagara Falls State Park, Niagara Falls, New York.

- USMC Security Forces Response facility, Naval Weapons Station Earle, Colts Neck, New Jersey, is dedicated to Lt. John Bobo.
- A main roadway through Marine Corps Base, Yuma, Arizona, is named Bobo Avenue.
- Niagara University's baseball field is named John P. Bobo Field.

One of the highest honors granted to any Navy or Marine veteran is the naming of a US Navy ship. The USS *2nd Lt. John P. Bobo* was christened by his mother, Jane Bobo, in 1985 at the General Dynamics Shipbuilding Yard in Quincy, Massachusetts. Mrs. Bobo died a year later.

Capt. John P. Bobo—USMC

Capt. John P. Bobo, USMC, nephew of the ship's namesake, visited the USNS *2nd Lt. John P. Bobo* while the ship was in Kuwait in July 2003. Ship and crew were participating in Operation ENDURING FREEDOM.

"I still get tears in my eyes when I think about it," Capt. Bobo said, referring to his uncle's heroic sacrifice. "His actions express the true core of values of the US Marine Corps."

Bobo's story is now known to generations of Marine second lieutenants going through training at Quantico, Virginia, and he has become a kind of "patron saint" to the new officers. Lieutenants fresh out of school are acutely aware of their vulnerability as they assume command of platoons filled with seasoned Marines. It is not for the faint of heart. It takes the grit and determination that John Bobo so perfectly personified. It helps to know someone like them went through it and accomplished amazing things. If Bobo did it, they can too. All it takes is heart.

> Let those who would handle
> Make sure they can wield
> His far-reaching sword
> And his close-guarding shield:
> For those who must journey
> Henceforward alone
> Have need of stout convoy
> Now Great-Heart is gone.
>
> "Great-Heart"
> Rudyard Kipling

CHAPTER 9

SAMUEL SWANN LINVILLE

Scout

Sam Linville—Christmas 1967

That suntanned, barefoot boy running down a country road in Piedmont North Carolina had few cares. Carolina summers in the early 1950s were laid back and easy going if you were eight years old and on your way to your favorite fishing hole. That was doubly true if you could take a shortcut through your aunt's kitchen on the way there. Aunt Becky always had fresh-made doughnuts or leftover biscuits slathered with sweet churned butter and honey, along with a bright smile and a hearty welcome when he hit the stoop of her shaded, front porch. Life was good.

Sammy Linville daydreamed of being a soldier. His father, mother, and stepfather had all served in the Army during WWII. His mama, Mary Elizabeth, had been a nurse in the Women's Army Corps achieving the rank of Tec5 (tec corporal) by the time she got out in 1945. She had met his father, Harry, during the war, and they had gotten married shortly after the war ended. Sam was born on Friday, November 22, 1946.

In 1950, Sammy's father died. The boy was five years old. His mother remarried in August 1953, and his stepfather was a good man from Winston-Salem named Ray Davis. Ray had given Sammy a bag full of toy soldiers their first Christmas together in 1953, and the boy loved them. He spent hours playing with the small troops in his sand box. It was built between two large maple trees behind their house on West Ray Street in High Point. He would dig foxholes and practice throwing clods of dirt like artillery shells. Davis had been a mechanic in the Army Air Corps during WWII; however, Sammy was more inclined toward ground action. His real dad had been an artilleryman. Sammy preferred "GI Joe" to "Steve Canyon" any day.

Sammy came by his love for the military honestly. He was too young to know it, but the blood of three Revolutionary War generals from North Carolina flowed through his veins. His fifth great-grandfather, Brig. Gen. Francis Nash, had marched his Carolina Brigade of two thousand troops to Germantown, Pennsylvania, in 1777 to join George Washington in the defense of Philadelphia. On October 4, 1777, as Nash and his troops marched along behind Washington's company, a cannon ball flew over the column, narrowly missing Washington's head. The six pound ball hit Nash's horse in the neck and Nash's thigh was crushed as the horse fell on top of him. Tended by Washington's personal physician, Gen. Nash died three days later. He was thirty-five years old.

Sammy's little sister came along in the fall of 1954. She was named Mary Raye, and she was soon the apple of everyone's eye—

well, almost everyone. Sammy was not sure he really needed a baby sister, and he did not recall being asked about it in advance.

"It was just kind of boom! And there she was," the boy thought. "Stinky diapers, spit-up, and all. Think I'll go 'n' see if the fish are bitin'."

In the summer of 1959, Sam's mother began to consider sending him to private school. The boy had a speech impediment that was causing him problems at school, both socially and educationally. He had performed reasonably well in the lower grades, and they had hoped he would "grow out of it," but as he approached high school, his grades plummeted. Mary and Ray had grown concerned. After careful financial considerations and seeing what schools were available, they decided to send Sam to Hargrave Military Academy in Chatham, Virginia.

Hargrave was an all-male boarding school that offered structure, discipline, and small class size, averaging ten students per class. The Davis's were not wealthy, but they had been putting aside money toward Sam's college. If they could use the money now to salvage the youngster's future, it would be worth the investment. Sammy had always loved the military. Now he would get his first real taste of it at the ripe old age of thirteen. He was enrolled as a cadet in the Military Junior School as a seventh grader and spent two years at the military school in Virginia.

Cadet Sammy Linville at Hargrave Military Academy 1959–1961
Photo 1—Seventh-Grade Junior School, 1959
Photo 2—Eighth-Grade Glee Club, 1960
Photo 3—Right In Formation, 1960
Photo 4—Eighth-Grade Chorus, 1961

Besides all things military, Sam loved fishing. He would come walking down the road with a grin on his face and have a new lure in his hand, or a new rod he wanted to try out. He spent many hot summer days "drownin' worms" in the local streams and reservoirs. There were a number of lakes in the Greensboro/High Point area, and he would ride his bicycle or hitch a ride with a friend. He was always looking for a new "fishin' hole."

Sam was known for always having a smile on his face. He loved to crack jokes and make people laugh. His speech impediment was referred to as "cluttering"; he tended to speak too rapidly or too jerky (or both). The more excited he got, the worse it was, and the more difficult it was to understand him. He often made fun of his speech problem to make people laugh. His hero was a new country singing star named Mel Tillis. Tillis would crack jokes about his stutter and then sing with a beautiful baritone voice. Sam had bought several of his records.

Everyone knew when Sam got serious, it was time to stop and listen to what he had to say. Around Halloween, he would gather a group of his friends, borrow Ray's old GMC truck, and they would head for the woods. They would spend the day cutting, splitting and loading wood for his grandmother, Anna Swann Grimes. She lived on Spring Garden Street in Greensboro and had been a widow for over thirty years. She had come to rely on her grandson. He always made sure Grannie Swann (as he called her) had whatever she needed, and he spent as much time with her as he could. Some days he would borrow his mother's Chevy, stop by the Boar and Castle Restaurant in Greensboro for butter-steak sandwiches, and drive on to her house for lunch. Grannie Swann adored Sammy.

PART 2

After graduating high school, Sam was unsure of the future. He was not into the college scene, and after two years of military school, joining the Army had lost some of its appeal. He was more interested in hunting and fishing. He was working odd jobs but had not found anything steady. The war in Vietnam was beginning to crank up.

The Marines had landed at Danang on March 8, 1965. Vietnam was in all the newspapers and on the evening television news. Walter Cronkite would drone on and on about it every night.

Sam knew if he was not in college he would soon be drafted, but he was hesitant. Grannie Swann passed away in March 1966, and Sam missed her terribly, which contributed to his indecision. Ray had taken a job as a printer in Salisbury, North Carolina. He was working odd hours and was gone most of the week. It was too far away for him to commute daily, so he had rented an apartment there. That also contributed to Sam's indecisiveness. He hated the thought of his mother and Mary Raye being alone at night. God he detested being an adult. Everything had gotten so damned complicated. He just wanted to go fishin' and forget it all.

At the end of September 1966, Sam received the dreaded envelope in the mail. He opened it and read, "The President of the United States to Samuel Swann Linville, Greetings: You are hereby ordered for induction into the Armed Forces of the United States, and to report to the Carolina Trailways Bus Station in Greensboro, North Carolina, on October 31, 1966, at 6:30 a.m. for forwarding to the Armed Forces Induction Station in Charlotte, North Carolina." He stared at the notice, reread it, and then took it in to show his mother.

"Shit fire," he thought to himself. "Happy f***in' Halloween!"

On Monday morning, October 31, Mary Davis drove her son to the bus station in Greensboro. Neither of them could think of anything to say. She gave him a kiss, he ducked his head shyly looking at the pavement, mumbled a "Bye, Mama," and he was off on his next adventure.

At the bus terminal in Charlotte, Sam joined up with a couple dozen inductees who had arrived from other parts of the state. They were herded onto another bus and driven to the induction center. After physical and psychological tests, the men were ushered into a large conference room for their swearing-in ceremony. When that concluded, they were loaded onto another bus and headed south to Fort Jackson, South Carolina.

It was late at night when they arrived at the fort, and it was very dark. It had already been a long day. The men had managed to doze some on the bus, but they arrived stiff-legged and tired. The weather was cold for October. Temperatures were in the upper forties, but the youngsters had little time to think about the weather. The screaming drill instructors met their bus and had them running everywhere they needed to go. First came the military barbers. The new troops were formed into a "sort of" military formation and ran to the barbershop for haircuts which took all of five seconds each. Then they ran through a warehouse-type building where they were issued PT shorts and ill-fitting fatigues.

The men were then trotted to a nearby WWII-style barracks where they were permitted to stow away their gear before double-timing to a nearby chow hall for their first meal. It was an unidentifiable gray mess that was slopped on their trays, along with powdered eggs, and they were given about three minutes to eat it.

"What is this stuff?" Sam whispered to the man sitting next to him.

"SOS," the other recruit replied. "You know what that means, right?"

It was the infamous chipped beef gravy on toast, known fondly as "shit on a shingle."

"It really wasn't bad," Sam said later. "Course, I was so hungry. I'd have eaten anything."

The men then ran to another large processing center for additional aptitude tests and inprocessing. Sam had always been skinny as a rail, but at this rate, he mused, "I'll lose a few more pounds before this is over with."

The men finally jogged back to their barracks at about 0500.

"Lights out!" one of the DIs screamed. "Reveille at 0600!"

Once he had adjusted to the Army system and his DI's way of doing things, Sam had few problems. He was still plagued by the speech impediment and took some ribbing at first, but his time in military school stood him in good stead. Guys who had prior service or had attended military school were identified and designated platoon leaders. A speech teacher at Hargrave had also worked with him, teaching him to concentrate and speak slower, and that helped his confidence.

Sam's twentieth birthday on November 22 found him on the rifle range, sprawled in three inches of cold, muddy water and pouring rain. The temperature that morning when "Reveille" had sounded was thirty-seven degrees. His platoon had double-timed to breakfast, followed by PT and drill, and then more PT. After lunch came more PT and then double-time to the rifle range.

"So much for the sunny South," Sam thought. He had not expected a party on his birthday, but "warm and dry" would have been nice. "If I were home, Mama would have barbecued ribs baking in the oven and a pig-pickin' cake in the fridge," he said to himself. At that moment his rifle range sojourn came to an abrupt end.

"Fall in, ladies!" the sergeant screamed. "Time for your immunizations. We gotta get those shot records up to date." The men were given shots in both arms as they passed between the medics. After the "shooting gallery," they double-timed to the uniform shop where they were issued Army greens. In between every event was more double-time, PT, and close-order drill.

Sam's most trying times were enduring the teargas in the gas house, making it up Tank Hill in full battle gear, and climbing "Drag-Ass Hill." It was a large sand dune on Fort Jackson—with a full backpack and rifle, the men took two steps forward and slid back one. The DIs loved it.

The eight weeks flew by, and it was soon time to ship out for advanced individual training (AIT) at Fort Polk, Louisiana. Linville reported there in early January 1967.

"We arrived in buses and were assigned to our barracks at Fort Polk," Linville said. "The barracks were the same WWII-style wooden buildings we had at Fort Jackson with open bays full of military-style bunk beds, wide-open latrines, and showers. It no longer makes any difference to me that there are no partitions between the toilets or showers. Most of us have lost any inhibitions we ever had or any sense of privacy a long time before now." He laughed.

"Some things are different from basic," Linville continued, "but not much we'd notice on a daily basis. We run every morning before breakfast. We run and have PT after breakfast. We run to every training area, every event we are involved in all day, and any other goddamned place they wanted us to go all goddamned day. We get maybe three or four hours sleep a night.

"It is warmer than Carolina, but it's so humid, and it rained about every other f***in' day. It's no wonder the 'brown-hats' called it Camp Swampy. Anything we don't polish, oil, or wipe down every day molds, rusts, or corrodes. After the first couple of weeks, if we keep our noses clean, we actually get a weekend pass, which is sweet, but there's no place to go. The closest town is Leesville, which doesn't have shit, but at least it's off post. We can go there, grab a burger, drink a beer or two, and just hang out for a while.

"Did you know there're four kinds of poisonous snakes in the US? Did you know Fort Polk has 'em all? Did you know I hate f***in' snakes so damned bad? Does anyone give a shit?"

Training was intense. "We all knew we were going to Vietnam when we finished—and in case we happened to forget that fact, our training instructors reminded us of it several times a day, every day," Linville said. "Each day seemed endless, but all together the time went by really fast. They kept us so busy we didn't have time to think about time, if that makes any sense."

Linville graduated from AIT on April 14 and flew home to Greensboro that afternoon for twelve days leave. Mary and Mary Raye met his Eastern flight and welcomed him home. Mary thought Sam had gained weight. He looked fit and handsome in his green uniform. Mary Raye blushed and said, "All my girlfriends will want to date my brother." Sam laughed and gave his little sister a hug. Mary Raye was thirteen ("going on eighteen," Sam thought to himself).

"There is no place more beautiful on God's green earth than North Carolina in the spring," Sam said. It had always been his favorite time of year. He enjoyed the drive home along streets lined with blooming dogwoods, flowering crabapple trees, weeping cherry trees, brilliant azaleas, and beds of narcissus and tulips. Sam drank it all in like it was the first time he'd seen it.

The young man was not home long before he found his favorite pair of ragged Blue Bell jeans, rescued his fishing gear from the garage, and headed for High Point Lake. He planned to enjoy every minute of his brief vacation. Ray would be driving in from Salisbury for the weekend, and Mama had planned his favorite dinner: barbecued ribs, spicy baked beans, slaw, 'n' hushpuppies. There was rumored to be a pecan pie or two hidden away for dessert. It couldn't get much better than that, unless there was homemade banana ice cream to go with the pie.

On Saturday, April 15, a group of twenty US veterans marched at the forefront of a parade from New York's Central Park to the UN Plaza, behind a banner Vietnam Veterans Against the War. The men were part of a hundred thousand protesters in a demonstration organized by the Spring Mobilization Committee to End the War in Vietnam. This marked a new development in which American vets joined the anti-war movement. Six of the veterans would form an organization of the same name after the march. What was described as "the largest peace demonstration in decades" in Manhattan lasted four hours. Later in the day, a group called Veterans for Peace in Viet-Nam would be among sixty thousand protesting the war at Kezar Stadium in San Francisco.

On Monday, Sam heard Chuck Bowles, one of his High Point fishing buddies, had caught a twelve-pound bass at Lake Brandt, the week before he got home. He called Chuck, convinced him to take the afternoon off, and they drove to Lake Brandt in Greensboro. Chuck had recently gotten married, so the two would not be spending as much time together as they had in the past.

Sam called a couple old girlfriends, but they were "involved," so he spent most of his evenings at home with Mama and Mary Raye. His mother continued to fix all his favorite meals, so he was usually too stuffed with fried chicken, or ribs, or country-fried steak, along with black-eyed peas, pinto beans, fried apples, and fresh-baked cornbread to go out and drink anyway. He'd just collapse on the couch in front of the TV to watch *Jackie Gleason*, *Bewitched*, *Gomer Pyle USMC*, or whatever else was on the tube. He usually dozed off by 9:00 p.m.

As the time drew near for Sam to deploy, he became somber and dreaded the thought of leaving home. One of his cousins, Walt Reese, came by to see him and they talked for a while. "Sammy had changed," Walt said. "I'd known him my whole life—he'd always been optimistic and upbeat about everything—that was just Sammy—but that was gone. He told me he didn't think he'd make it home from Vietnam. He'd already started giving his belongings away. He offered me his favorite rod 'n' reel, but I wouldn't take it. I told him to hush his mouth, and we'd go fishin' together when he got back."

On the morning of April 26, Mary took Sam to the airport in Greensboro to catch his flight west. It was the middle of the week, so Ray was back on the job in Salisbury, and Mary Raye was in school. It was always difficult for Mary to tell Sam goodbye. It was even tougher when she knew he did not want to go. They were sitting in the airport restaurant drinking coffee, and what little conversation she had managed to elicit from Sam had ceased once again. He just sat and stared at the floor.

With a slight smile on her face, Mary said, "You could always drive to Canada. I hear they have some great fishing up there."

With a quizzical look on his face, as if trying to determine how serious she was, Sam smiled at her and said, "Nah Mama—I'd better go 'n' do the job I'm gettin' paid to do. There's no tellin' when I could come home without goin' to jail. Y'all'd miss me if I was gone too long."

Then with a grin, he added, "B'sides, this Southern boy'd freeze his lily-white ass off the first winter he spent up there," and they both laughed.

Rising from their chairs, Sam leaned over and kissed his mother on the cheek. He picked up the small backpack he was carrying, and they walked together to the boarding gate.

PART 3

The 1st Battalion, 5th Mechanized Infantry was one of the few mechanized units to serve in Vietnam. It had earned a Valorous Unit Award as part of the 2nd Brigade Task Force, which had distinguished itself in ground combat against the Việt Cộng in 1966. Ordered to secure a base of operations for itself and the remainder of the 25th Infantry Division in the vicinity of the town of Tân An Hội in the Củ Chi District, the Task Force had embarked on two months of continuous combat operations in an area that was completely dominated and fiercely defended by the VC. After sixty-six days of continuous combat, the Brigade succeeded in seizing, clearing and securing their base of operations and the surrounding area, severely disrupting the Việt Cộng operation and discrediting the VC in the eyes of the local population.

In January 1967, the battalion shifted operations from Củ Chi to Tây Ninh Province, some thirty miles to the northwest. Tây Ninh was an exit point for the Ho Chi Minh Trail, and Units of the 25th Division were placed there to plug the hole. The 5th Infantry participated in daily search and destroy operations in an effort to interdict the movement of supplies to the Saigon area.

Linville arrived at Tan Son Nhut Air Base amidst a tropical downpour. The date was April 29, 1967. He was assigned to the 4th Squad, 4rd Platoon, Alpha Company, 1/5th Mechanized Infantry Regiment "Bobcats" at Tay Ninh Combat Base. There was some improvement in the weather, so after checking in, Linville boarded a chopper and was transported to join his unit at Tây Ninh.

Tay Ninh Combat Base, Tây Ninh Province

As the helicopter descended through the fog, Linville got his first glimpse of what would be his new home for a brief time. All he could see through the mist was a sea of red mud, dozens of large tents, a few scraggly palms, and a runway. After landing, Linville was escorted to Alpha Company HQ to sign in and then was shown to his quarters to unload his gear.

Sam tossed his duffel bag on a bare cot in the large tent and heard the rain begin to fall again, striking the top of the tent with loud, sharp reports. His squad was out on a search and destroy operation, so there would be no one around for the rest of the day. Heading back to headquarters to be briefed and processed in, he looked up at the dark clouds looming overhead.

"Man," Sam said to himself, "I thought Polk was a shit hole. It can't hold a candle to this."

That afternoon, the supply sergeant issued Linville his M16, jungle fatigues, poncho, boots, and the basic supplies he would need in the field. Sam was also able to store his duffel bag with his extra uniforms and the gear he would not need in the company area.

In the following days, Linville joined his fellow soldiers in their daily routine of search and destroy and RIF (reconnaissance in force) missions in the area along the Cambodian border. On May 3, the 1/5th commenced a two-day sweep of the Hố Bò Woods, north of Củ Chi, as part of Operation MANHATTAN.

The woods area consisted of old rubber plantations, sparse to dense forest, and open rice paddies with large dikes. The area was used by the Việt Cộng as a base area and was laced with trenches and tunnels. It was riddled with long rows of jagged bomb craters left by waves of B-52 bombers, and its destroyed plantations were overgrown with head-high vegetation and dense, thorny brush. Battle debris littered the countryside, and a massive array of tank-tread tracks gave it the appearance of an abandoned training area for armored vehicles. Hidden beneath the tropical overgrowth were the bunkers and fighting positions of the VC and several NVA main force units, the principal one being the 101st Infantry Regiment which had first entered the area from North Vietnam in 1966. The NVA had been more or less constant residents of the Tây Ninh-Hậu Nghĩa-Bình Dương region since that time.

At 9:25 a.m., Alpha Company made contact with an unknown number of VC, and there was intermittent contact and sniper-fire throughout the day. The battalion continued the operation on the following day, and six Bobcats were killed by mines and booby traps. Four were from HQ Company, one from Bravo Company, and one was from Alpha Company, although Sam Linville did not know him.

"We stayed in the area for the next week," Linville said. "The Cu Chi Base Camp wasn't far from where we were located, so our commander moved us there. It was a secure location—we could perform maintenance on our APCs and equipment, get some rest, have some decent hot meals, and prepare for our next op. I hadn't had much chance to get to know the guys in my squad, so it was good down-time for me.

"We still had to pull guard duty on the company perimeter, which wasn't fun. Man, it was always raining, and it was so dark. I always had the feeling someone was watching me watching them. And the f***in' skeeters didn't mind the rain at all. They just attacked in swarms, and even if the bug juice had been worth a shit, the rain washed it off as fast as I smeared it on. I was happy when my relief man showed up."

1/5th Mech leaves Cu Chi Combat Base. 1967

During the rest of May and the month of June the 1/5th conducted a variety of operations in the Bàu Trai, Đức Hòa and Củ Chi areas. Much of the time, the battalion combined operations with various elements of the South Vietnamese Army, and on June 24, there was a ceremony celebrating the reopening of Highway10 between Đức Hòa and Bàu Trai.

Sam made friends with Davis Franklin, a fellow Carolinian in his squad. "Dave's from Duck, North Carolina," Sam said. "I was there once on a fishin' trip with Ray, my stepdad. We stayed in a cheap-assed motel right on the beach. I just remember the whole place was paneled in knotty pine. I think it was under about ten feet of water the next September when Hurricane Donna hit the coast. Dave's a short-timer. He's been here almost a year, so he's great to talk to."

"I only knew Sam for a short time," Davis Franklin says. "He and I pulled some roadside security details together. Sam's a character. We were both from Carolina, so we could always find stuff to talk about, like fishin' and basketball. Sam's a UNC fan, and I pull for Duke, but we don't hold that against each other—much," he said, laughing. I shipped back to the World 'bout a month after he arrived."

In mid-July, Cu Chi Base Camp came under mortar attack during the night. Sixteen rounds of 82mm mortar fire impacted the camp in less than a minute. Fifteen soldiers were wounded.

"Man, I couldn't believe it," Linville said. "It was about 9:30 p.m. and pouring rain, as usual. A bunch of us were sittin' in the mess tent drinkin' warm Falstaff, eatin' popcorn, playin' pinochle, and listenin' to the Supremes on a Sony tape recorder when all hell broke loose. We heard loud explosions, and then the lights went out. We all hit the deck. It didn't last long, but it scared the shit outa me. The lights soon flickered back on, and we headed for our hootches to see if they were still standing. The party was over for that night."

During the fall months, the 1/5th Mech was tasked with protecting Rome Plow operations west of Củ Chi, and also, along with elements of the Thirty-Fourth ARVN Rangers, providing protection for engineer and construction activities along Highway 10 between Đông Hòa and Lộc Thành. This activity was part of a long-term pacification op called Operation BARKING SANDS.

Sam Linville celebrated his twenty-first birthday on November 22, and a good time was had by all—more warm Falstaff and popcorn. "Shit-fire, man," Linville said. "I'm free, white, and twenty-one—well, I'm not exactly free."

From December 1 to December 7, the 1/5th participated in the close of Operation BARKING SANDS with the 1st Brigade.

At 11:00 a.m. on December 16, the battalion forward base camp was attacked by an estimated platoon-sized VC force. The enemy struck from the west, southwest and southeast. Approximately twenty to thirty RPG rounds were fired along with AK-47 fire. At 11:20, the VC broke contact. Two Bobcats from Charlie Company were killed, and sixteen were wounded. Two other troops were burned to death inside an APC that was hit by an RPG round. Their remains had to be removed by Graves Registration personnel. Two APCs were destroyed in the attack. Three dead VC were found after the attack was over.

Two new men joined the 4th Squad in mid-December. Jack Hawley was from New Jersey and Mateo Lopez was from Oklahoma. Linville had become the "old guy" in the squad, having been there for almost eight months. He was also one of the few who was over twenty-one. Jack and Mateo were both eighteen.

"It didn't take long for us to get acquainted with Sammy Linville," Jack Hawley said. He was a character. He would tell these long drawn-out stories, and I had trouble understanding him at first. It was partly my problem. He had this speech condition that made him hard to understand. The more excited he got, the worse it was and the faster he would talk. And he got excited often. Combine that with his Carolina accent and my Jersey ears, and we had a communication problem, but he was such a good guy, we made it work.

Hawley continued, "Our top sergeant, Luis Nadal, was from Puerto Rico, and he was not easy to understand either. Sarge thought Linville was some kind of an alien because they could not communicate at all, even though they were supposed to be speaking the same language. Sgt. Nadal would have to get one of us to translate for him when he needed to talk to Sam."

"Mat Lopez was a quiet kid," Linville said. "He and 'Jersey Jack' hung around together. They were the two FNGs in the squad, so I guess that was normal, but they were cool guys, and they fit in pretty quickly. I had become the primary point man for our squad and also for our platoon. I liked doing it, and most of the guys hated it, so it worked out for me. Traditionally, they would make FNGs walk point, so if one of them was ordered to do it, I would walk point with him. That seemed to make everyone feel better."

For the remainder of December, the 1/5th Mech remained at Cu Chi Combat Base, making routine search and destroy forays into the surrounding countryside. Christmas day was just another day for Alpha Company. The men did have a hot meal, but in spite of a so-called truce, someone forgot to tell the VC.

Bob Hope and his beauties visit
Cu Chi Combat Base, December 1967

PART 4

On January 10, the battalion began conducting cordon and search operations in the area of the Michelin Rubber Plantation. The plantation was located near Dầu Tiếng, approximately halfway between the Cambodian border and Saigon and, at thirty-one thousand acres, it was the largest rubber plantation in Vietnam. It was an important base and staging area for the VC and the NVA. The plantation was also an important source of revenue for the South Vietnamese Government, and it was believed the Michelin Company paid off the VC in order to keep the plantation operating during the war. US forces were obliged to compensate Michelin for damage caused to the rubber trees during operations in the plantation, and those operations were frequent.

On January 12, elements of the Task Force continued company size operations in the plantation, primarily in the area of Bến Củi. At 7:55 a.m., Alpha Company received five RPG rounds along with small arms and automatic weapons fire near the Ben Cui Rubber Plantation, which was part of the Michelin Plantation. Fire was returned, but one tank and two APCs received minor damage.

"How close did Sammy come to shooting me that night?" Jack Hawley asks no one in particular. "It was just another Army screw-up that nearly cost me my life. We were together on LP [listening post] duty one night when our radio went dead. Mat Lopez and I were working together while Sam napped. I told Lopez to stay awake while I went for a working radio. Instead Lopez woke Linville, and then went to sleep without telling him where I had gone. When Sam heard me returning from behind the position, he was scared and ready to shoot. Thank God he was cautious and spared my life. He and I didn't sleep the rest of the night. We were too scared about what had just happened and what could have happened. We spent the night shoulder to shoulder looking out into that dark, foggy Vietnam night saying very little. As the sun broke through the fog and crept into the morning sky, we were still trembling and trying to find a way to handle our emotions. It would have been nice if we could have found a way to pass on to Lopez what we suffered through that night, but he never understood why we were so upset. He didn't have a clue what he had done. He just thought no harm, no foul—so f***in' stupid, man."

The sweep of the plantation and the Dầu Tiếng area continued for the next ten days, and then on New Year's Eve, January 31, 1968, an intelligence report indicated a force of eight hundred VC was headed for the Tây Ninh market.

Offensive activity by the Việt Cộng had increased during the month of January. The large number of attacks was conducted to cover the movement of VC forces to the Saigon area. This was in preparation for the Tet Offensive of 1968.

On February 1, the 1/5th base camp was located at Tay Ninh West. At 10:00 p.m., an intelligence report was received from brigade headquarters indicating that two VC battalions were located fifteen miles south of Tây Ninh, two miles inside South Vietnam from the Cambodian border.

On February 2, a mortar attack was launched on Cu Chi Base Camp at 6:55 a.m. The 4/23rd Infantry ammo dump was hit, and the resulting explosions destroyed the 1/5th Headquarters and Bravo Company areas. Bravo Company and HQ Company mess halls were totaled, and Alpha Company and Charlie mess halls were damaged.

Throughout the month of February, the 1/5th companies were involved in continued RIF operations across the Củ Chi, Tây Ninh, Dầu Tiếng area. The Battalion Forward Base had been located three miles east of Hóc Môn (six miles northeast of Saigon).

On March 6, Alpha and Bravo Cos., along with the Recon Platoon from 1/5th, and Alpha Company, 2/34th Armor conducted a sweep northeast of Hóc Môn. At 4:00 p.m., the units made heavy contact. At 4:15 p.m., Alpha Company, 2/34th Armor reported one killed and one wounded. A soldier from Bravo Company was moving along a tree line when he was shot in the head. Two men from Bravo went to check on him and both were shot. One was killed—the other wounded in the leg and hip.

Alpha Company was moving with men walking in front of the APCs. The 3rd Platoon was in the middle and got hit first. Sam Linville was walking point.

"We were gettin' some sniper fire from the trees," Linville said, "so our sergeant turned us on line and advanced us toward the sniper fire. An M60 machine-gunner named Mike Shaughnessy got shot in the stomach and called out for help. The man next to him turned and got shot in the head. Someone called for a medic, and as Doc Pollock moved forward to help Shaughnessy, he was shot and killed. Our sergeant ordered us to pull back. Shaughnessy was still alive, but there was no way any of us could get to him without losing more men. The Cong snipers had us cold.

"Air strikes with napalm were called in during the night," Linville continued. "At 8:00 the next morning, the body of Doc Pollock was recovered. And then, the bodies of the other two were located. Shaughnessy was found with a rosary wrapped around his hands. He probably was praying right up to the minute he died.

"In addition to the three dead, we had eight wounded," Linville continued. Then, looking at the ground, he added softly, "We lost some good men. Tough to take, man—tough to take."

In addition to the men lost, one APC was destroyed when it hit a mine. A second APC and a tank were also damaged by mines in the area.

APCs clear way through brush as infantry follows

A week later, the battalion moved back to Cu Chi Base Camp and then proceeded to a new forward base in the northwest corner of the Filhol Rubber Plantation. It was located by the Saigon River, ten miles northeast of CCBC. In an Alpha Company reorganization, Sam Linville and his 4th Squad were moved from the 3rd Platoon to the 1st Platoon, 1/5th Mech.

On March 14, Alpha was conducting a RIF operation in the early afternoon. Sam Linville was walking point with "Jersey Jack" Hawley.

"We trusted Sam with our lives every time he walked point," Hawley said. "He was so good at it. He had the keenest eye. We called him Scout. He carried a big Bowie knife he had brought from Carolina, and it hung in a sheath from his belt. Some elephant-ear cuttings adorned his belt as well. Sam was definitely a character, but he was our character, and he was our scout."

"Our platoon was moving with men on the ground in front of the tracks when we started receiving enemy sniper fire," Linville said, "One Bobcat was shot in the chest and died before a dust-off could get him out. We were ordered to take cover as artillery was called in. Jack and I hunkered down behind the nearest M113 and waited for the barrage to begin.

"Man!" Linville cried. "Our arty blew the hell out of us. The assholes dropped rounds right on top of us. Two of our guys were killed—twenty were injured. Friendly fire's a real bitch."

On March 20, Alpha and Bravo Cos. Conducted RIF operations near the junction of Rach Son Creek and the Saigon River. During the day, miscellaneous items of equipment and ammunition were found and destroyed. About 3:00 p.m., they discovered a cache containing twenty-nine rounds of 82mm mortar, CS gas rounds (tear gas), thirteen tons of rice, along with peas, peanuts, and beans. The food stuffs were stacked and covered with plastic sheets. Vegetation from the area was cut and placed on top of the plastic in an effort to camouflage the material, and two platoons remained with the cache to guard it overnight.

The following day, an extensive search of the cache-site was conducted, and we located twenty-four mines, twenty additional mortar rounds, over two hundred RPG rounds, and twenty-five hundred rounds of small arms ammunition, other equipment, and weapons. An additional fifteen tons of rice, two tons of salt and a thousand pounds of canned food were also located.

The overall cache site consisted of four different complexes containing almost a hundred underground bunkers and tunnels. One tunnel was over two hundred yards in length and ran under Highway

TL15. Ten pound packs of CS gas rounds were placed inside the tunnel complex spaced about sixty feet apart. All demolition charges and CS packs were connected and detonated simultaneously. This method sealed the tunnel, trapping the CS gas inside.

By nightfall, all the bunkers and tunnels had been destroyed and the material from the cache site had been transferred to the battalion forward base site at Filhol. On March 22, the 1/5th, along with Alpha Company 2/34th Armor prepared to move back to CCBC. A convoy of ten five-ton trucks arrived at Filhol Plantation and was loaded with the captured materiel from the cache site. The battalion and the convoy then departed for Củ Chi, arriving there by 5:00 p.m.

On March 26, the 1/5th departed Cu Chi Base Camp and established a forward base about half-way between Tân Sơn Nhứt and Đức Hòa. During the last week of March and the first two weeks of April, the battalion conducted RIF and cordon and search operations in its AO. Then on April 19, the battalion moved to a new forward base located three miles south of Vĩnh Lộc.

The intelligence summary states, "VC/NVA activity during February and March consisted of trying to maintain a foothold in the Saigon area. They made a determined attempt to control areas adjacent to Saigon. After great manpower and equipment loss the enemy withdrew to base areas. Time period of March 15 to April 15 was characterized by little action. Period was used by the enemy to refit and receive replacements. During the last fifteen days of April enemy activity reached a peak. Large groups of replacements were identified in the TAOI [Tactical Area of Interest]. Supply caches with large amounts of food, ammunition, and arms were located."

On May 1, two platoons from Alpha Company, one platoon from Company A, 2/34th Armor and one company of Regional Force soldiers conducted a sweep operation. One platoon from Alpha Company secured the battalion's forward base area. Bravo Company established checkpoints in the area of Bình Hưng Hòa and Xóm Gò Me, and night ambushes were deployed throughout the area

During the next week, elements of the battalion conducted sweeps in the area of Ap Cu Lao, three miles west of Tân Sơn Nhứt, with negative contact. Alpha Company 1/5th Mech would spend the night at Tan Son Nhut Air Base.

"That night, we 'borrowed' a tin of bacon from the mess crew and Sammy fried it up for us on a steel plate over an open fire as an evening snack," Jack Hawley said. "Jim Antolini was a good-ole-boy from West Virginia. He had procured a couple bottles of scotch; another one of the guys brought chocolate-chip cookies his mother had sent him—I had the usual bag of popcorn. We were having a regular feast, and we all talked about home. We were all so far from home. Sam said cooking over the fire reminded him of his camping trips. He always had tales to tell about his boyhood hunting and fishing adventures in the Blue Ridge Mountains in Carolina."

"It was surprising how little we talked about each day of 'work' in Vietnam," Hawley continued. "Sam had been awarded a Bronze Star Medal a few weeks back for meritorious service, but he didn't think he deserved it. I don't think he even told his family. He was embarrassed by it. He was the best point man the company officers and NCOs had ever seen. Obviously they thought he deserved it. Someone put him in for it. Someone higher up approved it. Sam thought medals should be reserved for true heroes, and he didn't see himself in that role. Sam's first tour had been completed the last week of April, but he had extended another six months. He said he wasn't ready to go home yet. Sammy Linville was one of a kind, without a doubt, and for many of us, who knew him, lived with him, and fought with him. He was a hero."

Sam Linville's Bronze Star

On the morning of May 9, 1968, Alpha Company's twenty APCs were set to move out of the perimeter at Tan Son Nhut Air Base—it was a beautiful morning, which had been rare in past weeks. The sky was blue, the sun was shining, and birds were singing in the trees. For a moment, we could almost forget we were in the middle of a war. The troops had eaten breakfast, had mounted their tracks, and were formed up in a line, headed out of the base's secure area.

Spc.4 Jim Antolini was a track commander (TC). Sam Linville and three other troops were on top of the same APC. Doug Protz, who had just arrived as a replacement the night before, was occupying the turret containing the .50 cal machine gun. While moving down the perimeter road, the TC in charge of the APC directly behind Antolini's track observed an explosion, which occurred where Antolini was sitting. The massive blast threw the six troopers off the vehicle causing the column to come to a halt. Medics were called forward, and the rest of the company took up defensive positions. No one was sure what had transpired.

Sam Linville was found lying in the road behind the destroyed APC. He was unconscious and barely alive when the medics reached him. He died a few moments later. Jim Antolini was located deep in the tall grass near the road. He had suffered catastrophic injuries and had died instantly. Protz, his body protected inside the turret, had critical head injuries. He was alive but unconscious. He died at the Tan Son Nhut base hospital later that same day.

Ambulances arrived posthaste and carried away the dead and wounded. None of the troopers on the track were without injury, including the driver, who suffered a temporary loss of hearing. After order was restored, the APCs began moving out again to complete their day's mission.

The crewless, destroyed track was left behind, sitting alone in the middle of the road—mute testimony to the terrible tragedy that had occurred on that beautiful morning in May.

The Alpha Company report for that date simply states, "On May 9, 1968, three Bobcats from Company A were killed when an APC blew up from an accidental internal explosion." It was assumed a hand grenade accidentally blew up inside the track, causing a large secondary explosion of other ordnance and munitions.

The men who had served for months with Sam Linville and Jim Antolini were stunned by their sudden, tragic, and senseless deaths. Doug Protz's death was no less tragic. He had been with the 1/5th Mech for exactly two days.

Jack Hawley summed it up best: "Sam, we could never love you as your mother did or your wife and children would have in future years, yet all of us that have served with you during the past months have loved you. How else can we explain the pain we all felt when you were gone?"

Cpl. Samuel Swann Linville was buried on May 25, 1968, with full military honors, next to his Grannie Swann, in the Swann Family Cemetery in Harnett County, North Carolina. His grave was surrounded by blooming dogwoods, brilliant red azaleas and wild daisies. Masses of purple wisteria hung from large poplars and perfumed the air, along with pink peonies and wild magnolia—all the flowers Sammy loved so much.

Linville's military awards include the Bronze Star Medal, the Purple Heart, the Combat Infantryman's Badge, Vietnam Service Medal, Republic of Vietnam Campaign Service Medal, and National Defense Service Medal.

Mary and Ray Davis were devastated by the death of their son. Neither would ever fully recover from the emotional trauma they suffered with his untimely death. Ray passed away from a heart attack nineteen months later—Christmas Eve, December 24, 1969. He was fifty-two years old. He was buried in historic Salisbury National Cemetery in Salisbury, North Carolina. Mary Grimes Linville Davis passed away in 1992, and she is buried next to her son.

Swann Family Cemetery—near Swann Station, North Carolina

I know a pool where the waters cool
Rest under the brawling falls,
And the song and gleam of that mountain stream—
Oh, it calls, and calls, and calls!

"The Call of the Stream"
Charles H. Crandall

CHAPTER 10

MICHAEL DAVID HELMSTETLER

Twenty-Seven Days

Mike Helmstetler

Early in March 1966, Mike Helmstetler informed his supervisor at Eastern Air Lines in Greensboro, North Carolina, that he had been accepted for Marine pilot training and would report to Naval Air Station Pensacola the first week in April. Mike had enlisted in the Marine Corps Reserve and, while in boot camp, had taken flight aptitude tests and applied for the Marine Aviation Cadet (MarCad) Program. This was a dual-purpose course to qualify as a Marine officer and aviator.

A couple of weeks later, Dot Lewis, one of Eastern's senior agents threw a going-away party for Mike at her home in Guilford College. The Eastern crew was always ready for a party at Dot and Bill Lewis's home. Dot's parties were mythic, and Mike was popular, especially with the younger female agents. Most off-duty employees attended the blowout and more arrived after the airline closed its offices later that night. The affair turned into the party of a lifetime.

Among the party attendees were Lonnie Long, who had just completed an extended tour in Vietnam in November 1965 and been rehired by Eastern. Gary Blackburn, an Air Force veteran who had been hired by Eastern to fill Helmstetler's spot in the workforce was also in attendance.

The Marines, in coordination with the Navy, had created the Marine Cadet Program at Pensacola Naval Air Station in 1959. The program accepted enlisted Marines with two years of college, many of whom had already attended bootcamp and individual combat training before entering flight training. Helmstetler had spent two years at Guilford College in Guilford College, North Carolina. He had then gone through bootcamp at MCRD-Parris Island in December 1965, followed by four weeks of individual combat training and four weeks of specialist training at Camp Lejeune in January 1966.

> **MARINE AVIATION CADET MICHAEL D. HELMSTETLER,** son of Mr. and Mrs. Charles A. Helmstetler of 116 Greenview Terrace, High Point, is attending Naval Pre-Flight School at the Naval Air Station in Pensacola, Fla.

High Point Enterprise—April 6, 1966

In the 1960s, MarCad was expanded to meet the growing needs in Vietnam—all pilot trainees, whether Navy or Marine Corps, had to meet the same standards to become a Naval Aviator. Likewise, MarCads were eligible for the same training pipelines as all other trainees; however, with helicopter requirements looming large for Vietnam, Helmstetler shifted from flying the T-28 after carrier qualification to the helicopter pipeline, where he trained on TH-13s and the larger H-34s. Mike soon discovered he loved to fly, and especially loved flying choppers.

After successfully completing training and earning his Naval Aviator wings in Pensacola, Second Lt. Helmstetler moved from Pensacola to Marine Corps Air Station New River in Jacksonville, North Carolina. At New River, he began the nine-month intensive training course in the CH-46D. The new helicopter was crewed by two pilots (pilot and co-pilot), along with a crew chief, two .50 caliber gunners, and if necessary, a corpsman. "It was a sweetheart to fly," Helmstetler said. "I loved it from the first day."

While in Pensacola, Mike had met Sue Schultheis. The had met during the summer of 1966 as Sue was preparing to finish her final year at Florida State, and during the year, they fell in love. When the time came for him to ship out to New River, they made the decision to get married. Their engagement was announced on March 26, 1967. Sue's father, Anthony, had been a Naval Reserve aviation cadet at Pensacola in 1939. During WWII, Anthony Schultheis had been a highly decorated pilot (Navy Cross) and had risen to the rank of lieutenant commander during his six years of active duty in the Navy.

The ceremony was planned for July 1, 1967. Mike took leave and drove to Pensacola for the wedding. The Helmstetler family caught an Eastern flight (and many "good wishes") from Greensboro to Pensacola, midweek. The groom's brother, Larry, was his best man. Sue's younger brother, Anthony Jr. along with various cousins and friends served as groomsmen and ushers. There was a luncheon honoring the bridal party at the Pensacola Country Club on Friday and a bridesmaid's luncheon on Saturday at Scenic Hills Country Club in Pensacola.

The Saturday evening service was at St. Christopher's Episcopal Church, and it was a special night. There were guests from North Carolina, Louisiana, Alabama, and Florida, and the church was decked with arrangements of white orchids and stephanotis, to match the bridal bouquet. Lt. Helmstetler wore his Marine dress blue uniform and Sue was resplendent in yards of white organza and French Chantilly lace. The bride had a Maid of Honor, a Matron of Honor, and seven bridesmaids wearing aquamarine gowns with illusion veils. Each carried a brandy snifter trimmed with orchids and containing a lighted aqua candle. After the ceremony, Sue's parents, Anthony and Ethel, hosted a reception at the Pensacola Country Club.

The couple drove to the Smoky Mountains in North Carolina and Tennessee for their honeymoon, and then drove to MCAS New River, where they would reside while Helmstetler resumed his training with Marine Medium Helicopter Squadron 161. The squadron had departed Vietnam at the end of 1966, relocating to New River. From December 18, 1966, until July 6, 1967, HMM-161 trained twenty-nine pilots in the CH-46D helicopter as replacements for Vietnam.

Lt. Col. Paul W. Niesen assumed command of HMM-161 on July 7, 1967. "Col. Niesen, was an inspirational leader," Helmstetler said. "He especially enjoyed working with us newly commissioned aviators, and we looked forward to working with him."

Knowing Vietnam loomed in the near future, Mike spent as much time with Sue as he could. If he was not training, he was with her. They drove to Pensacola for Thanksgiving with the Schultheis family, and in December, they drove to High Point for Christmas with the Helmstetlers. The two enjoyed Christmas-shopping together, and Mike introduced Sue to some of his hometown friends. Sunday morning, December 24, dawned clear and very cold for Carolina—it was twenty-one degrees in High Point, and Sue delighted in the frosty weather. Growing up in Florida, she had not experienced such cold temperatures, and she loved it. It made their first Christmas as husband and wife even more special.

After New Year's 1968, HMM-161 began to stabilize its authorized personnel, and extensive additional training was assigned in preparation for the April rotation of the unit back to Vietnam. On April 1, the newly promoted Marine Reserve pilots at New River included Jim Andrews, Chuck Songer, Jim Sweet, Bill Hitchcock, Bob Mullins, Mike McElwee, Al Doktor, Rudy Kaiser, Brent Blair,

Tom Collins, Charlie Galavitz, and Mike Helmstetler. They would deploy as copilots on the CH-46D helicopters in one month.

On the morning of April 20, Mike kissed Sue goodbye and reported in at headquarters. The wives were able to watch and wave proudly as the squadron and its twenty-four aircraft departed for the cross-country flight to MCAS El Toro. The base was located at Irvine, California, and was the home of Marine Corps aviation on the West Coast. Three days later, the squadron arrived at its destination, and on May 1, 1968, the unit boarded the USS *Princeton* for the seventeen-day voyage to Vietnam.

Standing: Jim Andrews, Chuck Songer, Jim Sweet,
Mike Helmstetler, Bill Hitchcock, Bob Mullins
Kneeling: Mike McElwee, Al Doktor, Rudy Kaiser, Brent
"BC" Blair, Tom Collins; Charlie Galavitz

Helmstetler said, "The trip across the Pacific gave the squadron a chance to test the sea-worthiness of the H-46D. Col. Niesen, performed a water rescue one afternoon when he landed his helo on the ocean to rescue a sailor who had fallen overboard. The seaman was none the worse for wear, although a bit soggy and embarrassed. He was also very grateful. That was the only excitement we had during an otherwise boring trip."

He continued, "At least it gave us something interesting to talk about for a few hours, and then it was back to the card games."

The squadron arrived in Vietnam on May 17 and began to unload the *Princeton* at its new home in Quảng Trị Province. Situated north of Phú Bài, the Quảng Trị strip was fifteen miles south of the DMZ and not far from the 3rd Marine Division command post at Đông Hà.

"When we arrived, there wasn't much there," Helmstetler said. "There was a kind of landing pad made of corrugated steel to land our choppers on—not much else. We built sandbag bunkers and lived in them until we were able to get tents. The Hilton, it was not. We had no running water, no electricity, and no latrines. We built our own base for the CH-46Ds, and then we built the buildings we needed to maintain the helicopters. And we did all that in our spare time."

Marine CH-46D prepares to land aboard USS Princeton

The squadron was incorporated as part of the Provisional Marine Aircraft Group 39 (ProvMAG-39), 1st Aircraft Wing. The following day all HMM-161 personnel were given indoctrination briefings. From May 19 to 22, the squadron flew missions integrated with HMM-262 to become familiar with the area. Starting on May 23, the squadron began providing helicopter support as part of ProvMAG-39 and the 3rd Marine Division. The Third MD was supplying men, ammunition, and other materiel to Khe Sanh in support of the 26th Marine Regiment and the 1st Marine Regiment.

Helmstetler and fellow pilot, Capt. Lufkin Sharp, were assigned H-46D, tail number 153381, and immediately began flying Marines and supplies from the 3rd Marines post at Đông Hà to Khe Sanh Combat Base. The base had been under siege by the NVA for six months. Resupply and medevac aircraft were still coming under fire as they approached the landing strip there.

Due to its posture and appearance on the ground, the Marines affectionately called the CH-46D "the phrog"; however, it was anything but frog-like in the air. As the new primary assault helicopter, it brought a greatly increased payload, increased air speed, and ease of loading and unloading people and cargo. In generally bad weather and from bases near the coastline, H-46Ds shuttled throughout the mountainous Khe Sanh area. They constantly moved medevacs, Marines, and materiel as the tactical situation required, often under IFR (instrument) conditions, all the while being strenuously opposed by the NVA. All pretense of the war being fought by indigenous Việt Cộng guerillas with home-made weapons had long since vanished.

"In the first few days after we began operations, it seemed as if Lance Cpl. Bill Graeber, a gunner on board Jimmie Sweet's chopper, was determined to win the war all by himself," Mike Helmstetler said. "On June 3, he was credited with killing twelve NVA soldiers and destroying two enemy .50 cal. machine guns. Two days later, he added four more enemy troops to his total kills," Helmstetler continued. "Sweet has started calling Graeber 'Wild Bill.' He says he's not taking his chopper off the ground if he doesn't have Wild Bill along for protection."

"Skeeter" Sharp was commander of their phrog, and Mike "Helms" Helmstetler was the copilot. Both were accomplished pilots, and the two young men made a great team. Sharp was twenty-six years old, from Gainesville, Georgia, and was one of the more popular members of the 161 team. He was married and had two little girls back in Georgia. Helmstetler was twenty-three.

1st Lt. Mike Helmstetler

"There was never a dull moment when Skeeter was around," Helmstetler said. "He had that dry Southern sense of humor. He could tell a story, never crack a smile, and we'd piss our pants laughing. We loved having him around."

Skeeter and Helms flew to Đông Hà early each morning. Their chopper was fully loaded with troops, ammo and/or supplies, and they headed west.

"Khe Sanh was a real shit-hole," Helmstetler said, "but the airstrip there was even worse. It was the bull's-eye for every mortar and rocket hidden in those goddamned hills surrounding the base, and it was the prime target for all the big Russian and Chinese guns parked seven miles away across the Laotian border. There was nothin' random about the shelling there. We would make our approach, and if the wind was right, we'd hear the NVA .50-cals starting up when we approached the strip, and the first incoming artillery would precede our landing by seconds."

"Y'all hang on," Skeeter would yell, with his Georgia twang, "Here comes the shit storm."

Helms continued, "Our crew-chief, 'Smitty' was from Louisiana. If we were haulin' grunts, he'd have the men place their gear on the floor beneath them to shield their butts from ground fire that might penetrate the underside of the phrog. It was definitely questionable how much good that would do, but Smitty insisted they do it. The men were nervous at the thought of .50-cal rounds coming up through the thin belly of the chopper. We had our own .50 cal. gunners, but it was difficult for them to see anything to shoot at. We'd circle down through the clouds and knew we'd only have a few seconds with the tailgate down to unload the Marines with their gear before the mortars zeroed in on us. As we began our descent, we'd see green tracers streaking up through the clouds past our windows. Smitty told the Marines they'd have less than ten seconds on the deck. He'd say, 'Y'all better be off that ramp in ten or know how to f***in' fly!'"

One of the grunts said laughing, "Shit! Cap'n Sharp didn't even land the chopper. The chief lowered that tailgate as the chopper hovered, and he dumped us out like bags'a garbage from the ass-end of a sanitation truck. And hell man, they were gone!"

Capt. Lufkin "Skeeter" Sharp

PART 2

Khe Sanh Combat Base had been built by US Special Forces in western Quảng Trị province in 1962. The base was located atop a plateau in the shadow of Dong Tri Mountain. It was surrounded by uninhabited jungle, impenetrable undergrowth, and trails hidden by seventy-foot trees, dense bamboo thickets, and ten-foot-tall elephant grass. It was a natural infiltration route for communist guerillas and NVA troops moving south and into the cities on the east coast of Quảng Trị Province.

"When you're at Khe Sanh, you're not really anywhere," Marine Brig. Gen. Lowell English once declared. "You could lose it and you haven't lost a goddamned thing," but as usual, MAC-V commander, Gen. Westmoreland disagreed with him. In the spring of 1966, Westmoreland had begun to think of Khe Sanh as part of a larger strategy. Considering the possibility of eventually gaining approval to advance Allied forces through Laos to interdict the Ho Chi Minh Trail, the general decided it was "absolutely essential to hold the base." He ordered substantial Marine units to take up positions at MCB Khe Sanh and ordered his staff at MAC-V to begin planning for an incursion into Laos.

Per Westmoreland's orders, the 1st Battalion, 1st Marines arrived at Khe Sanh in April 1966. Marines also secured three surrounding hills and built combat outposts. Construction of an airfield at Khe Sanh was completed in October. Late in 1967, the North Vietnamese appeared to be planning something big. Reconnaissance patrols reported large groups of NVA troops moving into the area. NVA reconnaissance patrols and ambushes became more frequent, and sniper fire increased. The Marines stopped running patrols and improved their fortifications as reinforcements arrived. Then, on January 21, 1968, nine days before Tet, "all hell broke loose." Hundreds of 82mm mortars, artillery shells, and 122 mm rockets slammed into the base. The Marines dove for cover in trenches and bunkers, a mess hall was destroyed, several helicopters and trucks were destroyed, and fuel storage areas were set ablaze. Roughly twenty thousand NVA troops had surrounded the combat base, which was manned by approximately 5,500 Marines. The Marines could not be reinforced or resupplied except by air, and the enemy had attacked during the monsoon season, when the weather limited flights.

One of the first enemy artillery rounds hit an ammunition dump near the eastern end of the runway setting off a series of horrendous explosions. Mortar and artillery shells stored in the dump were blasted into the air and exploded when they came down. Adding to the chaos, a large amount of tear gas was released making it impossible for the Marines to see without gasmasks.

The artillery barrage continued nonstop for seventy-seven days and nights. The men tried to stay underground as much as possible, but Marines were killed and wounded every day. The mental toll on the Marines based there is impossible to imagine.

Gen. Võ Nguyên Giáp, Hồ Chí Minh's top general, always aware of the value of negative publicity in the US media, hoped to repeat the same sort of victory he had won years earlier at Điện Biên Phủ. Similarly besieged French forces had been overrun and slaughtered by the thousands in 1954. In addition to 2,293 dead, over five thousand had been wounded and almost eleven thousand captured by Viet-Minh forces to end the First Indo-China War. With dreams of such a victory over the American quỷ (devils) dancing in their collective heads, communist generals were willing to commit almost anything to accomplish their purpose. And who could blame Gen. Giáp for wanting to reprise such a stunning victory?

Some have argued the Battle of Khe Sanh was merely a ruse to distract attention from the buildup in the south (preparation for the Tet Offensive 1968). It would seem, however, Gen. Giáp's commitment of three reinforced divisions during the opening stages of the Khe Sanh campaign was way more than necessary for a ruse. Giáp always had a sound reason for everything he did. This was not a miscalculation, nor was it overkill. Giáp wanted another coup.

Westmoreland ordered Marines to hold the base. He said, "[A] factor favoring the decision to hold Khe Sanh was the enemy's determination to take it. Our defense of the area ties down large numbers of North Vietnamese troops which otherwise could move against the vulnerable populated areas whose security was the heart of the Vietnamese pacification program."

Pres. Johnson agreed with Westmoreland and was said to have remarked to his advisors on numerous occasions, "I don't want no gawddammed Din-Bin-Foo!" The president installed a replica of the landscape around Khe Sanh in the Oval Office so he could follow the briefings on the action there. Johnson was not above making tactical suggestions during the war and loved to boast, "Mah generals can't bomb a gawddammed shithouse without askin' mah permission first."

In March, under cover of fog and darkness, NVA troops began to dig deep trenches around Khe Sanh, tunneling in toward the perimeter wire on the east end of the camp. They were undetected until F-4 Phantoms resumed tactical operations and spotted the enemy operation from the air. The NVA evidently hoped they could tunnel under the wire and the runway to plant mines or explosives that would destroy inbound aircraft or the runway surface. A US Air Force bombing run quickly doomed the effort after it was discovered.

The US public read media accounts of the besieged marines in their daily newspapers as the fighting unfolded and watched the news anchors every night on the evening news programs: "American servicemen bombarded by artillery and reliant on resupply from aircraft that come under heavy fire on approach and departure," was the daily report. After "Tet 1968," the major news story of the day was "Khe Sanh," and that continued in graphic detail for weeks.

A major US-South Vietnam counter-offensive had successfully repelled the Tet Offensive in February and March. Militarily, it had been a crushing defeat for the NVA and especially the Việt Cộng; however, it had hardly constituted a "victory" for US and ARVN forces, and it became a political nightmare for the Johnson administration. Tet demonstrated to skeptical Americans how weak the South Vietnamese military was and convinced many that the US government had misled them on the progress of the war—particularly Westmoreland's optimistic pronouncement that there was "light at the end of the tunnel." Tet dominated television coverage in early 1968. Pictures and video from "Battlefield Saigon" and "Battlefield Hue," crowned by the mythical "Cronkite moment," fueled pessimism and confirmed the beginning of a credibility gap between what the Johnson administration was telling the American people and the reality on the ground. The anti-war movement was quick to detect the burgeoning distrust and used it to their political advantage. Led by the major news networks, public support for the war plummeted. Within weeks, national polls indicated 78 percent of Americans believed the US was not making progress in Vietnam. Approval of

President Johnson's conduct of the war dropped to an all-time low of 26 percent, and that disapproval was reflected in the treatment many veterans received upon their return to the States. Those who hated the war felt compelled to express that hatred by attacking the young men being forced to fight it.

1ˢᵗ Cavalry—Operation PEGASUS—March 1968

In March 1968 Operation, PEGASUS was launched by a combined USMC-US Army/ARVN task force. It was on overland operation that fought its way through to the besieged Marines at Khe Sanh. American commanders considered the defense of Khe Sanh a success, but shortly after the siege was lifted, the decision was made to dismantle the base rather than risk similar battles in the future. On June 19, 1968, the evacuation and destruction of KSCB began.

PART 3

Sharp and Helmstetler reported in at Đông Hà on the morning of June 19. The weather was miserable at 6:00 a.m.—there was steady rain falling.

Mike had awakened early and remained on his cot listening to the sound of the rain on the tent where he was quartered. It was so damned hot. He was wearing only Marine-issue skivvie shorts but was bathed in sweat. It was still dark outside as he glanced at the illuminated hands of the Bulova Accutron watch Sue had given him for Christmas. It was 0400, so it would be 4:00 p.m. the afternoon before (June 18) in Pensacola. A slight smile crossed his face, and he felt a stir in his groin as he thought of his wife. He missed her so much. It was difficult to believe it had only been two months since he kissed her goodbye at New River. It seemed much longer. He wondered what she was doing. He needed to write to her. He tried to write often, but it was difficult when he was flying seven days a week. Reaching under his cot, he brought out a clipboard with a pen and a sheet of paper, along with a small penlight, and he began to write:

My darling, Sue,

How do I love thee? Let me count the ways… I guess that line has been used before, but it's still a pretty good line. I miss you.

It's very early morning here—I need to shower and prepare for another long and trying day of work, but all I think about is you.

Mike's eyes filled with tears, and he could no longer see to write. "Dammit!" he said, tossing the clipboard aside. He rose from the cot, dropped his shorts, and tied a towel around his waist. Grabbing his dopp kit, he headed out into the rain. "Marines don't cry," he said softly, shaking his head. He stopped and turned his face up into the dark, falling rain. Feeling the cool drops course down his cheeks and chest, he repeated softly and firmly, "Marines do not cry…" Clutching the towel at his waist, Mike trudged toward the showers. It was going to be that kind of day. "I'll finish the letter tonight," he thought sullenly, "and there's always tomorrow."

Skeeter and Helms reported and were advised they would be flying to Hill 881 South. Their first mission was to transport Marines of the 1st Platoon Kilo 3/9/3 from the Hill 881(South) Combat Outpost to Khe Sanh Combat Base.

What had become known as the Hill Fights, involving Hill 881 North, Hill 881 South, and Hill 861, which overlooked Khe Sanh, had seen some of the bloodiest fighting of the war. The 2/3 and 3/3 Marines had taken on six NVA battalions and eventually prevailed, but at a terrible cost. Now the Marines were being pulled from those blood-soaked hills they had fought so heroically to capture and were being transported to KSCB for evacuation and movement south.

Khe Sanh, 1968

Picking up half the platoon—seventeen Marines, along with their equipment, Skeeter and Helms lifted off and headed the short distance to Khe Sanh. They would return later for the rest of the platoon. The weather had gradually worsened during the morning. The heavier rain had stopped, but it had been replaced by dense fog and intermittent drizzle, which had settled into the valleys. The first approach was aborted at the LZ due to poor visibility. Sharp circled back over the camp and made a second attempt.

As the helicopter neared the ground, a large cargo parachute from a low-altitude cargo drop was sucked up by the rotor wash and caught in the aft rotor system of the H-46D. The huge chopper jerked violently as Capt. Sharp struggled to control it. The parachute wrapped around the rear rotor blades, causing their rotation to slow a miniscule amount—in a split second the synchronization of the two sets of overlapping rotor blades was destroyed. The rear blades instantly collided with the front blades, forcing the front rotor to tilt up in the back and down in the front, shearing off the forward half of the cockpit. In his book *1500 feet over Vietnam*: *A marine helicopter pilot's diary*, Bruce Lake wrote, "One of the front blades came down and scooped out the cockpit just like a scoop through ice cream. Both pilot's [sic] legs were severed."

Marine Sgt. Paul Dean Scott was on the ground and said, "I was at the LZ when the crash happened. I was a new guy in-country serving in the Marine Corps field artillery Lima/4/12. I watched in disbelief as the parachute was pulled up into the rotors. The co-pilot was killed instantly when the blades collapsed into the cockpit. The pilot tried to eject and was hanging upside down from the chopper, and there was so much blood, man. One of the corpsmen and several Marines went to the chopper and pulled the pilot out—we tried to stop the bleeding with tourniquets, but the injuries were too bad."

The area was total, bloody mayhem—a chaotic scene reminiscent of Picasso's *Guernica.*

One of the blades had hit Mike Helmstetler in the head, killing him instantly. Lufkin Sharp was removed from the wrecked chopper, rushed aboard another helicopter by Navy corpsmen and flown to "D" Med-Quang Tri, but he died en route from blood loss and shock due to the amputations sustained in the crash.

The seventeen Marines, two gunners, and crew chief on board were trapped in the rear of the H-46D due to the closure of the rear ramp. According to Roy "Doc" Fellows, the platoon corpsman on board, "Some of the men suffered relatively minor injuries: hot aviation fuel burns, contusions, and abrasions [due to the hard landing]." The Marines were treated by Navy corpsmen at the base upon their release from the chopper.

Mortars and artillery began to hit the west end of the camp. As the barrage worked its way methodically across the expanse of the base, the Marines and corpsmen moved the injured, along with the body of Lt. Helmstetler into a nearby bunker.

The only apparent damage to the helicopter was missing rotor blades, and the front half of the cockpit was gone. The Marines would salvage what they could after the shelling had let up.

Minor attacks on Khe Sanh Combat Base continued until the base was officially closed on July 5. Fighting continued in the vicinity of Khe Sanh until July 11, 1968, when the last Marine units were finally withdrawn from the area.

PART 4

The funeral service for 1st Lt. Michael Helmstetler was held at Springfield Friends Meeting in High Point, North Carolina, at 11:00 a.m. on July 5, 1968. (July 1 was the first anniversary of Mike and Sue's wedding in Pensacola.) Those attending included Mrs. Sue Helmstetler, her family, Mr. and Mrs. Anthony Schultheis, and brother, Anthony Jr. of Pensacola, Florida, Mike's parents, Mr. and Mrs. Charles Helmstetler of High Point, Mike's brother and wife, Mr. and Mrs. Larry Helmstetler, and son Gregg, along with dozens of additional family members. Many friends and former coworkers from Eastern Air Lines also attended the somber event.

There is no formal structure or order of service at a Quaker funeral. The meeting was introduced by pastor, Max Rees. The emphasis is on "simplicity and stillness." Anyone can speak about their loved one who has died. There are long periods of silence, which may be broken by someone saying a prayer, reading from the Bible, or sharing memories of the deceased. At the end of the service, one of the Friends signaled the coffin should be withdrawn and shook hands with the pastor. The funeral ended with mourners shaking hands with each other and with family members. Burial followed at Floral Garden Park Cemetery in High Point.

Mike Helmstetler began flying active support missions on May 23, 1968, and flew nearly every day for twenty-seven days—until his death on June 19, 1968. During the course of those twenty-seven days he earned three Air Medals. The final Air Medal was awarded posthumously for "Heroic Action" on September 3, 1968, by the office of Maj. Gen. Raymond G. Davis, Commanding General, US Marine Corps Forces—Pacific. His other awards included the following: the Purple Heart, Combat Action Ribbon, National Defense Service Medal, Vietnam Campaign Medal, Vietnam Service Medal,

Marine Corps Expeditionary Medal, the Vietnamese Gallantry Cross, and his proudest achievement: the US Navy Aviator Insignia.

Warm summer sun,
Shine kindly here,
Warm southern wind,
Blow softly here.
Green sod above,
Lie light, lie light.
Good night, dear heart,
Good night, good night.

"Warm Summer Sun"
Mark Twain

AUTHOR'S NOTE:

Of the newly promoted class of HMM-161 officers in the 1968 photograph, Charles "Chuck" Songer was wounded just south of the DMZ on August 19, 1968. He was medevaced first to Japan, and then to Bethesda Naval Hospital in Bethesda, Md., to recuperate; James "Jim" Sweet was KIA on October 17, 1968, when his medevac Ch-46D was shot down coming out of Cồn Tiên and crashed into a mountain, Mike Helmstetler was KIA at Khe Sanh on June 19, 1968, and Bob Mullins was killed in a C-130 crash in 1970 while undergoing transition training at El Toro, California. The 25 percent casualty rate embodied in that picture is fairly typical for any representative group of CH-46D pilots or aircrews in Vietnam during 1968.

CHAPTER 11

MARVIN GLENN SHIELDS

For His Friends

Marv Shields

Marvin Glenn Shields was born on December 30, 1939, near Port Townsend, Washington. Marv grew up in the family home on Discovery Bay, located at the northeastern edge of the Olympic Peninsula, one of the most spectacularly beautiful spots in the United States. Fishing, hunting, and camping were primary parts of life for any boy growing up there in the 1940s—kind of like breathing. When Marv reached his teenage years, he spent his summers working at the local sawmill. He attended school in Port Townsend, was a proud member of the "Redskins" football team, and graduated in 1958.

Shields was one of the first employees of Mineral Basin Mining Company, a gold mine development project in Hyder, Alaska, which was founded by a company in Port Townsend. He worked there the summer before his senior year and returned there to work fulltime as a construction worker in 1958. Moving back home after three years, he married Joan Elaine Murray, his high school sweetheart, and then enlisted in the Navy in January 1962. "He knew he was going to get drafted," Joan said later, "and he wanted to be a Seabee, [so enlistment was his only choice]." It was a natural fit for Marv.

After completing basic training, Shields was assigned to the Naval Air Station at Glynco, Georgia, for apprenticeship training. He completed his training in May 1963 and went home on leave. In September, he was assigned to take Construction Mechanic training at the Naval Construction Training Center at Port Hueneme, California. When that was finished, he was assigned to Alfa Company, Naval Mobile Construction Battalion 11 in Okinawa. He deployed in November 1963.

Joan had taken a job in Port Angeles, Wash., about forty-five miles west of Port Townsend. Port Angeles was a bustling community with ship building and commercial fishing. She was pregnant and expecting their first child around the first of the year. Marv received a much-anticipated phone call in the early morning hours of January 12, 1964, Okinawa time (it was still January 11 in Port Angeles). He was the father of a beautiful baby girl, and they named her Barbara Diane. In September 1964, Marv came home from Okinawa, saw his daughter for the first time, and was totally smitten. With thirty days leave, they had plenty of time to get acquainted, but he knew it would be a long time before he saw the baby and Joan again. A second overseas deployment loomed in his future.

Marv was assigned to Seabee Team 1104 (NCMB 11) and returned to Port Hueneme for Seabee team training. He completed that training on January 22, 1965. Little Barbara had celebrated her first birthday a few days before, and he had "talked" to her on the phone, listening to her coo as she responded to the sound of her daddy's voice. He shipped out for Vietnam a week later.

Shields now held the rank of construction machinist third class (petty officer third class). He and the other twelve members of Team 1104 arrived in Saigon on February 1, 1965, and were attached to the 5th Special Forces Group (Airborne).

Marvin Shields

After completing construction of a Special Forces camp at Bến Sỏi near the end of May, Seabee Team 1104 moved to a newly established Special Forces CIDG A-Camp at Đồng Xoài (pronounced "Dung Shwai"), fifty-five miles northwest of Saigon. The Civilian Irregular Defense Group camps were manned by irregular military units recruited from indigenous minority populations (usually Montagnards or Nùngs). The Seabee team's mission was to finish construction of the camp (A-342), extend the cleared fields of fire between the compounds and the surrounding jungle, reinforce the earthen berms on the camp's perimeter, and build interior bunkers that would offer the Green Berets better protection against mortars and rockets. Once the defenses were completed, the Seabee team would turn their attention to constructing additional basic facilities for the comfort of the occupants. Those would include a dining area, more secure sleeping accommodations, better sanitation, and a more dependable and secure power supply. Arriving on June 3, the nine-man advance team set to work. Four additional members of the team had been delayed by the incessant rain and would arrive in a few days with heavy equipment.

The day after they arrived, the Seabees began to gather the supplies they would need for their various construction projects. Some members of the team hauled in loads of gravel from a nearby airfield and began to build up the defensive positions. They also started work on a latrine, a shower, and a water purification system. The latrine was finished in two days.

"We actually built an American-style head [toilet] for the special forces troops," CPO Johnny McCully said, laughing. "That was one thing we wanted to do—keep the Green Berets happy, so when we went out on patrol [with them], they'd take care of us." McCully was assistant commander of the Seabee unit.

During the ensuing days the Seabees occasionally heard small arms fire, and a few mortar rounds landed near the camp, but it just served to remind them they were in the middle of a war. There were no casualties or significant damage. There did not appear to be undue cause for alarm, and the Seabees continued with their various projects uninterrupted.

104—L to R Standing: J. Klepher, D. Brakken, W. Hoover, *, L. Eyman, D. Mattick, J. Keenan, J. McCully, M. Shields* *ing: R. Supczak, F. Alexander, J. Wilson, J. Allen* *Supczak, Alexander, and Allen were not at A-342)*

The Special Forces camp's location was at the intersection of two basic, but important, country dirt roads. One road ran north and south with access to the mountainous jungle to the north, which was controlled by the communists. The other road ran east and west with access to the safe haven of the Cambodian border. Put quite simply, this intersection was of major strategic importance to both the Americans and the Việt Cộng. The VC wanted to control both roads to facilitate the movement of men, equipment, and materiel coming down the Ho Chi Minh Trail. Their forces near Saigon and the Mekong Delta to the south relied on that flow of men and supplies. Enemy commanders had good reason to destroy the encampment before it was finished. For the South Vietnamese military and their American support, controlling the roads was critical to stopping the Việt Cộng from accomplishing their goals, or at least slowing them down.

The camp consisted of two adjacent compounds. Each compound covered roughly eighty yards square. The northern compound was the CIDG camp, housing the Green Berets and their contingent of two hundred Montagnards (two companies), along with their families. Although the CIDG troops were technically under command of the South Vietnamese Special Forces (LLDB), they were housed separately from the Vietnamese. There was no love lost between the Montagnards and the Vietnamese, who considered them inferior, referring to them as "moi" (savages). In response, the Montagnards showed only nominal support for the South Vietnamese Army, or for that matter, the Saigon government. In practice, only Special Forces, who recruited, trained, paid, and led the "Yards" actually exercised control over them and inspired their loyalty.

The adjoining compound was District Headquarters for the local ARVN forces and served as their command post. Within the ARVN compound was a unit of two hundred Vietnamese soldiers, along with a Vietnamese Special Forces company, an artillery battery, a reinforced howitzer position, and an armored car platoon. The buildings in the Vietnamese compound were older, but were more permanent and solid, having been constructed of stucco-covered brick.

Across the road was the village of Đồng Xoài, which was a district capital in Phước Long Province. Overnight, the twenty Americans usually divided between the two compounds, and an American was always on watch in each area. The Green Berets did not trust their Vietnamese allies to stay alert during the night. ARVN troops had a penchant for sleeping on the job.

It was generally known the Việt Cộng in the area were mobilizing a force to attack A-342. Green Beret patrols and reports from friendly indigenous tribes had resulted in that intelligence, but the size of the force they were massing and when they might attack remained a mystery.

In Vietnam, the southwest monsoon runs roughly from April to September with June, July, and August typically being the rainiest months. Rain had poured down all day on June 9, and the red mud was ankle deep. The dark and dismal day turned to the inky blackness of a moonless night with dense fog and the continuing drum of steady rainfall. The Seabees ate their cold c-rations, headed to their assigned quarters in the north compound, and had orders to sleep with their clothes on. It was going to be a long night with little or no sleep. The Việt Cộng thrived on this kind of miserable weather, and Charlie was unlikely to miss a night like this.

Later that night, without warning, a VC mortar round hit the CIDG camp. The time was about 11:45 p.m., and Chief McCully was on guard duty. He had just finished making the rounds of the compounds with one of the Montagnard troops and had stepped into the barracks in the CIDG camp. He was drinking coffee with Green Beret Sgt. 1st Class James Taylor, the Special Forces senior medic, when the first explosion rocked the camp. That was followed by a barrage of 57mm recoilless rifle fire and 60mm mortars that exploded inside the Montagnard compound. The mortars were being fired from the jungle just beyond the cleared fields of fire to the west. During the previous day, under cover of the fog and drizzle, the VC had assembled their forces undetected in the dense jungle and thick undergrowth.

VC mortars rained down, creating chaos and injuring many of the Montagnards who had rushed from their barracks upon hearing the noise of the attack. The bombardment destroyed the camp's dispensary, filled with its store of medical supplies, along with the radio equipment in the communications shack. One of the first US casualties was the Special Forces commander, Capt. William Stokes, who sustained shrapnel wounds to both legs as he tried to reach the commo shack to call for help. He was near the building when it exploded. Most of the other Green Berets in the CIDG compound also suffered shrapnel wounds but were still fighting. For the next three hours, the VC poured mortar, recoilless rifle, machine gun, and small arms fire into the camp.

Yelling for everyone to take up defensive positions, McCully grabbed his M14 and three hundred rounds of ammo and ran toward the northwest berm surrounding the northern camp. PO2 William Hoover, PO2 Lawrence Eyman, and PO3 Shields were there returning fire. Hoover was already injured from shrapnel to his arm, leg, and back, and Shields had shrapnel wounds to his head. During a brief lull in the barrage, Shields sprinted to a burning shed, retrieved ammo, and distributed it to his teammates.

McCully took a .50-cal round through his shoulder but still managed to operate a 57mm recoilless rifle. Seabees were not specifically trained on recoilless rifles or howitzers, but during the battle the Green Berets provided quick basic instruction in the worst possible environment, and the Seabees literally learned on the fly.

The ARVN compound was also taking mortar fire, but with stronger buildings and more secure bunkers, they were less vulnerable to the attack. After a long siege of steady mortar fire, the shelling gradually slowed and then ceased. For a brief moment, the stormy night was completely quiet as the inhabitants of the compounds hunkered down in the darkness. Then the silence was broken by the screech of a tinny bugle and a screaming horde of uniformed Việt Cộng burst from the jungle. In the rainy darkness, the enemy soldiers charged across the muddy clearing toward the perimeter berms, illuminated by flickering flames from the ruins of several burning buildings. As the enemy soldiers got to the concertina wire surrounding the camp, those first to reach the wire threw themselves on it, face down; those who followed stepped on their backs and continued the charge.

These troops were not farmers. They comprised elements of the Việt Cộng's 272nd Regiment. They were well-trained and armed with recoilless rifles, Chinese potato-masher hand grenades, machine guns, and flame throwers. The VC 272nd units, part of the VC 9th Division, had attacked the village of Đồng Xoài and Camp A-342. Meanwhile, the VC 273rd Regiment was covering the roads and setting up ambushes at landing zones ARVN or US relief forces would likely use to assist the camp once the attack had begun.

The CIDG and ARVN defenders fought courageously, but when one VC went down, he was replaced by two more of the advancing host. Human waves of Việt Cộng reached the Montagnard perimeter berms and soon pushed their way over. The enemy also poured over the berms into the South Vietnamese Army compound, forced over by sheer numbers. It was later estimated the size of the VC force attacking the camp was in excess of two thousand troops. The horrendous noise and extreme violence of the attack was beyond anything the Seabees or even the Green Berets had experienced. It was quite simply beyond comprehension.

Despite heavy losses, once inside the compounds, the Việt Cộng created total chaos. Flame throwers were terrifying to the Montagnards and many of them scattered in an attempt to save themselves. The Special Forces primary radios were knocked out when the VC destroyed the communications hut, but their radio man, S. Sgt. Harold Crowe, finally got a PRC-10 infantry radio working (the old faithful "prick 10") and made a desperate call for air support. Helicopters arrived and dropped flares to light up the battlefield. It was not difficult to find enemy targets. The VC continued to push forward, and as the flares slowly drifted down, filtered through the rain and fog, they cast an eerie light on the swarming masses of enemy soldiers encircling the two compounds. It was what has been called a target-rich environment.

About 1:30 a.m., two UH-1B Huey helicopters from the 3rd Flight Platoon, 118th Aviation Company, arrived overhead. They immediately spotted seven enemy .50 caliber machine gun positions firing into the camp and opened fire on them with rockets and machine guns, but it did little to slow the attack. The choppers began to take enemy ground fire, and one of their fire-team leaders was wounded, but they remained on site until they expended all their rockets and ammunition.

The Việt Cộng followed their initial assault with another two-hundred-round mortar barrage. Then, about 2:30 a.m. they launched a second ground attack supported by artillery, rockets and heavy machine guns. Employing AK-47s, grenades and flame throwers, the massive force assaulted the north end of the L-shaped CIDG compound.

Lt. (j.g.) Frank Peterlin, the Seabee commander, four of his Seabees: McCully, Hoover, Eyman, and Shields, along with several Green Berets: Medic James Taylor, radio man Harold Crowe, Pvt. 1st Class Michael Hand, S. Sgt. Donald Dedmon, Sgt. Charles Jenkins, and Sgt. Robert Russell were manning the defenses. They were supported by the surviving Montagnards.

Hundreds of enemy fighters were pouring over the berm and overwhelming the defenders. Demolitions and flame-thrower teams made up the vanguard of the VC companies attacking the camp. The enemy troops would mass, come over the berms with grenades and flame throwers—then reassemble, mass and come over the berms again. Just before each assault the VC troops started yelling and screaming, and once they got inside, there was total chaos.

"A VC fired at me with a flamethrower," McCully said, "but it went over my head. Peterlin shot him at close range and killed him. Then a grenade knocked me down—I dropped my rifle and as I reached for it another VC flamethrower set it on fire and burned my arm. Man, it was a world of shit. I climbed over the berm to the east with a couple of Yards and headed for cover."

Capt. Stokes was incapacitated by his wounds but was still in charge. He gave the order for all Americans to fall back to the District Headquarters where they would make what might be their final stand. Green Berets Russell and Jenkins were killed while returning fire amidst the melee. The Montagnard compound was lost. Seabees Shields and Eyman, and Green Berets Taylor, Crowe, and Hand withdrew, fighting every step of the way. Making their way across a hundred-yard gauntlet of enemy fire, they headed for the ARVN compound. Shields and medic Taylor carried Capt. Stokes who could not walk. Crowe carried their weapons while firing his own M14. All were wounded. Shields had back and neck wounds, and a broken jaw from a bullet to the side of his head. Eyman was seriously wounded during their escape.

Peterlin, Hoover, and Dedmon were cut off from the rest of the group. The three began evasive maneuvers toward the eastern side of camp until a grenade explosion knocked Peterlin to the ground, and he was wounded in the right foot by a bullet. Unable to walk, Peterlin became separated from Hoover and Dedmon. He low-crawled through the concertina wire, found a foxhole outside the eastern berm, and dragged himself into it.

William Hoover and Don Dedmon saw no way out. They were completely surrounded by hundreds of enemy troops, and both were wounded. The men stood back to back, Seabee and Green Beret, and fought heroically until they were killed on the northern berm.

William Hoover   *Donald Dedmon*

"At that point, the northern camp was under VC control," Peterlin recalled. And the danger did not come only from the enemy. "Our planes bombed and strafed the entire area. They assumed we were all dead. [At that point], the worst danger we faced was probably from the US and South Vietnamese planes staging their bombing and strafing runs."

Also separated from the rest of the Americans, McCully and his two Yards withdrew to the east. They hoped to locate a buried cache of weapons and a radio located outside the compound, but they could not reach the secret cache. The area was swarming with VC who would shoot them on sight.

PART 2

Like the Texians in the Alamo, the surviving Green Berets, Seabees, and about twenty Montagnards fought their way to the brick headquarters building and awaited their fate. The Seabees who were already in the lower camp were Jim Wilson, Dale Bracken, medic Jim "Doc" Keenan, and Matt Mattick. Larry Eyman and Marv Shields were the only Seabees to make it from the CIDG compound down to the lower camp.

Capt. Stokes now turned over command to his executive officer, 2nd Lt. Charles Quincy Williams. Lt. Williams was not a typical second lieutenant. He was a "mustang," having been promoted from the enlisted ranks. He had been an NCO in the 82nd Airborne. Williams had been wounded in the thigh, left leg, left arm, and stomach, but he was tough as nails, and was now in charge. The building and its defensive wall was surrounded by the Việt Cộng and taking a continuous barrage of AK-47 fire and grenade blasts. There were eight Green Berets and Seabees along the wall trying to fight them off, but there were too many of the enemy, and they came pouring over. The Americans were finally forced to move back into the headquarters building and began firing from the open windows. They hit the VC with everything they had and barely avoided being routed from the masonry structure through the rest of the night.

When daylight began to creep across the blasted and bloody landscape, Lt. Williams discovered a VC .30 caliber machine gun set up 150 yards from their "fortress." The gun began to deliver a withering barrage of fire into the headquarters building, causing all the occupants to hug the concrete floor as bullets ricocheted off the stucco walls and ceiling. It seemed as if the gun might soon reduce the brick building to a pile of terracotta chips. Williams quickly concluded they had to silence the machine gun or they would all die.

A weapons expert, the lieutenant grabbed a 3.5 inch rocket launcher and asked for a volunteer to carry two rockets. It appeared to be a suicide mission, but the lieutenant knew it had to be done to save the rest of the team. Every man was bandaged and bloody; some were wounded more seriously than others. Williams had been wounded four times. Shields, who had been wounded three times by bullets and shrapnel, had never fired such a weapon, but he immediately held up his hand.

"Let's do it, Lieutenant," Shields mumbled with his broken jaw, spitting out a glob of bloody phlegm.

To get into a somewhat-protected firing position with a clear shot, Shields and the lieutenant had to navigate across about sixty feet of open area. Sneaking out a side door, the two Americans caught the VC off guard. They had not expected any kind of offensive attack from người Mỹ (the Americans). Moving quickly and quietly through the dim, foggy morning light, the two managed to cross the area without attracting fire.

Crouching low, Williams put the launcher to his shoulder. Shields loaded a rocket, stepped to the side to avoid the back blast, and tapped Williams' helmet to signal all was ready. The lieutenant took careful aim; the rocket was fired and right on target. With a violent explosion, the enemy machinegun was silenced for good.

"…right on target."

The Seabee and the Green Beret had accomplished their mission, but now they had to get back across the open area to the comparative safety of their brick citadel. And the VC knew exactly where they were. Every enemy weapon for hundreds of yards was trained on the area they needed to get across. As the two men began to move, they were engulfed in a hailstorm of bullets and machinegun fire. Both men were hit. Williams was wounded again in the right arm and leg but was still mobile. Shields was not so lucky. He was hit by machinegun fire and went down hard. The bullets had shattered the femur in his right leg. He was bleeding profusely and could not move. Williams grabbed him by the arm, dragging him into a somewhat protected slough near the building but was unable to haul him further. Two Green Berets jumped out of the door and hauled both of them inside. Medics tended to both men, but Shields was unconscious and in bad shape.

There had been continuing efforts to get relief to the Green Beret camp during the night. With some improvement in the weather, elements of the 1st Battalion, 7th ARVN Regiment were inserted into two landing zones about 8:00 a.m. One helicopter with seven Americans aboard was hit with a rocket-propelled grenade, and everyone on board was killed. The ARVN units which made it onto the ground were hit with a deadly ambush by the VC 273rd Regiment and were rapidly destroyed as well. No one survived the onslaught. With hundreds of ARVN troops killed in the attempted helicopter landings, further rescue efforts were temporarily halted.

Marv Shields was bandaged and regained consciousness. Though seriously wounded and in a lot of pain, nothing could keep him down for long. With his good nature and determination, he was soon helping the other defenders. He tossed clips of ammo to the men as they called for them and was instrumental in keeping up everyone's spirits by laughing and making jokes throughout the morning. But the tough young sailor gradually grew weaker due to blood loss and eventually fell silent. Jim Keenan, the Seabee hospital corpsman, covered him with a poncho and tried to keep him warm, but there was little else he could do. Most of the camp's medical supplies had been destroyed in the first mortar barrage the night before.

The bandages from Shields' many wounds continued to ooze blood as they had for hours. He was sweating heavily but had bouts of extreme shivering, was clammy, and cold. Shields would open his eyes, mumble softly as if he were speaking to Joan or his baby daughter, then a slight smile would cross his face and he would close his eyes again as Keenan cared for him.

The gunfire and grenade blasts stopped only long enough for the enemy to regroup, and then a new attack was launched. The VC seemed to have an endless supply of both ammunition and bodies to inflict on the small camp. Lt. Williams maintained radio contact with the Air Force using the patched-up PRC-10. He and Sgt. Crowe called in air strikes against VC positions and tried to break up troop concentrations. With the helicopter flights in abeyance, the defenders of the Special Forces camp were not sure how much longer they could hold out. They were running dangerously low on ammunition, and their brick stronghold was falling in around them. Every mortar blast brought down more of the crumbling structure. There was no rescue operation in sight, and the VC were massing for another human-wave attack, hoping to finally overwhelm the building's defenders.

In preparation for the final assault, Williams withdrew his combined team, along with their wounded from the destroyed headquarters building. The building was threatening to collapse on top of them, and he was afraid it could not withstand another bombardment. He moved the men to a nearby fortified howitzer position. It was a hazardous fifty-yard trek across a ditch and barbed-wire barriers amid steady gunfire. The trip was especially difficult because every man was wounded, but they leaned on each other, helped each other, and limped their way across. It took four Green Berets to carry Capt. Stokes, who could not bear to put any weight on his legs. Keenan hoisted Shields on his back and carried him most of the way, but one of the other Seabees had to help him maneuver the injured man over the ditch and barbed wire. Wilson found twenty ARVN troops holding their own within the fortification. He dispensed the remaining ammo and grenades, and they prepared to make their final stand. The men were firing their M14s semi-automatically (one shot at a time) when they had a visible target to conserve ammunition.

Most of the VC troops were moving into position for their final coup de grâce. Their commanders had decided this battle had gone on long enough. The battalion had wasted enough time, ammunition, and men. It was time for the final kill shot. It was time to teach these quỷ ngoại bang xấc xược (insolent foreign devils) a lesson they would not forget—time to end it.

At noon, the 118th Aviation headquarters in Bien Hoa received a chilling radio message from Đồng Xoài. It was sent by radioman Crowe. "I'm using my last battery for the radio and there is no more ammunition," the message said. "We are all wounded. Some of the more serious are holding grenades with the safety pins already pulled. The VC are attacking in human waves. The last wave was stopped but we are expecting the next wave now, and we cannot withstand it."

The 118th Aviation's commanding officer Maj. Harvey Stewart heard the message and said, "I cannot just sit here. I'm going in." Stewart, five pilots, and their crewmen boarded three Hueys and lifted off to try and rescue any survivors still holding out on the ground. As the three choppers and a gunship escort closed in, the camp was designated a "free strike" zone, meaning American aircraft and artillery had free reign to pound it with everything at their disposal. Air Force crews used napalm, bombs, and rockets to buy time for the defenders.

About 1:00 p.m., Stewart's helicopters swooped in through heavy enemy fire and landed. Working amid a blizzard of gunfire, they loaded the Americans and several ARVN fighters onto the waiting choppers. Maj. Stewart's bravery and command of the rescue operation was later recognized with the Distinguished Service Cross, the Army's second-highest award for valor.

Marvin Shields, with his severe wounds, continued to slip in and out of consciousness. Corpsmen Keenan hauled him on board the chopper and immediately began to administer fluids in a desperate attempt to save his life. He worked feverishly, but Shields had lost too much blood. Any effort was futile.

"Marv tried to laugh and joke to the end," Keenan said. "The last thing he did was thank everyone who'd helped him. When he finally went under, it was very quiet—nothing dramatic," Keenan concluded with tears in his eyes. "He just went to sleep—Marv just went to sleep."

The rest of the wounded made it to a Saigon hospital and the medical treatment they needed. All of them survived.

PART 3

Destroyed ARVN District Headquarters at Đồng Xoài—June 1965

Helicopter gunships continued to fire on the VC within the area surrounding the two compounds. Fixed-wing aircraft dropped their ordinance and strafed the enemy troops outside the berms. Huge swathes of flaming napalm blackened the jungle surrounding the camp. The two Việt Cộng regiments began to scatter and melt back into the jungle to the north from whence they had come. The Battle of Đồng Xoài was over.

Vietnamese relief forces arrived, and the remaining Americans, including Seabees Peterlin and McCully, were rescued later that day. This battle was one of the bloodiest engagements of the war to that date. The village of Đồng Xoài was hit hard during the fight with the civilian death toll totaling over 150 men, women, and children. The number of wounded was many times that. The VC had torched the town with flame throwers. Forty-three of the Montagnards and ARVN troops were killed in the battle. The remainder had escaped into the jungle, including the Montagnard family members. Over 130 Việt Cộng bodies were found in the area of the camp, but VC dead were always carried off the battlefield, if possible. Their losses were later estimated to have been over seven hundred.

Outside the camp, American deaths included eight helicopter crewmen, four each from Blue Tail One, 118th Aviation Company, and Alpha Company, 82nd Aviation Battalion. Five US Army advisers died, three of whom had been passengers on Blue Tail One and two were killed elsewhere attached to ARVN units. More than four hundred ARVN soldiers died in the landing zone ambushes.

For the twenty Americans directly involved in the battle, their actions during that long night and day were the very definition of valor. The Special Forces camp at Đồng Xoài was one of the first times a team comprised of US Marine-trained Seabees and Special Forces Green Berets was created, and for a limited time, served and fought together. The result was an amazingly cohesive fighting unit, and the results speak for themselves. Two Seabees and three Green Berets were killed during the fourteen-hour battle. That is too many, but realistically all could and should have died, considering the overwhelming enemy numbers and the violence of the attack.

As a result of this battle, three Distinguished Service Crosses, six Silver Star Medals, nine Bronze Star Medals with "V" device for Valor, twenty Purple Heart Medals, and one Navy Unit Commendation (for Team 1104) were presented to this Army/Navy team. In addition, two Medals of Honor were awarded.

On September 13, 1966, the Shields family, including Marvin's wife, Joan and their two-year-old daughter, Barbara Diane, Marv's father, William Glen Shields of Mariana, California; his mother, Victoria Casselery of Port Townsend, Wash., and a brother, Ronald M. Shields, US Army, convened in the office of President Lyndon

B. Johnson as US Navy Secretary Paul H. Nitze read the citation for Marvin Glen Shields' Medal of Honor.

For conspicuous gallantry and intrepidity at the risk of his life above and beyond the call of duty. Although wounded when the compound of Detachment A342, 5th Special Forces Group (Airborne), 1st Special Forces, came under intense fire from an estimated reinforced Viet Cong regiment employing machineguns, heavy weapons and small arms, Shields continued to resupply his fellow Americans who needed ammunition and to return the enemy fire for a period of approximately three hours, at which time the Viet Cong launched a massive attack at close range with flame-throwers, hand grenades and small-arms fire. Wounded a second time during this attack, Shields nevertheless assisted in carrying a more critically wounded man to safety, and then resumed firing at the enemy for four more hours. When the commander asked for a volunteer to accompany him in an attempt to knock out an enemy machinegun emplacement which was endangering the lives of all personnel in the compound because of the accuracy of its fire, Shields unhesitatingly volunteered for this extremely hazardous mission. Proceeding toward their objective with a 3.5-inch rocket launcher, they succeeded in destroying the enemy machinegun emplacement, thus undoubtedly saving the lives of many of their fellow servicemen. Shields was mortally wounded by hostile fire while returning to his defensive position. His heroic initiative and great personal valor in the face of intense enemy fire sustain and enhance the finest traditions of the US Naval Service.

Also attending the ceremony was Army 1st Lt. Charles Q. Williams, the Green Beret commander at Đồng Xoài. He had received his Medal of Honor two months earlier.

2nd Lt. Charles Q. Williams

Marvin Shields' additional military decorations included: the Purple Heart Medal with two Gold Stars, National Defense Service Medal, Vietnam Service Medal with two campaign stars, the Vietnamese Gallantry Cross with Palm, the Vietnamese Military Merit Medal, and the Vietnamese Campaign Medal with 1960 device. Shields had been in Vietnam four months and nine days. He was twenty-five years old.

The Gardiner Community Church in Gardiner, Washington, was standing room only on June 19, 1965, as Marv Shields was laid to rest. Many of the attendees had to stand outside and listen to the service on hastily erected speakers. The weather was beautiful with bright sunshine and temperatures in the midsixties. After the service, most of the congregation walked the half-mile to the gravesite. Marvin was buried in "the most beautiful spot in the cemetery." Banked in sprays of summer flowers, his grave overlooked his beloved Discovery Bay. An honor guard of white-gloved Marines fired three volleys over his casket, as would befit any military hero. But Marv Shields was not just any hero. He was the first member of the US Navy to be awarded a Medal of Honor in Vietnam and the only Seabee to ever be awarded the Medal of Honor. The Navy wanted to bury Marvin at Arlington National Cemetery, but Joan insisted he be buried at home.

Following the sounding of "Taps" by a Navy bugler, there were few dry eyes among the assembled multitude. The American flag which had draped the casket was folded by two of the Navy men and presented to Marvin's widow by Melville Williams, USN. Mel had accompanied Marv's body home from San Francisco. He was also from Discovery Bay and was a close friend of both Marv and Joan. They had known each other since high school, and when he heard about Marvin's death, he had called Joan, asking if he could bring Marv home.

EPILOGUE

HONORING MARVIN GLEN SHIELDS

The Seabees have always moved quickly to honor their dead heroes. Before the end of 1965, with their usual "can do" spirit, the Seabees had already named their new camp at Chu Lai, RVN, "Camp Marvin Shields." Shortly after that, they named another new camp at Đà Nẵng, "Camp Hoover," after SWF2 William C. Hoover, the other Seabee killed at Đồng Xoài.

On April 10, 1971, the USS *Marvin G. Shields* (FF-1066), the fifteenth *Knox*-class frigate, was commissioned at Puget Sound Naval Shipyard with Commander William J. Hunter in command. Like all US Navy destroyers and frigates, the ship was named after a Navy or Marine Corps hero. By 1971, its namesake, Marvin Glenn Shields had become a Seabee legend.

Launch of the USS Marvin G. Shields

The *Marvin Shields* was built at Todd Shipyards in Seattle, Washington. With a design based around the large AN/SQS-26CX sonar, she was armed with an eight round ASROC (anti-submarine rocket) launcher forward. She also carried an Mk 42 5"/54 caliber naval gun for air and surface targets. The *Shields* and her sisters were designed to provide the US Navy with a potent antisubmarine warfare platform. *Knox*-class frigates also carried the SH-2 Seasprite Helicopter, which included LAMPS (Light Airborne Multi-Purpose System), an advanced antisubmarine and antiship scouting and attack system, which added to the already potent anti-submarine warfare suite contained on the ship.

- The *Marvin Shields* deployed to support US forces fighting in Vietnam in 1971 and supported Coalition forces during Operations Desert Shield and Desert Storm.
- In 1974, the US Navy created the Shields Medal in honor of CM3 Marvin G. Shields. It is presented each year to an active duty enlisted member of the US Navy in Occupational Field 13 for outstanding contributions to facility construction and/or maintenance by demonstrated technical and leadership ability.
- The Naval Construction Battalion Center is an eleven-hundred-acre US Navy complex located in Gulfport, Mississippi. It is home base for the Atlantic Fleet Seabees. Address: 4902 Marvin Shields Boulevard.
- Camp Marvin Glen Shields in Okinawa is located in the northwestern part of Okinawa City. It is equipped with a construction equipment repair facility and resource storage facility. It also has barracks, residential housing, and leisure/recreational facilities.
- Shields Hall—the enlisted men's bachelor living quarters, Puget Sound Naval Shipyard—Dedicated June 14, 1996.

[Marv] was a people person, although if he were alive today he would be very uncomfortable with all the attention. But he was a hero. Remember him for what he died for and why he died: For his friends, he died as he lived, for his friends. He sacrificed himself for his friends and for that reason he's a hero in the truest sense of the word.

—Joan Shields-Bennett
Widow of Marvin Shields
Launch of the USS *Marvin G. Shields*

In slumbers of midnight the sailor boy lay;
His hammock swung loose at the sport of the wind;
But watch-worn and weary, his cares flew away,
And visions of happiness danced o'er his mind.

"The Mariner's Dream"
William Dimond

CHAPTER 12

JOHN CHARLES YATES

This Marine

John "Butch" Yates

"Butch Yates was my buddy," Arvie Byers said. "We lived on this little hard-scrabble farm outside Garrison, North Dakota—about one hundred miles south of the Canadian border. The Yates family was our only neighbor. My house was 'bout a mile down this narrow dirt road, and the Yates place was just over a little knoll and across a creek. Butch and I'd walk together to the main highway to catch the school bus. Man, it was so damned cold in the wintertime. Snow'd be ass-deep on a shaved-tail mule, and the temp would be 'bout twenty below. We didn't think much about it. It was all we'd ever known. I slept in the loft with my little brother—the snow'd sift in through the siding on the house during the night, and there'd be a layer of snow on our quilts when I dragged my ass outa bed in the mornin'. I'd break the ice on the water bucket in the kitchen when I got downstairs, and I'd heat water on the cook stove to wash up while my mom fixed my breakfast.

"All Butch talked 'bout was bein' a soldier, even when we were nine years old. He had a bunch'a toy soldiers his daddy'd bought him for his birthday, and he'd play with'em all day long. His dad, Louie, had been a soldier in WWII. We played 'war' in the creek all summer. Butch moved away to Minnesota after we finished eighth grade in 1956. I sure missed him. My mom and Mariana, Butch's mom, wrote back 'n' forth, so I kept track of him, but I really missed havin' him to play ball with and talk to. I wasn't surprised when I heard he'd enlisted in the Marines after high school. That was just, Butch."

Louie and Mariana Yates, along with their sons, Butch and Joe, moved from North Dakota to Fergus Falls, Minnesota in the summer of 1956. Louie and Mariana had struggled to make ends meet on the farm before the war. And after being drafted and absent for two years, Lou had struggled even more in the decade after the war was over. Farm economies had once again faced the challenge of overproduction during the war years and then returning to peacetime production and markets when the war was over. Technological advances, such as the introduction of gasoline and electric-powered machinery during the war, and the widespread use of pesticides and chemical fertilizers meant production per acre across the northern plains was higher than ever. That was depressing prices and costing farmers money. Mariana had family in Fergus Falls who told her the economy there was booming and jobs were abundant, especially for veterans. With thirteen thousand people, Fergus Falls was seven times the size of Garrison and offered a variety of employment, so they sold the farm and moved 320 miles east.

Lou Yates soon found a good-paying job with Otter Tail Power Company, and the family moved into a small house near Fergus Falls High School. Butch was a rising freshman and Joe was just a year behind him. Over the next several years, the family embraced life in the city of Fergus Falls—Louie and Mariana became involved in the community both socially and politically accepting leadership roles in the Federated Church, where they were members, and in the local affiliates of the Minnesota Republican Party.

Butch graduated from high school in 1960 and went on to Fergus Falls Junior College. He was one of the first one hundred students at the new junior college, and his parents were very proud of him. No one in their family had attended college before, but Butch was smart—Louie and Mariana thought it would help to ensure a good-paying job for him in the future. In addition, unlike his younger brother, Butch had always been a bit shy and immature, so it was a way to keep him around home a little longer. "Butch just needed some more time to ripen," Louie said, laughing. "Two years of college will help him grow up."

"I finished my second year of FFJC in June 1962," Yates said. "My dad and mother and my Grandma Hazel Larson were going on a trip west, and they had delayed their departure so I could go along. My brother Joey had to work, so he was unable to go with us. He was also 'in love' again [as usual], so he wasn't really interested in being gone for three weeks, anyway.

"We were going to visit my Uncle John Yates, whom I was named for," Butch continued. "I was twenty years old—I was eight the last time I had seen Uncle John, so it was a special trip. We headed for South Dakota, drove through the Black Hills, and then on to Yellowstone Park in Wyoming. What an amazing place with herds of buffalo and antelope roaming the hills, beautiful waterfalls, and all the geysers and hot springs. From there, we drove through the Teton Mountains and made our way on to Salt Lake City. From the Great Salt Lake, it was a four-hundred-mile drive across Utah to my uncle's home in Farmington, New Mexico. We stayed a week in Farmington and then drove to Colorado Springs and Denver. We spent a day in Rocky Mountain National Park. There was still snow at fourteen thousand feet elevation on Trail Ridge Road, along with spectacular scenery. We had bowls of hot chili at a little chalet overlooking a snow-covered valley. It was hard to believe it was mid-July. Minnesota was calling, so we headed home.

"I had gone along with my parents' wishes to this point in my life. I had graduated from FFJC with honors in June and had gone on the family trip in July. Now it was time to fulfill my own dreams and follow the path that would define my life.

"I enlisted in the Marine Corps in August 1962. As a resident of a state west of the Mississippi River, I went through bootcamp at MCRD San Diego in California.

"Boot camp wasn't as bad as I expected," Yates said, "but I'd really prepared myself for it both physically and mentally. The fact that I was in better physical shape and was two or three years older than most of the other recruits was a big help. Most of the guys were right out of high school, and there were several who hadn't finished high school. My dad knew what he was doing when he insisted I attend junior college before enlisting. It definitely paid off for me.

"The Quonset huts that served as our billets and the training facilities we used during the day were located parallel to one of the runways at San Diego airport. The two areas were separated by a tall chain link fence. My third week of boot camp I was assigned to walk guard duty from 2000 hours [8:00 p.m.] to midnight. I had to march up and down the fence line, making sure no one sneaked in [or tried to escape].

"From my vantage point, I could see the lights of fancy homes on a bluff that looked out over the ocean and watch the traffic as it moved along a highway not far from the base. It was Saturday night, and I could imagine guys taking their dates to park somewhere on that bluff, watching the moon light sparkling out on the ocean, before taking the girls home to their parents in one of those big houses. It wasn't long before I was totally homesick, and yearning to see the moon rise over one of the gorgeous lakes back home. There are eleven hundred lakes in Otter Tail County, Minnesota, so I'd had a few dates watching the moon rise over the water."

Butch Yates

"Yatesy was one of my billet-mates during boot camp," Will Wilburn said. "Man, if there was ever a man born to be a Marine, it was Yates. To be honest, Yatesy didn't look like much. He was little, about five foot six or seven and wiry with horn-rimmed glasses. He looked a lot like the kid in those Charles Atlas ads that's gettin' the sand kicked in his face. But man! What a man he was. He didn't have an ounce of fat on him, and he was so tough.

"Yates was older," Wilburn continued. "Most of us were right out of high school and green as hell. He had a couple years of college, which was rare for guys in our platoon. He was a hell of a lot smarter than most of us, and was the most competitive man I've ever met. He could run faster, jump higher, climb better, you name it—he didn't wear a cape, but this man was a Marine before he became a Marine. On top of that, he was a great guy. What more could you ask for? Ya just had to hate a guy that seemed to have a handful of aces. The DIs picked up right quick this man was special. They made him a squad leader and continually gave him more responsibilities. I think they wanted to see how much he could handle, but he never backed down, he never quit, and he never disappointed."

After completing the ten-week course at San Diego, Yates and his fellow boots moved on to Marine Combat Training at SOI-W (School of Infantry-West) Camp Pendleton. It was located an hour north, traveling by Marine Corps bus up the California coast.

While at SOI-W, Yates completed two weeks of training under simulated combat conditions in the fundamentals of day and night patrolling, employment of infantry weapons, survival methods, and assault tactics. He was taught how to use hand grenades, a compass, and the principles of map reading and land navigation. He also learned how to detect and disarm mines and booby traps, and while being exposed to live machine gun fire, he learned to advance safely from one point to another. After this course, he was scheduled to go on to more advanced training before being assigned to his permanent unit.

With high test scores in both math and electronics, Yates was sent to the Communication-Electronics School Battalion at Twentynine Palms, California. He would be trained as a Ground Radio Repairman, MOS 2841.

It has been said that Twentynine Palms is "50 miles from water and three feet from hell." Needless to say, for a boy from the green hills and pristine lakes of western Minnesota, "three feet from hell" was an apt description. Located in the high desert region of Southern California's Mojave Desert, Twentynine Palms receives very little rain and has practically no plant life at all.

"The old hands call this place 'The Stumps,' which is giving it the benefit of the doubt," Butch said upon first seeing the landscape at Twentynine Palms. "I have my doubts anything has ever grown in this god-forsaken place big enough to leave a stump, let alone twenty-nine of them," he said, laughing. "I thought Uncle John's place in New Mexico was barren, but it can't hold a candle to this Mojave moonscape."

Near Twentynine Palms, California, 1960s

"I had several different schools to go through," Yates said, "so sometimes I'd finish one course, and then sit around waiting for the next school to start. We started with basic stuff, and the first classes were pretty straightforward. As long as I paid attention, the courses were easy for me, and I began to learn how electronics work. I had to study, pay attention, and work within my group. I couldn't screw around.

"There was a high dropout rate," Butch continued. "The number of different subjects we had to learn in a short time contributed to that. We learned about four years' worth of college or tech-school level stuff in ten months, and that meant some intense studying for all of us. Some of the guys who picked up transistor theory struggled when they got to binary. Some who got the book stuff fell apart when we began to do the hands on stuff. For me—man, I just loved it all."

"About midway through July, it was so damned hot. We were all pulled into a conference room and depending on what our ranking was in our class, and the MOS and duty station availability, we were designated what specialty we were going to continue in. We knew the 5000 series guys were only gonna be around through part of the school anyway, but some guys got cool MOS courses because of how well they had done in school and the needs of the Corps at the time. Most of us would go to GRRC (Ground Radio Repair Course) and become 2841s. The school was a combination of everything we had learned about finding and fixing problems, but the course would be targeted to the radio systems used by fleet marine units.

"While we were going through this last school, the Corps was still processing our security clearances. If we didn't get our clearance we couldn't remain in school and would be bumped to another MOS. All those stories about the stuff guys didn't tell their recruiter 'cause it was no big deal—well maybe it was a big deal. Some of the boots in my class didn't get clearances because something came up during their background checks, and it really sucked. After all the hard work they had put in—it happened just a couple of weeks before we graduated.

"During those times between the different classes, we had some down time. Of course, it was the Marine Corps, so we still had PT and some drill, barracks duty, cleaning details, and other day-to-day stuff, but we also found time to visit Joshua Tree National monument, and we could camp, hike and rock climb if it wasn't hot as hell."

After graduating from GRRC near the top of his class in December 1963, Butch Yates went home to Fergus Falls on leave. President John Kennedy had been assassinated three weeks before, and the country was still in a state of mourning. Flags everywhere were at half-staff.

Pfc. Yates—home for Christmas 1963

Christmas morning dawned cold and clear, with a brisk Arctic wind blowing in from the northwest. With wind-chill temperatures in the teens, Butch's "summer from hell" in Twentynine Palms seemed to be in the distant past.

"We were expecting subzero temperatures to move into the area in a couple days," Butch said, "so after church on Christmas morning and dinner with my Grandma Hazel, Joey and I, and our parents, made the rounds of family and friends to make sure they had adequate supplies of food and fuel oil or wood to stay warm. The forecasters were predicting below-zero temperatures for at least a week. That was colder than normal for December, even in western Minnesota."

By mid-January, Butch had purchased a used 1960 Dodge Dart. It was tan in color with a white top, loaded with chrome, and looked brand-new. It was his first car, and he was very proud of it. He loaded up his duffel bag, a suitcase packed with "civvies," and a picnic basket full of food prepared by his mother and grandmother. Leaving for North Carolina early on January 17, 1964, the temperature was nineteen degrees, the sky was clear, and the road was straight and dry. One could not ask for more in Minnesota in January.

Yates arrived in Jacksonville, North Carolina, in the afternoon of January 20. The temperature was a balmy sixty-three degrees. The young man rolled down the car window, feeling the wind ruffle his short Marine haircut. He smelled the ocean breeze blowing in off Onslow Beach as it swayed the fronds of the stubby palmettos and the branches of the longleaf pines lining Highway 24.

Butch approached the main gate of Camp Lejeune and watched the Marine sentries as they checked the identification of the drivers ahead of him. As he waited, he reflected on the seventeen months of training and study that had brought him to this place and pondered what might lie ahead in the weeks and months to come.

PART 2

Sgt. John Yates arrived at Da Nang Air Base on January 6, 1967. He was assigned as the communications chief for Bravo Company, First Amphibian Tractor Battalion, 3rd Marine Division; however, his duties and interests covered a much wider range than just supervising radio repairmen or overseeing the radio maintenance shop. He was continually looking for ways to improve himself and the Marines he worked with.

By April 1967, the First AMTRAC Battalion was relocated north to the Marine combat base at Cửa Việt. The base was located at the mouth of the Cửa Việt/Thạch Hán River, approximately ten miles north of Quảng Trị and only six miles south of the DMZ. Under Operation NAPOLEON, First AMTRAC, along with 1st Battalion,

3rd Marines, was tasked with keeping the waterways around the base open for the transport of Allied commerce and supplies.

Leaving Da Nang for Cửa Việt—April 1967

Yates had been reassigned to Alpha Company, 1st AMTRAC Battalion and made the move to Cửa Việt with his new company. "We're right on the beach at the mouth of the river," Yates said. "There's nothing here but sand, scrubby pines, and a few small fishing villages. There's no soil fit to grow anything other than sand fleas. There's a great crop of those bastards, and they can really get under your skin. Good news is there's usually a breeze from the sea. The heat doesn't seem as stifling as it does inland."

The 1st AMTRAC Battalion had barely finished setting up their tents at Cua Viet Combat Base when Operation HICKORY was launched on May 18, 1967. The 2nd and 3rd Platoons of Bravo Company, along with elements of Alpha Company provided direct support to the amphibious assault force in the opening stages of the operation.

During the evening of June 12, 1967, the North Vietnamese Army launched a barrage of 130mm rockets and artillery shells against the First AMTRAC base area. Some 225 rockets and artillery shells rained down in and around the battalion camp. Every unit in the perimeter wire was hit, and many of the troop tents were knocked down. Supplies were destroyed and shrapnel ripped through the entire area, damaging communications, mowing down trees, shattering windshields, and puncturing barrels of fuel and petroleum. Casualties included one Marine killed and thirty-three others wounded. The dead Marine was Sgt. James Kistler. He was a member of the Maintenance Platoon from Headquarters Company, and he had been the patrol leader of two fire teams of Marines on guard duty that evening. One of the first 130mm rockets fired at the compound overshot the position and impacted just a few yards behind Kistler, killing him instantly. A month after the attack, the base camp was designated Camp Kistler in his memory.

During the ceremony dedicating the camp in honor of Sgt. Kistler, a portion of a letter he had written was read, "Now I'm no hero, nor a philosopher, nor a historian, but I think I'd rather die tomorrow than know that my friends and relatives or their children would have to live someday under the communists. And it will happen if we let them have their way in Asia."

Throughout the ensuing months, Camp Kistler continued to be subjected to frequent NVA artillery and rocket fire from north of the DMZ. "There's nothing we can do about it," Yates said. "As much as we'd love to go after the SOBs, we can't cross the DMZ. The NVA come south all the time, whenever they feel like it, but the politicians won't allow us to go back north after them. They're afraid we might start a war," he concluded with a wry smile.

Early on the morning of July 14, 1967, nearly half of 1st AMTRAC Battalion departed Camp Kistler on Operation HICKORY II. Capt. Leo Jamieson, Alpha Company commander led an interesting collection of troops and vehicles into battle. Alpha Company served as the infantry unit with ninety-five Marines on the ground, leaving the 4th Platoon (still operating as an AMTRAC platoon) behind at the CP as the reserve force. Bravo Company supplied twenty-seven AMTRACs, while H&S Company supplied three, and to provide more firepower in the field, two HOW-6s (tractors with 105mm howitzers) from 3rd Platoon, 1st Armored AMTRAC Company (also based at Cua Viet CB) accompanied Jamieson on HICKORY II. Besides their M14 rifles, other weapons available to the AMTRAC Marines were the .30 cal machine guns atop the tractors or carried by teams on the ground, two M79 grenade launchers, and an Indochina-War-vintage 60mm mortar that had no base plate.

Alpha Company had no mortars, so an earlier commander, upon spotting the aging 60mm tube on board a South Vietnamese naval junk had made a deal for it. There was no base, bipod, or sighting equipment in the bargain, but the company had the mortar tube and ammunition. It would serve in an emergency. The total strength of Jamieson's force in the field was thirty-two AMTRACs and 225 Marines.

Sgt. Yates had previously been the comms chief for Bravo Company, but after joining Alpha Company, he had taken on the role of field radio operator with the leadership team in Capt. Jamieson's command tractor. He handled communications with the battalion command post for Jamieson. His friend, Sgt. Hugh Connelly (Alpha Company radioman), handled communications between Jamieson and the platoons, as well as comms with the AO, gunships, and fixed wing air support.

Crossing the Cửa Việt River was a time-consuming process for a large number of AMTRACs. They had to cross one at a time, but no vehicles hit mines, and none were attacked or otherwise disabled during the crossing, so that part of the operation was completed in about ninety minutes. Capt. Jamieson had sent a small force across the river the night before to secure the northern bank and provide security for the next morning's crossing.

The force was then split in two for the advance north, with about half the AMTRACs moving along the tree line and the remainder moving in the surf along the beach, where there was less danger of encountering land mines. As soon as the AMTRACs began the sweep north along the tree line, the NVA initiated a series of hit and run attacks. Small groups of enemy troops would strike with small arms fire, quickly retreat northward, and then repeat the process. By 11:00 a.m., as the AMTRAC force started to cross an area of open terrain, it came under attack again by small arms fire, mortars, and RPGs. Two AMTRACs were hit by RPG rounds and another struck a 40–60 lb. antitank mine. Artillery and air strikes were called in, and once the strikes were completed, Jamieson was able to medevac three Marines who had been wounded during the attack. At 11:45, uniformed NVA were spotted to the north and another airstrike was called in. Jamieson set off a smoke grenade, and an A-4E Skyhawk quickly appeared overhead.

"You're pretty close," the pilot said. "You better keep your heads down."

Butch Yates remarked, "Man, that Marine pilot came in at tree-top level. We were so close we could see the writing on his helmet. He had a sun visor, or I could probably tell you the color of his eyes. There was a deafening roar that made our ears ring and vibrated our teeth. He came back around for a second pass with his 20mm cannon blazing, and this guy was an artist. He had no idea of the size or capabilities of the enemy force he faced, but he just came in like a bat outta hell. He took 'em to school and taught 'em a real tough lesson—made me proud to be a Marine."

There was no additional enemy contact as Capt. Jamieson and his unit turned west and moved along the DMZ. When he got closer to the western edge of the "desert" (the sand dunes comprising much of the coastal plain), Jamieson headed south toward Hill 31. A long sand dune ridge extended to the north from Hill 31 and marked the western edge of the desert. To the west of the desert, the terrain had jungle vegetation and was dotted with abandoned villages adjacent to Jones Creek, a rivulet running from the Bến Hải River (the actual border between North and South Vietnam) south to the Cửa Việt River. It was along this western series of dunes just NNW of Hill 31 and about a mile south of the DMZ that the unit's first major engagement with a large NVA force occurred at around 4:00 p.m.

As the AMTRAC force headed south, it came under heavy attack from the dune line to the west, and the Alpha command tractor stalled. Those on board included Jamieson, Yates, Connelly, and the tractor crew. While the rest of the force pulled back, unaware the command tractor was being left behind, the stalled tractor came under heavy RPG, mortar and small arms fire from the ridgeline to the right front. Jamieson and his team were totally pinned down. They jumped from the tractor and moved behind the engine for cover as the radiomen tried to establish communications with the rest of the force. One of the tractor crewmen had already been wounded in the shoulder.

Realizing the seriousness of the situation, Yates handed his radio to Connelly and, braving heavy machine-gun fire, ran twenty yards to the stalled tractor. Completely disregarding his own safety, he scrambled to the top of the vehicle and manned the .30-cal. machine gun, firing into the dune line where most of the enemy fire was coming from. As the NVA concentrated their fire on the offending American gun, Yates was forced to abandon the position, which offered him little protection. Throwing the ancient 60mm mortar tube to the ground, he tossed down four boxes of mortar ammo and jumped off the beleaguered vehicle.

Grabbing the mortar, dragging the ammo boxes, and ignoring the barrage of enemy fire, Yates quickly moved back across the exposed area to a more sheltered position. He observed the Marine squads in contact with the NVA and saw some enemy movement as the NVA sought to improve their position. Removing his helmet, Yates stuck the butt-end of the mortar tube in the helmet, held the weapon in his bare hands, and fired. The first round went long, but his second round landed directly on the NVA positions. He began to walk the mortar rounds across the enemy fighting positions so effectively that the NVA fire dropped to almost nothing within a few minutes. Taking advantage of this lull, Yates ran back to the tractor. He once again clambered on top of the idled machine and threw down more ammunition. When the tube became so hot it burned his hands, Yates tugged the green towel from around his neck, quickly wiped the sweat from his face, wrapped it around the tube, and continued to fire into the NVA positions.

The NVA tried to flank the Marines, but now they were met not only with well-aimed rifle fire, but with 60mm high-explosive and "Willie Pete" (white phosphorus) rounds. And one of the HOW-6 AMTRACs arrived on the scene, moving along the ridge firing its 105mm howitzer directly into the NVA line with devastating effect. The combined barrage of rifle, mortar, and howitzer fire proved too much for the NVA. The enemy survivors broke contact and headed north toward the DMZ under the cover of dusk.

"One of the prettiest sights I've ever seen was that HOW-6 moving back and forth in front of that ridgeline destroying the NVA unit that had us trapped," Hugh Connelly said. "Our helpless little group would certainly have all been killed had it not been for the courageous action of both Butch Yates and the HOW-6 crew."

Butch Yates, Hugh Connelly, Dan Reeves—Alpha Company

"Sgt. Yates was trained as a communications specialist," Capt. Jamieson said, "but he proved the fundamental necessity for solid combat training, determination in the face of the enemy, and bold initiative under fire."

After the area was worked over by Army gunships, three fixed-wing airstrikes and several artillery missions, the Marines assaulted the ridgeline and thoroughly searched the undulating dunes to be certain there were no active enemy troops still hidden there. The battle ended with twenty-five confirmed NVA troops killed. The 1st AMTRAC Battalion had two vehicles damaged and had to medevac sixteen of the twenty-nine wounded Marines to a Naval Support Hospital. Thanks to Yates, the Marines had no one killed.

"Butch Yates's actions kept us alive until one of the HOW-6's got here," Jamieson said. "Without his courage and initiative, many of us would not have survived to fight another day."

The area was nearly dark as Jamieson moved his force a mile east into the desert and set up defensive positions. From that location, his listening posts could monitor both the dune ridgeline and Hill 31 to the southwest.

On July 15, day two of the operation, Capt. Jamieson's primary objective was to clear the NVA force known to be present on Hill 31. The attack and bloody fight up the hill began at 8:30 a.m. and was over by 2:00 p.m. with fourteen Marines wounded and two killed. From Hill 31, Jamieson and his troops headed toward the abandoned village of Nhi Thương, which was nearby. From his vantage point on the hill, Jamieson had observed enemy troops, along with some artillery pieces within the village confines.

Around 3:30 that afternoon, Alpha Company's reserve unit (4th Platoon) arrived from the CP to resupply the AMTRAC force with food and ammunition. The platoon was then employed to provide additional support for the sweep through the village, and it brought the overall strength of Jamieson's force back up to near the original 225 Marines, as well as thirty-four AMTRACs, two more than the commander had started out with.

The village was cleared with eight additional Marines wounded. Total NVA confirmed killed for the day was twenty-seven. The AMTRAC force headed back to base, arriving about midnight, and Operation HICKORY II was over.

Body counts were a sensitive issue with Lt. Col. E. R. Toner, the 1st AMTRAC Battalion Commander. Early in his command, the colonel had advised the company commanders that the accepted old method of accounting for enemy KIAs and "probables" was not acceptable to him. Soon after the meeting, he made himself even clearer. If a company commander reported five NVA troops as KIA, he had better be prepared to load five whole bodies into an AMTRAC and ship them back to headquarters as the colonel might request.

During HICKORY II, Capt. Jamieson reported a number of NVA killed and a large quantity of weapons and ammunition captured. The BC said, "Tell Leo to send the whole mess in by tractor." Within an hour, an AMTRAC crew chief walked into the Battalion Combat Ops Center, saluted the colonel, and reported, "Sir, I've delivered the bodies and weapons as ordered." Jamieson's count was correct with all of the dead NVA troops delivered and down to the last bullet of ammunition as had been reported.

After the operation, Jamieson was told his AMTRAC force faced an entire NVA regiment during HICKORY II. Intel reports included in Op Order (#39-67) indicated the 31st Regiment of the 341st NVA Division (estimated strength 620 men) was operating in the area.

Capt. *Leo Jamieson takes a break—Operation HICKORY II*

For his actions on the afternoon of July 14, Sgt. John "Butch" Yates was nominated for and awarded a Silver Star. Yates was presented the award by Lt. Col. Toner on November 10, 1967, the 192nd anniversary of the Marine Corps. He was promoted to staff sergeant a few days later. Capt. Jamieson and the HOW-6 section chief also received Silver Stars for their service on day one of Operation HICKORY II.

Sgt. Dick Roberts, who was in Yates' company said, "Butch Yates leads seven-man recons during the night. That's definitely outside the purview of his job description, but he sees a need for it, so he does it. He goes above and beyond what is required or demanded, or even expected, every day and night. His recons are well organized, and he's always careful with the lives of the Marines he has with him. He may be a comm chief by MOS, but his real calling is 0311 (Marine Infantry Rifleman). That's why AMTRACers are called amgrunts.

"Yates is a natural leader," Roberts continued. "He takes E-4 corporals out on his recon patrols and mentors them on leading patrols, map reading, everything they will need when they are promoted to sergeant E-5. There's no telling how many Marine lives he's going to save in the months ahead due to the training he is doing now. I extended my tour in December '67 because of him. I wanted to learn from him."

Mariana Yates had tried her best not to worry about Butch. She knew her son and had full confidence in his intelligence and physical abilities. He wrote to her and Lou every week, sending photographs of the seascape and beach near his base, the sand dunes, the Vietnamese fishing boats, and the children. He rarely mentioned anything of a military nature, although she obviously knew he was involved in combat to some degree. He was a Marine, after all; however, her self-imposed "blindness" came to an abrupt end with the arrival of the November 24 edition of the *Fergus Falls Daily Journal*. The headline for the paper's front-page story read "Fergus Falls Man Cited for Bravery in Vietnam War." The lengthy accompanying article, based on a Department of Defense press release, described in detail the actions that had earned their son his Silver Star Medal "in the face of extreme danger." Staring at the article and the photo of Butch in his Marine dress uniform, Mariana's vision began to blur, tears welled and trickled down her cheeks. "Oh Butch," she whispered to herself. "What am I going to do with you?"

Butch Yates with his Silver Star—November 1967

PART 3

By January 1968, the 1st AMTRAC Battalion had become one of the most unique US Marine battalions in Vietnam. In addition to its normal complement of AMTRAC Marines and materiel, the battalion had attached to it: regular Marine infantry, Marine tanks, Marine combat engineers, and Marine reconnaissance elements. There were also US Army armored personnel and South Vietnamese Popular Force troops (part-time South Vietnamese militia). If there was a battalion for all seasons and all situations, this was it.

One evening in early January, a US Army artillery advisor with the ARVN unit atop Hill 31 alerted the 1st AMTRAC Battalion operations officer that a major NVA force was crossing "Oceanview," a large cleared area six miles north of Camp Kistler. Oceanview was located right on the DMZ and approximately three hundred NVA had moved past the outpost in less than fifteen minutes. Using a Starlight night vision scope, the advisor had counted the column of three men abreast as they were silhouetted against the phosphorescent waves breaking on the beach.

The Battalion CO notified the Twelfth Marines fire support coordination center (FSCC) in Đông Hà and the division direct air support center (DASC) quickly set up a time on target. When the signal came to fire, a combination of bombs from A6 Intruders, and 175mm, eight-inch howitzer, 105mm and 4.2-inch mortar fire rained down on the selected target area for twelve minutes. At first light, an ARVN company nearest to the enemy position, along with its US Army advisors, swarmed over the carnage. The advisors watched as the ARVN troops picked their way through bodies and body parts in search of vital intelligence information that would explain why such a large force was secretly moving south.

The Americans were rewarded after two hours when a battle plan for the TET Offensive 1968 was found on the remains of an NVA officer. The advisors called for an Army helicopter and hand-carried the captured document to the 1st ARVN Division HQ in Quảng Trị. This amazing discovery was only made known to the 1st AMTRAC Battalion several days later, but it seemed to have gone no further. This information arrived about the same time as increased NVA contacts kicked into high gear on January 15, 1968.

Massive NVA units were on the move. Sightings day and night streamed into battalion, regimental and divisional communication centers across I Corps. NVA forces were moving en masse, and they were all headed south.

US intelligence was not entirely in the dark. On January 5, 1968, US 4th Infantry troops operating near Pleiku had captured a copy of Urgent Order Number One. This highly classified NVA order outlined a planned attack on Pleiku during TET by a VC battalion and an NVA regiment. The documents were forwarded to MACV HQ in Saigon.

On January 17, NSA had sent out the first of a series of intelligence bulletins regarding recent SIGINT (signals intelligence) analysis. According to the bulletin, it was "likely" various NVA units were preparing to attack Kontum, Pleiku, Darlac, Quảng Nam, Quảng Ngãi, and Bình Định Provinces, as well as the city of Huế. On January 20, additional documents were captured containing plans for attacks on the cities of Buôn Ma Thuột and Qui Nhơn, and there were indications of increased enemy activity in the areas around Saigon. NSA's warnings were based on analysis of VC and NVA communications intercepted by ASA (Army Security Agency), USAFSS (Air Force Security Service), and the Marines' 1st Radio Battalion intercept site atop the Rockpile, ten miles south of the DMZ. In spite of mounting evidence, Gen. Westmoreland, and his cadre in Saigon remained skeptical the North Vietnamese were capable of mounting such an offensive.

Those dealing directly with the influx of enemy forces, however, had little doubt something was afoot. Marine and Army units across northern I Corps were reporting increased movement and more frequent contacts on a daily basis. Enemy artillery and mortar attacks were more frequent all along the DMZ. Larger numbers of NVA were being sighted in broad daylight west of Highway 1. Marine/ Naval Aerial Observers were picking up larger units moving in along the Laos/Vietnam border, and that was just the tip of the iceberg.

"On January 20, 1968, Alpha Company left Camp Kistler and moved up the north side of the Cửa Việt River," Yates said. "We soon found ourselves engaged in an all-out battle with hundreds of NVA troops near the village of Mỹ Lộc. By the end of the day, First AMTRAC had suffered thirteen Marines killed and fifty wounded. The average age of those thirteen dead Marines was just a little less than nineteen years old—such a waste, man, such a waste. There was obviously something going on over and above the enemy activity we normally had to deal with."

By mid-February, Yates was nearing the end of his thirteen-month tour in Vietnam, and he made the decision to extend his time for an additional six months. There was too much going on along the Cửa Việt, and he was too sorely needed to leave. His commander needed him; his company needed him and especially the young corporals he continued to mentor. He wrote his parents, told them of his decision, and promised he would be home in the summer.

Butch Yates—always teaching

The 3rd Battalion 1st Marine Division had been involved in Operation NAPOLEON-SALINE since January 20. On February 27, operational control of Three/One Marines was transferred to the 1st AMTRAC Battalion. On that same night, radar-guided bombs struck the village of Lâm Xuân, and at 8:00 a.m. the following morning, the village was hit by a barrage of US Naval gunfire coming in from the China Sea. The attacks, however, had done little damage to the NVA bunkers. When Lima Company Three/One Marines attacked the village later that morning, they encountered heavy gunfire, and three of their tanks were disabled by land mines. The Marines pulled back for further air and artillery strikes and in the afternoon resumed their attack as a second Marine company established a blocking position. At dusk, the NVA withdrew under cover of NVA artillery coming from across the DMZ. When the Marines entered Lâm Xuân on February 29, they found sixty-nine dead NVA and captured two wounded NVA troops. Marine losses were eight dead.

On March 1, Mike Company Three/One Marines supported by two AMTRACS and two HOW-6s from 1st AMTRAC Battalion conducted a sweep of Mai Xá Thi. The AMTRACs shot line charges into the hamlet to clear the houses along the riverbank while the H6 operators used their howitzers to fire canister shot into the village. As the LVTs moved into the hamlet, they were met by heavy weapons fire from the west. India Company was ordered to support the west flank of Mike Company, and they engaged the NVA until dark, killing thirty-six and capturing three. Sweeping the area over the next two days the Marines found eighty-three additional NVA bodies and captured another wounded soldier. Marines had twenty-seven dead and many wounded. The prisoners were interrogated and revealed that the 52nd Regiment of the 320th NVA Division had moved south of the DMZ to replace the 803rd NVA Regiment, which had moved south into Thừa Thiên Province.

On March 10, Cửa Việt Base was hit by NVA artillery from across the DMZ, destroying 150 tons of ammunition, damaging numerous buildings and killing one Marine. "We thought all hell had broken loose," Yates said. "The arty and rockets coming in were loud enough, but man, when that ammo went off, it was like the end of the world. Our ears were still ringing two days later. We lost one man and had a bunch wounded. It's a wonder we didn't lose more than we did. The force of the blast knocked down tents and hooches for a hundred yards in every direction."

On March 18, as a platoon of two/four Marines patrolled an abandoned hamlet a mile south of Mai Xá Thi, they were engaged by heavy weapons and artillery fire. The Marines called in air and artillery support and on entering the hamlet the next day found seventy-two dead enemy troops. They also captured four wounded troops who had been left behind. The Marines lost thirteen dead. March was a bloody month. The Marines killed more than 440 NVA, but their losses were heavy, too: sixty-five Marines lost their lives during the month.

On April 11, NVA artillery, firing from across the DMZ, hit the Cua Viet Combat Base fuel farm destroying forty thousand gallons of petroleum. Yates had just returned from a night patrol with a half-dozen young corporals and was near his hooch at Camp Kistler when the artillery barrage began. He instinctively dived into a nearby bunker and then realized not all his Marines had made it to cover and crawled back out into the melee. Yates saw several figures running, but one was lying inert on the ground twenty yards from him. Bending low, Butch raced to the Marine and recognized him as a newly arrived corporal named Carlisle. He determined the youngster was alive but unconscious. The man had lost his helmet, had deep gashes on the side of his head above his ear, and was bleeding heavily. Grabbing the man by the arm-holes of his flak vest, Yates began to move backward, dragging Carlisle toward the nearest bunker. And then another shell exploded some thirty yards behind him. Yates was slammed to the ground, bleeding from his nose and ears, and from multiple shrapnel wounds covering his buttocks, thighs, and legs.

"I just remember dragging Carlisle, and then I was lying there in the dirt," Yates said. "It took some time to realize what had happened. I wasn't sure where I was or what was going on. My ass and legs were on fire. I heard explosions all around me, and my vision began to clear."

Yates soon regained his senses. Shaking his head to clear away the fog, he slowly rose to his feet, gained his balance, and resumed dragging the still unconscious corporal into a nearby bunker. A Navy corpsman tended to the many wounds of both men and remarked that without treatment, Carlisle would have died. After the artillery siege ended, Carlisle was medevaced by chopper to a naval hospital, and Yates was moved to the base infirmary for treatment of his myriad flesh wounds and a severe concussion.

Camp Kistler had been hit by sixty-four rounds of 100mm artillery. It had sustained damage to two of the unit's LTVs. In addition, a maintenance building, a storage facility, and a mess hall had been seriously damaged. One squad tent had been completely destroyed.

Two days later, Yates was visited by the 1st AMTRAC Battalion Commander, Lt. Col. G. F. Meyers. Meyers thanked Yates for his exemplary service to the battalion over the past fifteen months and then presented him with a Purple Heart and a Bronze Star for saving the life of Cpl. Carlisle. Butch wrote to his parents, putting his own spin on the incident, downplaying the details of it and then changing the subject to his impending trip home in ten weeks.

Near the end of April the Navy's Task Force CLEARWATER received intelligence that the NVA were planning to block the Cửa Việt River again. Four NVA battalions, including two from the 320th Division, infiltrated past an ARVN Regiment to occupy the area around Đại Độ. The NVA troops moved into a series of prebuilt bunkers surrounded by barbed wire, which had been built over the preceding weeks. The ARVN force that had responsibility for security in the area was completely oblivious of the enemy activity or the existence of the bunkers.

At 3:30 a.m. on April 30, NVA troops fired on a Navy patrol boat, which returned fire, and then returned to Đông Hà Base. At 4:00 a.m. the same NVA unit opened fire on a US Naval landing craft causing major damaged, killing one American sailor and the US Navy ordered all traffic on the Cửa Việt River to cease. Some three hours later, a patrol was dispatched by Two/Four Marines to investigate the area. The unit became heavily engaged by the NVA force and additional companies from Two/Four and One/Three Marines joined the action throughout the day. Marine losses were sixteen dead—NVA known losses totaled ninety dead. The NVA force withdrew, but for the time being, the enemy unit had achieved the objective Task Force CLEARWATER had warned about. The river was closed to all Allied traffic.

Contact with NVA forces remained heavy across I Corps throughout the month of May. The Cửa Việt River was reopened, and 1st AMTRAC Battalion was out on patrol nearly every day attempting to keep it clear and safe for Allied commerce and supply shipments. Yates was transferred back to Bravo Company when the communications chief there was seriously wounded and medevaced to the US Naval Station Hospital, Subic Bay, Philippines.

The NVA generally avoided contact with the Marines during the month of June, although NVA artillery hit the combat base at Cửa Việt on June 21 and 24, destroying an ammo dump.

On July 15, 1968, Butch Yates told his Marine buddies, "Gặp lại sau!" (See ya!), and he boarded a chopper for Da Nang Air Base. He was heading home on thirty days leave. He had not told his family he had already processed the paperwork to extend his time in Vietnam another six months. He would be coming back to the 1st AMTRAC Battalion in mid-August. He would broach the subject with Lou and Mariana after he got home to Fergus Falls.

PART 4

Butch emerged from his North Central Airlines flight at Hector Airport in Fargo, North Dakota. It was early in the morning— Thursday, July 18, 1968. He shivered as he took a deep breath of the clean, fresh air. There was a brisk wind blowing out of the west at 15 mph, and his Marine service uniform was not quite warm enough in the cool breeze. It had been a long time since he had been in weather like this. The sky was clouded over but seemed bright after the dim interior of the aircraft. There was also the fact that he had slept little in the last seventy-two hours. Blinking his eyes to clear his vision, he adjusted his glasses, slipped his garrison cap on his head, and descended the metal steps of the CV-580.

Walking toward the small crowd of people meeting the flight, Yates suddenly heard a shout, "Hey, Butch, welcome home!" Joe came on the run, wrapping his arms around his brother in a bear hug that almost knocked Butch to the ground. Laughing, with tears in his eyes, Butch pushed his "little" brother back and looked up at him.

"Joey," Butch said, "I'd swear you are still growing," and the two brothers hugged each other again. Joe, who was a sergeant in the 94th Armor Battalion, Minnesota Army National Guard, was almost five inches taller than his older brother and outweighed him by forty pounds. At that moment, Mariana and Lou walked up and wrapped their arms around both of their sons. They were so proud of these two young men.

Turning to kiss his mother, Butch said, "Hey, Mom, did you miss me?"

Smiling through her tears, Mariana replied, "Butch, what am I going to do with you?"

Loading Butch's bags into the back of his Jeep Super Wagoneer, Lou Yates could not stop smiling. It had been so long since the family had been together. Joe was working in Benson, Minnesota, which was about eighty miles south of Fergus Falls. He came home for a weekend occasionally, but with his social life and Guard obligations, they did not see him nearly as often as they would like. And of course, they had not seen Butch in eighteen months.

As always, the weeks flew by. Butch drove his dad's Wagoneer down to Benson for a weekend ("Man, do I love this Jeep!"). There was not much to do in Benson, which was much smaller than Fergus Falls, so on Saturday afternoon, the two brothers drove to St. Cloud, Minnesota, which was seventy-five miles east. With a population of thirty-five thousand people, St. Cloud had a significant nightlife with clubs, restaurants, theaters, and St. Cloud State College. Joe frequented the city regularly. Joe and Butch finally decided to get a motel room about 2:00 a.m. on Sunday. Neither was in any condition to drive back to Benson.

"Joey, you have corrupted me!" Butch complained, laughing; however, he and Joe made a return trip to St. Cloud two weeks later.

Mariana's mother, Grandma Hazel, had remarried and moved back to Illinois, but she and her husband, Bill, drove to Fergus Falls to spend a few days and see her grandsons. Joe, who worked as an aircraft mechanic at Benson Municipal Airport, came in for another long weekend, and the two ladies cooked some of the family's favorite dishes. Among them were Swedish meatballs, wild rice-crusted walleye, and lefse (a traditional Norwegian potato flatbread). Scandinavian cooking was standard fare in Fergus Falls.

On Sunday, August 11, the Yates family went to church together. Joe and Lou had both taken vacation over the coming week. Butch would be leaving on Thursday afternoon, and the family planned to spend as much time together as possible. Butch had told Joe he was returning to Vietnam, but he had not told his parents. They may have suspected, but they had not pressed the issue regarding his next duty assignment, and he had not volunteered the information.

After church, Mariana fried a skillet of crispy chicken and made milk gravy to serve over the fluffy biscuits baking in the oven. A pan of succotash and another skillet of fried Jonathan apples simmered on the stove. She loved cooking for her men and watching them enjoy her food.

After Sunday dinner was finished and the dishes done, the family adjourned to the front porch with thick slices of chocolate cake and mugs of hot coffee. Following Lou's promotion to manager at Otter Tail Power Company, he and Mariana had sold their house in town and moved to a small Victorian farmhouse that had come available on the edge of town. It sat on five acres of wooded land and bordered a small lake. The house was blessed with a wide front porch which ran the length of the house, and they had furnished it with a variety of rocking chairs and a porch swing that looked out over the lake. The temperature was in the low eighties, but there was a cool breeze coming in off the lake.

Butch had dreaded this moment, but he had delayed it as long as he could. He had to tell his parents his decision to return to Vietnam. Clearing his throat in an effort to swallow away the lump that was there, Butch said, "Mom and Dad, there's something we need to discuss."

"You are going back to Vietnam," Mariana volunteered—and the silence was deafening.

There was only the slight tinkle of a small brass wind chime Butch had brought his mother from Japan, the sough of the wind in the white paper birch trees that surrounded the lake, and in the distance, the soft cooing of a mourning dove.

Butch looked at Joey who shook his head with a slight smile and looked down at the floor.

"I have known you for a number of years, Butch Yates," Mariana said softly. "When you had not mentioned your next duty station, it didn't take me long to figure out why. Your father and I have talked about it. You are twenty-six years old and dedicated to the work you are doing. There is no way we would ever consider trying to influence you or stand in your way. You have our blessing, son. May God go with you, and may He keep you safe in the palm of His hand."

Butch rose from his rocker and walked to the swing where his parents were seated. Embracing his mother, and facing his father, he said, "Thank you. You have no idea how much this means to me. I'm doing what I need to do. I believe totally in the fight we are waging against communism. I'd be miserable if I left my buddies and the other men I work with and rotated back stateside. Many of them are extending their time in Vietnam too, so we can continue the work we're doing there. I love you, and I promise I'll be careful."

Pushing her son out at arm's length, blinking back tears, and shaking her head, Mariana said, "Butch Yates, what am I going to do with you?" and everyone laughed.

"Just love me, Mom," Butch replied softly. "Just love me."

On Thursday afternoon, the family found itself back at the airport in Fargo. Butch had checked his bags through to Seattle. He would retrieve them there, take a military shuttle to McChord AFB, and catch one of the military charters leaving for Da Nang AB in Vietnam.

Upon his arrival in Da Nang, Yates presented a copy of his leave orders and caught a Marine chopper to Cua Viet Combat Base. It was almost like being home again.

PART 5

Upon his arrival at 1st AMTRAC Battalion headquarters, Yates signed in and met with Maj. Stefansson, the Bravo Company commander. The major welcomed him back and briefed him regarding ongoing operations and the continuing effort to keep the Cửa Việt

River open and navigable. Bravo Company had been divided into three units with 1st and 2nd Platoons moved to the company outpost at Oceanview; Third Platoon manning Base Area C-4 to the west of Cửa Việt; and Bravo Company 4th Platoon remaining on reserve at Camp Kistler.

During the remainder of August and September, Sgt. Yates continued to serve as the Bravo Company communications chief. In September, he was awarded the Vietnamese Cross of Gallantry with Bronze Star. The medal was awarded by the Vietnamese government to military personnel who had accomplished deeds of valor or displayed heroic conduct while fighting the enemy Well into his third tour in Vietnam, Yates served wherever he was needed, and in his free time, he continued to work with the young corporals in the battalion, preparing them for their roles as Marine sergeants. Yates's performance evaluations were exemplary in every area, and when the time came for him to be considered for promotion to technical sergeant, his company commander, Maj. Stefansson made an unusual proposal. He presented the paperwork to Lt. Col. Meyers that would bestow a battlefield commission on the sergeant. If approved, effective October 15, 1968, Sgt. Butch Yates would become 2nd Lt. John Charles Yates.

Col. Meyers was well aware of Sgt. Yates and had been impressed with him since the day he had pinned the Bronze Star on his chest in the Camp Kistler infirmary six months earlier. The colonel signed the paperwork and returned it to Stephansson. The Bravo Company commander would deliver the news when Sgt. Yates returned to camp.

Yates, along with his buddy, Gunnery Sgt. Mark Avery, was away from Camp Kistler with Bravo Company 3rd Platoon. Avery was the B/3 platoon sergeant. He had arrived at First AMTRAC in mid-April and was a former drill instructor from Camp LeJeune. Avery was a born-teacher and loved instructing the younger Marines. He had pitched in to help Yates with his nightly patrols. Gunny Avery had kept Yates's "sergeant school" going while Butch was home on leave, and the two Marine sergeants had become close friends.

Bravo/3 was operating in support of two platoons from Alpha Company near Giêm Hà Trung, three miles south of Oceanview. The AMTRACs, which were transporting Marine infantry, had not seen much action and were headed down toward Cửa Việt when they ran into trouble.

Two of the Alpha Company LVTs (Alpha-11 and Alpha-04) detonated antitank mines almost simultaneously, and one of the AMTRACs caught fire. The crewmen were struggling to get out of the vehicles as the column of tractors ground to a halt. Yates, the Bravo comm chief, was in the Bravo command AMTRAC with Mark Avery, serving as radio liaison between the three platoon sergeants. Yates and Avery jumped out of their tractor and ran to the vehicle that was ablaze in an effort to rescue anyone who might still be on board. As the two men climbed on top of the vehicle, the fuel cells exploded violently in a huge ball of flame. Gunny Avery was blown into the air and off the vehicle, landing dazed some twenty feet away. Butch Yates, who had reached the crew chief's hatch and was attempting to enter it, was blown inside the vehicle. Three crewmen on the ground near the AMTRAC were seriously injured in the blast.

Navy corpsmen and other AMTRAC crewmen came on the run, but there was nothing they could do for Yates. The heat from the flames was so intense; no one could get near the destroyed vehicle for long. The corpsmen managed to drag the wounded crew members to a safe distance so they could tend to their wounds until a medevac chopper arrived on the scene. Avery, although in shock and suffering from minor burns, was not seriously injured.

When the platoons arrived back at Camp Kistler, word spread like wildfire. No one could believe Sgt. Yates was dead. He had been such a prominent and popular figure among the men for so long. It was difficult to believe in a place with so much death and destruction all around, the death of one man could have such an impact. The mourning was real and deep and palpable. The young Marines knew they had lost their leader, and they were hurting.

ırly on Monday morning, Lou Yates was sitting at the dining ble looking at the sports page, finishing his second cup of coffee, and preparing to leave for work. Mariana was in the kitchen filling the sink with hot soapy water when the doorbell rang.

Lou said, "Who could that be at this hour?" and went to the door. His heart sank when he saw two Marine sergeants in their dress blue uniforms. Lou invited the NCOs in, and Mariana came into the room drying her hands on her apron. The sergeants then proceeded to inform Lou and Mariana of the death of 2nd Lt. John Yates. For a fleeting moment, there was a glimmer of hope. They must have the wrong house. They are informing the wrong family.

"You must be mistaken," Lou said. "Our son is not an officer. He is a staff sergeant."

The senior NCO double-checked the folder of papers he had with him, and assured them he was "so sorry," but he had been directed to inform "Louis and Mariana Yates of Fergus Falls, Minnesota, that your son, 2nd Lt. John Charles Yates was killed in action on October 17, 1968, in Quang Tri Province, South Vietnam. There is no mistake."

Mariana fainted. Lou managed to catch her before she crumpled to the floor and one of the sergeants helped him carry her to a nearby couch. Lou called Joe in Benson, called his boss, their pastor, Rev. Van Dyken, and the grandparents in Illinois and Florida. In between calls, he tried to comfort Mariana, who was inconsolable, and deal with his own shock and grief. The Marine NCOs remained at the house as long as they could be of service to the family.

Joe arrived home as soon as he could get there safely and took charge of his mother. Mariana seemed comforted by Joe's presence as he wrapped his arms around her and pulled her in close to his chest. Joe still had not processed his own feelings regarding the loss of his brother and best friend. Butch and Joey, Joey and Butch—the two had been so dissimilar physically, but so close in every other aspect of their beings. For Joe, it was like losing half of himself—he had not had time to consider how he was going to deal with it. That would come later.

Friends arrived with food and condolences, and the house was soon in a hushed turmoil. Rev. Van Dyken, their pastor, and ladies from the church came in, took charge of the food, and brought some semblance of order to the overwhelming grief that had impacted the family. Neighbors made arrangements to pick up the grandparents who would be arriving at the airport in Fargo that evening.

The body of 2nd Lt. Butch Yates arrived home in a sealed casket on November 6. His funeral was held at 11:00 a.m. on Friday, November 8, at Federated Church in Fergus Falls. The service was standing room only with a large crowd standing outside. It had snowed the night before, and the temperature was twenty degrees with a stiff wind blowing out of the northwest. A squad of Marines from the reserve unit in Fargo served as pallbearers and bestowed full military honors on one of their own. Military rites at the cemetery in Laporte were brief, solemn, and bitterly cold. With the sharp crack of the M16s and the crystal clear notes of "Taps" echoing across the frozen landscape, there were few dry eyes among those sturdy souls who braved the frigid wind.

For the first time, Mayor Wenino of Fergus Falls requested all flags flown at half-staff in honor of Lt. Yates. After the funeral, family and friends returned to the church fellowship hall for hot chocolate, coffee, and a hot meal provided by the ladies of the church. The family requested in place of flowers, checks be sent to the John Charles Yates Scholarship Fund at Fergus Falls Junior College. Butch had been among its first students when the college opened.

In December, Lou, Mariana, and Joe Yates were invited to the Marine Recruiting Center in Fargo, North Dakota, where they were presented with Lt. Yates's Navy Cross. His other decorations included the Silver Star Medal, the Bronze Star Medal, the Purple Heart w/ Gold Star, the Vietnamese Cross of Gallantry with Bronze Star, the Vietnam Military Merit Medal, the Vietnamese Gallantry Cross with Palm, and numerous other awards. Lt. John Charles "Butch" Yates was twenty-six years old.

Dark clouds are smoldering into red
While down the craters morning burns.
The dying soldier shifts his head
To watch the glory that returns;
He lifts his fingers toward the skies
Where holy brightness breaks in flame;
Radiance reflected in his eyes,
And on his lips a whispered name.

"How to Die"
Siegfried Sassoon

EPILOGUE

ADDENDUM FOR TWO WARRIORS

Gunnery Sgt. John Mark Avery

On October 25, 1968, eight days after the death of his friend, Butch Yates, Gunnery Sgt. Mark Avery was aboard the command vehicle in a column of Bravo Company AMTRACs. Bravo was transporting a Marine infantry unit when it was attacked by a large NVA force. Exposing himself to the intense barrage of gunfire, Avery manned a machine gun and commenced firing on the enemy gun emplacements. Ignoring enemy rounds impacting near him, he maneuvered his vehicle to the flank of the NVA position and continued to deliver a heavy volume of fire which forced the NVA troops to retreat. Later that day, his tractor detonated an antitank mine and burst into flames, seriously wounding Sgt. Avery. Disregarding his injuries, he directed his men to establish a defensive perimeter and provide security for the remaining vehicles. He then supervised them in assisting a Marine that was trapped inside the burning tractor. Avery continued his determined efforts until he was medically evacuated. Mark Avery died from his wounds at the US Navy Hospital in Yokohama, Japan, on October 30, 1968.

His awards included a Silver Star Medal, Bronze Star Medal with "V" device, Purple Heart w/Gold Star, and numerous other awards. Gunnery Sgt. Mark Avery was thirty-one years old.

Capt. Leo Jamieson, USMC

Capt. Leo Jamieson, who was Butch Yates's commanding officer when he was awarded his Silver Star, referred to Yates as "the biggest Marine I ever knew," although Butch was five foot seven. "Yates saved my life on a few occasions," Jamieson said. "Several months after I left my command and rotated to Camp LeJeune, North Carolina, a casualty report came across my desk with Yates's name on it. I was stunned. What a terrible loss—to the Corps—to the world. He was such a special young man. I stopped what I was doing and wrote a long letter to his parents. I wanted to tell them exactly who their son was. I had the opportunity to meet them a few years later, and they had the letter framed, along with a photograph of Butch. Semper Fi, my friend. Semper Fi!"

Alpha Company radio ops prepare to go on patrol—September 1967

Ken Kindrick, who was a radio op in the 1st AMTRAC Battalion said, "I was among those privileged to have known Yatesy. He was an inspiration to those who served as radio operators in Alpha Company. The citations for his Silver Star and Navy Cross are awe-inspiring, but they do not do justice to the true measure of this man—this Marine."

CHAPTER 13

DELBERT RAY PETERSON

Renaissance Man

Del Peterson

It was cool and blustery in northwestern Iowa on May 11, 1939. That was the day Delbert Ray Peterson was born. His parents Bernice and Raymond "Pete" Peterson were both from Manson, Iowa. They had graduated from Manson High School in 1937 and married in 1938. Pete was employed at B&B Super Service in Manson, which had a population of some 1,400 people.

Three of Del's six siblings, Jolene, Denzil (Denny), and Robert (Bob), were born during the next four years, and then Pete was drafted into the Army. The year was 1944. He served honorably in the European Theater of Operations and was awarded a Purple Heart for being wounded in action. When he returned to Manson in 1945, he purchased his own service station and named it Pete's Mobil Service.

That is where Delbert grew up. He started kindergarten in 1944 and was so excited to be going to school. On the first day, when the kids went out for recess, Delbert thought the day was over, and he walked home. He was disappointed the day had gone by so quickly but discovered his error the following day when the teacher inquired as to why had had disappeared the day before. Delbert loved school. He memorized and gave the Gettysburg Address at the Memorial Day program one year and did such a good job, he was asked to do it for several years, sometimes dressed as Abraham Lincoln.

Three additional siblings came along from 1945 to 1948, Charles (Chuck), Judy, and Joel, and Del helped his mother care for the younger ones.

Delbert said, "We live in a big old farmhouse, and all seven of us kids sleep upstairs in three bedrooms: Judy and Jolene sleep in one, Denny and Bob sleep in another one, and I sleep in the largest room with Chuck and Joel. I spend most of my time trying to keep the peace, which is not easy. I also get up early to work at Dad's gas station on weekends and during the summer."

"Chuck, Denny, and Bob are always fighting," Del continued. "They fight all the time—I mean knock-down-drag-out, take-no-prisoners, kill-or-be-killed, all-ashore-that's-going-ashore, with fists and legs flailing and fists flying. The punches may not do that much damage, but they just put their heads down and swing away."

The Petersons would fight among themselves, but woe to any outsider who dared to pick on anyone in the family. There would be hell to pay. The older brothers always came to the rescue of the younger brothers and sisters no matter what. If a neighbor kid took a bike or called them names or threw a punch, he (or she) faced retribution and/or retaliation from all six siblings.

Delbert Peterson and his family—early 50s

Peterson graduated from eighth grade in May 1953 and enjoyed the blessings of growing up in a small Midwestern town. He pumped gas and fixed tires at his dad's gas station to earn spending money and was involved in everything from glee club, band, debate, and drama to basketball and football. He lettered in both sports all four years of high school and was captain of the football team. At six feet four, 225 pounds, his teammates called him "Bull."

Betty Jansson, one of Del's schoolmates, said, "The girls all had a crush on Delbert Peterson. He was so cool! He was tall and handsome and always had a smile. He was so good-natured and kind. His singing voice surprised me—he sang beautifully in the school programs."

Every student was involved in almost every activity because if they were not, the activity did not happen, but Del Peterson was a step ahead of his peers. As a junior, the American Legion sent him to Hawkeye Boys State where he was elected a state senator. He was class president two years, and his senior year, he was student council vice president and on the yearbook staff. He worked hard, and when he graduated in 1957, he was valedictorian of his class, a sort of rural Renaissance man.

Delbert entered Iowa State College in the fall of 1957 and left for school in Ames. The younger members of the Peterson family were devastated. Del had always been their mediator and their protector. He was their hero, and his departure left a large hole in the family hierarchy. The big old house suddenly became very quiet without his presence.

At Iowa State, Peterson continued to excel. His major was mechanical engineering, and in addition to his difficult studies, he sang with the college chorus and men's glee club, was a member of the Lutheran Student Association, and appeared in two college musicals. He also worked in the dorm cafeteria and taught ballroom dancing. During summers, he drove trucks, worked construction, and was an engineering aid for the US Forest Service in Washington State. During one summer, Del worked as a publication technician at Caterpillar Corp. in Peoria, Illinois. He also worked there during a semester he took off to earn additional money. He earned 80 percent of the money required to pay for his tuition while maintaining dean's list grades. This was a special young man with a bright future.

The summer before Del graduated he took Air Force ROTC training at Fairchild AFB near Spokane, Washington, and in October 1961, he was initiated into the O'Neil Squadron of Iowa State's Arnold Air Society. On July 12, 1962, Delbert graduated from ISU with a degree in Mechanical Engineering and was commissioned a second lieutenant in the US Air Force Reserve.

Peterson's formidable drive and dedication now switched from studies at Iowa State to the US Air Force. He loved flying. He went on active duty in January 1963, training at Vance AFB in Oklahoma before going on to McGuire AFB in New Jersey until August 1965.

One of Del's dreams since high school had been to own a sports car, so shortly after going on active duty, he purchased a new ivy-gold Ford Mustang. He had an active social life and was popular with the ladies, but he also understood he could not make any long-term commitments. US Marine ground forces had landed in Vietnam in

March 1965 and Del knew the air war was going to be heating up soon. In some capacity—in some form—Vietnam was in his future.

Del Peterson with his Mustang

In August 1965 Delbert was assigned to the First Air Commando Wing at Forbes AFB in Kansas for special training on the AC-47, a DC-3 airliner that was converted for military use. In November, Del was assigned to the 4th Air Commando Squadron, 14th Air Commando Wing. The Four/Fourteenth was the first operational AC-47 unit and was deployed to Tan Son Nhut Air Base near Saigon, South Vietnam, on November 14, 1965. The unit used the callsign "Spooky." Lt. Peterson was going to be the co-pilot on an AC-47 gunship.

Arriving at Tan Son Nhut in October, Peterson was excited about the role he and his crewmates were going to play in the struggle against the communists. They had a few weeks to get settled and prepare for the arrival of the Four/Fourteenth and their aircraft in mid-November.

"We've been training for months," Peterson said. "The troops on the ground have no idea what we are bringing to the fight, but we are going to make a big difference in this war."

AC-47D "Spooky"

The Douglas AC-47 or AC-47D, nicknamed "Spooky," was the first in a series of fixed wing gunships developed by the Air Force to provide more firepower when ground forces called for close air support. The plane had a row of 7.62mm General Electric miniguns (M134) mounted along the left (pilot's) side of its fuselage and could fire a barrage of extremely precise gunfire through two rear window openings and the side cargo door. The miniguns were activated by a control on the pilot's yoke whereby he could control the guns either individually or together. There were "gunners" among the crewmen, but their job was to assist with gun failures and similar issues. Each of the three miniguns could selectively fire either fifty or one hundred rounds per second. Cruising at 120 knots air speed at an altitude of three thousand feet, the gunship could put a bullet or red tracer (every fifth round) into every square yard of a football field-sized target in less than ten seconds. As long as its forty-five flare and twenty-four-thousand-round load of ammunition held out, it could do this intermittently while circling over the target for hours.

For night missions, the aircraft carried approximately forty-eight MK-24 flares. Each flare lasted up to three minutes (Mod-three version) and produced a light of two million candlepower. The delivery system was extremely simple: the loadmaster armed and dropped the flare out of the cargo door when the pilot signaled by flashing a cargo compartment light. The flares illuminated the combat area and exposed Việt Cộng and NVA forces as they prepared to attack in the darkness, usually sending them scurrying for cover like rats.

Ground troops welcomed the sight of Spooky because of its ability to put a heavy dose of defensive fire into a well-defined predetermined area. The AC-47 was a savior to American and Allied troops at besieged outposts up and down the length of South Vietnam, and during the ensuing years there would be countless reports from both civilians and military personnel of Spookys coming to their rescue and saving their lives.

When the first AC-47 gunships arrived at Tan Son Nhut, their guns had been removed in order to lighten the aircraft for the flight across the Pacific. The guns did not arrive until late December. In the meantime the planes were put to work on courier and cargo flights. The 4th Air Commando Squadron (ACS) lost their first aircraft, an AC-47D, on a courier flight between Tan Son Nhut and Phan Rang on December 17, 1965. The plane was struck by ground fire and crashed into a mountain sixteen miles south-southeast of Phan Rang. The wreckage was located on December 23, and the bodies of the nine men on board (four Fourth ACS flight crew members and five passengers) were recovered.

As the number of aircraft and flight crews increased, the fourth ACS deployed planes to Nha Trang, Đà Nẵng, Pleiku, Biên Hòa, and Bình Thủy. During January and February, the flight crews saw action nearly every night. Seventh Air Force Order No. 411-65 gave the Fourth ACS the mission to "respond with flares and firepower in support of hamlets under night attack, supplement strike aircraft in the defense of friendly forces, and provide long endurance escort for convoys." The Fourth ACS performed all of those tasks and more with exceptional style and remarkable success. When the Spookys first arrived in Vietnam, the VC viewed the lumbering planes as mythological beasts that appeared in the dark of night and spewed out a dragon's fiery breath filled with thousands of deadly bullets. They would say, "Đừng chọc giận con thú, và có thể nó sẽ không trở lại!" (Do not anger the beast, and maybe it will not return!)

"We rarely have a night off," Peterson said, I'm flying with Capt. Bill Collins. Bill is from Quincy, Illinois, so it's like old home week around here. We've been flying raids out of Da Nang AB almost every night. We drop flares to light up the area—then blast the targets with our miniguns. The Cong return fire and sometimes hit our plane, but we've been lucky, so far."

Del wrote home often. He knew his parents worried about him, so he did not write much about his combat missions. Bernice and Pete obviously knew he was not in Vietnam for a vacation. He had mentioned going out on night missions and trying to sleep during the day.

"Delbert could never sleep in the daytime," Bernice said, "He wouldn't even take afternoon naps when he was a baby. The doc said Delbert 'doesn't know he's supposed to sleep during the day. He's afraid he might miss something.' Jolene came along a year later and Delbert was a real pain in the butt when I was trying to take care of her. He was so curious about everything and was on the go from early in the morning until late at night. He never stopped to take a breath. He didn't even want to stop long enough to eat, or to let anyone else eat. Makes me tired to remember those days, but he was a happy baby. Delbert was a character."

PART 2

The A Sầu (A Shau) Valley was a narrow twenty-five-mile-long valley in Thừa Thiên Province. Located in I Corps, it was the second-most northerly province in South Vietnam, close to the DMZ. The A Shau Special Forces Camp was located in the A Sầu Valley, thirty miles southwest of Huế and a mile east of the Laotian border. The valley was strategically important for the North Vietnamese as a major infiltration route because it served as a bridge from the Ho Chi Minh Trail in Laos into the populated coastal areas of South Vietnam, which included the cities of Huế and Đà Nẵng. The Special Forces camp had been established in 1963 to help interdict the flow of troops and materiel from North Vietnam. Defending the camp were ten Green Berets from the Fifth Special Forces and two hundred CIDG troops. They were supported by Air Commando units equipped with vintage A-1 Skyraiders and AC-47 Spooky gunships.

Two ARVN camps at A Lưới and Ta Bat in the A Sầu valley had been abandoned on December 8, 1965. The Special Forces camp was routinely harassed by small Việt Cộng bands. Throughout February and March 1966, platoon-sized units of twenty to twenty-five troops from the camp were sent out to conduct reconnaissance patrols in the surrounding area. On March 5, two VC defectors turned up at the camp. Under interrogation, they indicated that four battalions of the NVA 325th Division were being deployed into the valley, and there was a plan to attack the camp. Based on that information, night patrols were dispatched to confirm the enemy positions. No sightings were made; however, Air Commandos conducting reconnaissance flights observed large build-ups of enemy troops along with anti-aircraft emplacements. As a result, airstrikes were ordered against the enemy positions.

The detachment had requested assistance from the Fifth Special Forces Group Mike Force in Nha Trang. On March 8, the camp was placed on general alert and the camp's defenders took up their defensive positions. The camps total strength, including reinforcements, was 220 CIDG troops, 141 Mike Force soldiers, nine Interpreters, forty-one civilians, six ARVN Special Forces soldiers, and seventeen Green Berets. They faced some two thousand NVA troops. The enemy assault was launched during the night but was beaten back with heavy losses. Because of poor weather conditions that hindered US tactical air and resupply efforts, the North Vietnamese commanders decided to continue despite their casualties. The second attack began during the early morning hours of March 9 with a mortar bombardment that damaged communications and reduced many defensive positions to rubble. The entire area was shrouded in dense fog.

At 11:20 a.m., Capt. Collins and his crew, just in from a night mission, were rousted from their beds and dispatched to support the garrison at the besieged camp. Del Peterson was the copilot, navigator was Capt. Jerry Meek, and flight engineer was S. Sgt. John Brown. Gunners were S. Sgt. James Turner and S. Sgt. Robert Foster.

Weather conditions were far from ideal when Collins and his "Spooky 70" crew reached the camp in their AC-47D aircraft. There was a four-hundred-foot ceiling and a steady barrage of enemy mortar and artillery fire that had torn up the landing strip and pinned down the defenders. The camp was in danger of being overrun. Air support and air evacuation were needed desperately. Two unsuccessful attempts were made to get under the clouds. Finally, flying at treetop height, Collins flew into the valley located the outpost and made a firing pass at the attacking forces. The aircraft took hits as it flew much lower than its usual altitude of three thousand feet.

"We could hear the .50 Cal rounds hitting the undercarriage of the aircraft," Peterson said. "We knew we were really vulnerable, but we had to try and help the guys on the ground. They were in big trouble and were depending on us to help them out."

The second pass was through a gauntlet of gunfire. Enemy gunners were waiting for them, and as they approached the camp, the sky exploded. The aircraft's right engine was torn from its mounts by savage .50 cal anti-aircraft fire. Seconds later the left engine was lost.

"God help us," Bill Collins yelled. "We are goin' down."

With superb airmanship, Collins crash-landed the bullet-riddled aircraft on a rugged mountain slope about five miles north of the Special Forces camp. All of the crewmembers survived with minor injuries except Sgt. Foster whose legs were broken by the impact. Peterson began first aid trying to make Foster comfortable, and Collins worked the survival radio. Collins and Peterson knew an enemy attack was inevitable and likely to happen soon. Since Foster could not be moved, they would set up a defensive perimeter at the site. They would not leave the injured gunner. Jerry Meek set up the defenses outside the aircraft and made sure all the M16s were loaded. About ten minutes later, they began to receive incoming fire and Meek was wounded by a VC sniper who was closing in on the downed aircraft. The crew, confident a rescue helicopter would answer their call, repulsed the first attack. Minutes later, a second attack began. It was also turned back, but as machine gun fire raked the side of the crippled aircraft, Collins was mortally wounded, and Foster was killed. With only four men left to defend the perimeter, the chances of holding out against another concerted attack and remaining alive until a rescue chopper arrived seemed remote.

Capt. Willard "Bill" Collins

As the third attack began, the distinctive sound of an Air Force HH-43 rescue helicopter was heard. Capt. Meek was now in command of the crew and ordered Peterson to guard the rear of the aircraft. He needed to ensure enemy troops were not approaching from that direction, unseen. Peterson donned his survival vest and crawled past the tail into the undergrowth with his M16.

Suddenly a hush fell over the area. After the gunfire and chaos, it was as if the world had stopped to take a breath. Lying in the thick jungle growth, Peterson felt the sweat coursing down the side of his face and soaking into the blue scarf he wore at the neck of his flight suit. He had operated on pure adrenalin since the crash-landing—now for a brief second his mind wandered back to his family in Iowa and his mother. He longed to see her face one more time.

"It's about three o'clock in the morning at home," Del said to himself. "Dad will be getting up in a couple hours to go to work at the garage." His eyes began to fill with tears, and he shook his head. "You can't do this, Peterson!" he said, swiping his face with the sleeve of his flight suit.

Then, out of the corner of his eye, Peterson saw muzzle flashes from an enemy machine gun that had been moved within a few yards of their destroyed gunship, and he knew what he had to do. If the enemy gun was not silenced, the chopper would be shot down before it could land and rescue the flight crew. It was up to him. Switching the selector on his M16 to full auto, Peterson crawled closer—then he rose up out of the brush and charged the machine gun, spraying fire from his rifle. The hostile fire diminished as two rescue choppers arrived over the crash scene. One descended to a ground hover—the other remained on guard overhead. Meek called to Brown and Peterson. Brown responded and came on the run. There was no response from Peterson. Meek continued to yell Peterson's name as he, Brown, and Turner ran for the chopper and piled aboard. As the chopper rose into the air, those on board scanned the area around the AC-47 for Peterson, but they saw no sign of him.

Lt. *Del Peterson*

Thirty minutes later, a Special Forces ground team arrived at the crash site. They found the bodies of Collins and Foster near their aircraft. The Green Berets fanned out and quickly made a thorough search of the area surrounding the plane and the scene of the fight that had ensued, but they found no sign they were certain was related to Peterson. They found drops of blood or blood trails leading away from the crash site, but the blood could have come from wounded or dead VC. The Americans had no way of ascertaining where the blood had come from.

Because of heavy enemy presence, the Special Forces team was unable to bring the bodies of Collins and Foster out with them. The two airmen were immediately listed as KIA/BNR. Because there was a strong probability Delbert Peterson was captured alive, he was listed as MIA. The location of the loss placed the gunship six miles north of the A Sầu Valley and two miles south of the Special Forces camp.

Both Peterson and Collins were awarded the Air Force Cross posthumously. This is one of the rare times during the Vietnam War when both pilots of an aircraft were awarded the nation's second-highest decoration for valor, and it is the only time in which the awards were made for extraordinary heroism in both air and ground combat.

Chuck Peterson was attending Fort Dodge Junior College in Fort Dodge, Iowa. He was working in a local grocery store when he received a call from an Air Force chaplain who was at his parent's home in Manson. The chaplain informed him his brother was missing-in-action. His mother wanted him to contact a sister who was also in Fort Dodge and come home to Manson.

"I'll never forget the look on my mother's face," Chuck said. "Dad handled things a little better. He'd seen war and was himself missing-in-action for a short period during WWII, so he knew things could change for the better." The family was still hopeful they would find Del alive.

From 1969 to 1972, Chuck and other members of the Peterson family met several times with a group called Iowans Care, an organization working to maintain awareness of the need for a full accounting of those MIA in Vietnam. The family members were asked to view pictures obtained from propaganda films or smuggled out of North Vietnam, but Del Peterson was not identified in any of them. In the mid-1990s, villagers near the crash site found Delbert's ID tag, a chain and key, and later excavations found a military ID and a religious medal, but no remains.

Peterson remained listed as MIA until February 1978, when his status was changed to KIA/BNR. During that period, he was promoted to major.

Chuck said, "While in Washington, DC, a few years ago, I placed my hand on Delbert's name on the Vietnam War Memorial. Although the Wall seems cold since it is black granite, it is nevertheless very impressive. I had the feeling that I think only a family member can feel. I wondered about Delbert's last moments and what he really felt because he knew he was in a war and was in a bad place with unfriendly people trying to do him harm. But I knew my brother, and I am confident, that when Capt. Collins died, Del's training took over. He focused on the survival of his crew, and he gave the ultimate sacrifice in doing so. There are others alive because he is not. 'Greater love has no man than this that he lay down his life for his friends.' I am proud of my brother. He was a gentle, caring and patient man, and a loving son and brother."

Del's brother Bob said, "If God asked me the formula for making a big brother. I would simply reply, Delbert!"

Maj. Peterson's other awards included the Air Medal with "V" for Valor and three Oak Leaf Clusters, and the Purple Heart. At the time of his disappearance, he was twenty-six years old.

When I come home from dark to light,
And tread the roadways long and white,
And tramp the lanes I tramped of yore,
And see the village greens once more,
The tranquil farms, the meadows free,
The friendly trees that nod to me,
And hear the lark beneath the sun,
'Twill be good pay for what I've done,
When I come home!

"When I Come Home"
Sgt. Leslie Coulson

Maj. *Delbert Peterson*

CHAPTER 14

LAWRENCE
DAVID PETERS

Sarjah Pete

Larry Peters

The Scout leader asked the assembled congregation to stand, ordered the color guard to present the colors, and then everyone joined in the Pledge of Allegiance. The Pledge was followed by the recitation of the Scout Oath: "On my honor I will do my best to do my duty to God and my country and to obey the Scout Law; to help other people at all times; to keep myself physically strong, mentally awake, and morally straight."

Standing at attention on the dais, immaculately dressed in his Scout uniform, was fifteen-year-old Lawrence David Peters, and this ceremony in August 1961 was his Eagle Court of Honor. Larry Peters never forgot his Scout training, and he never forgot the oath he took to do his duty to God and his country.

"I loved Scouting," Larry Peters said. "I made so many great friends and I learned a lot about leadership during my journey to Eagle Scout. There is a famous quote that says, 'In the end, it doesn't matter how many breaths you take, but how many moments take your breath away,' and I had a lot of moments that took my breath away during my years in the BSA."

Larry attended Benjamin Franklin Elementary and Junior High School in Binghamton, New York. He graduated from Binghamton North High School in 1964. Playing lead trumpet in the band, a regular starter on their football team, and strikingly handsome, Peters was a popular figure on campus, especially with the ladies, but Gail Mason was his steady girlfriend. He enlisted in the Marine Corps Reserve in September 1963 (while still in high school for pay purposes) and was assigned to the Forty-Eighth Rifle Company in Binghamton.

He completed his recruit training with the 1st Recruit Training Battalion at Parris Island, South Carolina, in September 1964, and in October, completed individual combat training with the 1st Infantry Training Battalion at Camp Lejeune, North Carolina. That was followed by AIT in December with the 2nd Infantry Training Battalion, at the same installation.

"The good news was it was a heck of a lot cooler at LeJeune in October and December than it was at Paradise Island in September," Peters said. "It was so damned hot, and we ran everywhere. It didn't even cool down at night, and the sand fleas were the pits."

After completing his training, Pvt. Peters returned to Binghamton, where he remained with the Forty-Eighth Rifle Company until enlisting in the Regular Marine Corps on January 30, 1966. He was promoted to private first class on December 16, 1964, to lance corporal on July 1, 1965, and to corporal on January 1, 1966.

Cpl. Peters requested assignment to Fleet Marine Forces, Pacific, and in March 1966, joined Staging Battalion, Marine Corps Base Camp Pendleton, California, for transfer overseas.

In May 1966, he joined Delta Company, 1st Battalion, 3rd Marines, in the Republic of Vietnam, and served consecutively as fire team leader, squad leader, and NCOIC of a Combined Action Company (CAC).

The Combined Action Program had originated with the Marines in 1965 and grew as the top Marine command saw the need for a "winning hearts and minds" pacification program, as opposed to the "kill everything that moves" concept favored by MACV commander, Gen. Westmoreland. While accepting the possibilities of such a program, Westmoreland argued they "didn't have the time" for such a program, while the Marine commander, Lt. Gen. Krulak argued, "We don't have time to do it any other way."

Unfortunately, Secretary of Defense McNamara while thinking the program might be a good one, supported Westmoreland's concepts and notion that pacification would be "too slow."

Westmoreland's staff informed the Marines that if they wanted to do such a program, they would not be supported, and it would have to "come out of their own hide." Nevertheless, the Marine idea went forward, though it was often underfunded and lacked equipment.

In an attempt to secure the heavily populated area around the Hue-Phu Bai airfield, the Marines discovered a ready-made ally in the surrounding villages—the part-time soldiers of the Popular Forces (Ruff-Puffs), the lowest echelon of the South Vietnamese Armed Forces. Minimally trained, armed, and paid, the Ruff-Puffs had proven to be ineffective toward the basic mission of providing hamlet and village security against the Việt Cộng. From the beginning, however; Marines on patrol had taken members of the RF-PFs along as guides and interpreters. It was thought with proper support and training, they could relieve regular Marines from the local defensive mission and assist in weeding out the enemy from the surrounding villages. From this ad hoc effort in 1965, the Combined Action Program was born.

Each unit consisted (ideally) of a fifteen-man Marine rifle squad composed of a squad leader, M79 grenadier, Navy corpsman, and three fire teams of four men each. Together with a Popular Force platoon of approximately thirty-five men, the combined unit was assigned to defend one village or a group of small hamlets.

For the nineteen-year-old corporal, working with the CAC in Hòa Thành, a Vietnamese hamlet fifteen miles northwest of Đà Nẵng, was the most rewarding thing he had ever done.

"I love my job," Peters said. "I like what I'm doing. I like the Vietnamese people. They are hardworking and very proud. I show respect for them, and I want them to respect me. I'm trying to learn some of the language," Peters continued. "I've gotten to the point where I can converse a little and I've learned a couple of Vietnamese songs."

PART 2

During late June and early July 1966, Marine reconnaissance units operating south of the DMZ observed and engaged increasing numbers of uniformed regular NVA troops. Gen. Westmoreland approved a Marine effort to run the NVA intruders back across the DMZ. Immediately Task Force DELTA was set up and on the morning of July 15, the battle began with aerial bombardment of LZs Crow and Dove. Operation HASTINGS had begun.

Cpl. Peters's unit, along with most other 1/3 Marine units were mobilized as part of the operation. The largest and most violent operation of the war to that point, Operation HASTINGS involved eight thousand Marines and three thousand ARVN troops, the 3rd Marine Division and the ARVN 1st Infantry Division against the ten thousand seasoned troops of the NVA 324-B Division

From July 15 to August 3, I Corps saw some of the most horrendous fighting of the war. During those nineteen days, 126 Marines died, and hundreds were wounded. NVA losses were estimated to be eight hundred dead, with thousands of additional casualties. When it was over, remnants of the enemy units melted into the jungle to the west or limped back across the DMZ. Marine general Lew Walt said,

"The NVA were well-equipped, well-trained, and aggressive to the point of fanaticism. They attacked in massed formations and died by the hundreds."

"Hastings was absolute hell," Peters said, "but it was something that had to be done. Hearing about Marines getting overrun by the NVA scares the hell out of you, but you go. You know you are going to see a lot action when you go out on a big operation."

Larry Peters received two Purple Hearts for Operation HASTINGS: one for a gunshot wound to his left hand, and the other for grenade fragments in his back.

With his customary humility, Peters said the wounds "didn't amount to much. I've hurt myself worse shaving," the young Marine said, and he laughed.

After HASTINGS, Cpl. Peters and his platoon returned to Hòa Thành and were warmly welcomed by the people there. Peters was promoted to sergeant on September 1, 1966. In November 1966, he served on temporary additional duty as company gunnery sergeant with Headquarters Company, 7th Engineer Battalion (CAC). That December, he was transferred to CAC, Sub Unit #1, Service Company, Headquarters Battalion, where he served as NCOIC, until April 1967.

Peters had made the decision to extend his tour. "There's still so much to be done here," he said. "As long as I can make a difference in the lives of these people, this is where I need to be."

In Sub Unit #1, Peters's duties, as well as his unit was expanded. "I now have 248 Vietnamese and forty-two Marines working for me," he said. "We go from village to village setting up headquarters and teaching the villagers how to protect themselves from the VC."

In return for his friendliness, the villagers had begun to refer to Peters as "Sarjah Pete," and he was frequently invited into their homes. The village of Hòa Thành even surprised him with a dinner in his honor hosted by the village elders.

Sea Tiger, the newspaper of the Third Amphibious Force in Vietnam, had published an article about "Sarjah Pete" after his platoon captured fifteen VC and killed five more in one of the villages. Datelined "DA NANG," the article described how the twenty-man

VC unit, including an undercover agent, a political action team, and an assassination team, never got to carry out its assignment after "Sarjah Pete" was tipped off by a friendly villager. The article then went on to discuss how life for the "controlled action Marine" is different from that of a rifleman. The CAC Marines "become de facto members of the hamlet in which they live," the article continued. "Sgt. Larry Peters is a working executive officer of CAC. The villagers call him 'Sarjah Pete,' and in six months of operation, the company has achieved good will by the construction of a refugee camp, a market place and pigpens. It also plans additional classrooms for the refugee camp in conjunction with the US-Asian International Development Program."

Larry Peters went home on leave in April 1967. Binghamton had never looked more beautiful with beds of spring flowers and cherry trees in bloom, but after steamy Vietnam, it was frigid. Arriving at Broome County Airport, some ten miles north of Binghamton on the afternoon of April 10, the temperature was fifty degrees, and there was a northwesterly breeze gusting to thirty-five mph. His mother, Mildred and younger brother, Ralph, were there to meet his flight and rushed to greet him.

"My God it's cold," Larry exclaimed to his mother as they strolled into the terminal building. He was wearing his Class A uniform but had not anticipated the cold wind. Ralph, who was fifteen, was excited to have his brother home and could not wait for his buddies to meet his brother "the Marine," whom he talked about constantly. Larry could not believe how much Ralph had grown during the year he had been gone. Larry's "little" brother was now taller than him and would soon outweigh him too.

Larry was one of six children in his family, and almost all had some connection to the military, aside from Ralph, who was a junior at North High School. Larry's oldest sister, Shirley, was a lieutenant in the US Navy Nurse Corps. She was based in Bremerton, Washington, but expected to deploy to Vietnam aboard the hospital ship USS *Repose* within a few months. Another sister, Lynda, was a lance corporal in the Women's Marine Corps, and was stationed in San Diego, California. After graduating from high school, Lynda had attended

Kings College in Briarcliff, New York. While on semester break her senior year, she had driven Larry to the Marine recruiting office, and to their mother's dismay, the recruiter had talked Lynda into signing up, too. Larry's brother, Jack, was a civilian employee with the US Army Education Center in Germany. His oldest brother, Don, was an Air Force veteran and lived in Gainesville, Florida.

"We are hoping for a family reunion sometime next year," Mildred Peters said. "It's been far too long. The children have not all been home at the same time since their father died in 1963."

Larry Peters shows photos from Vietnam to his
"little" brother, Ralph (left), and mother, Mildred

Larry was interviewed by the local newspaper during his time at home and talked about his work with the Vietnamese people. He also discussed the other Marines in his CAC unit.

"The guys I work with don't mind being there," he said. "They see the value in what we are doing. Of course, knowing they only have to be there thirteen months helps," he added, laughing. "Morale is good. Everyone marks days off the calendar until they can go home. Seeing so much death and destruction during our operations makes you realize what's going on in the world. It's quite an experience and it definitely made me grow up a lot. The men in Vietnam think the peace demonstrators and draft card burners in the US are fools, and they don't let it bother them."

Most of Larry's friends from high school were away in college, including his girlfriend, Gail. John and Nicky, two buddies he had known from the 48th Rifle Company in Binghamton, were also home on leave, so he spent time with them. They went out for beers at Van's Tavern, their old hangout on Court Street. None of the three was twenty-one, but Frank "Van" Van Valen didn't ask for ID. He knew they were Marines and home on leave. Nicky was also heading back to Vietnam in a month, so Van was not about to give his boys a ration of shit and tell them he could not serve them beer.

Van had been with Col. Bob Taplett's 3/5th Marines at Chosin Reservoir in Korea in December 1950. With temperatures plummeting to thirty below zero and howling Siberian winds buffeting their positions, the Marines spent four days and nights fighting wave after wave of screaming Chinese troops. Fighting, marching, and fighting some more, eighteen hundred Marines had left Yudam-ni. When the last of the units arrived in Hagaru-ri four days later, only 320 were left. The rest were dead, wounded, or missing. It had been sixteen years, but Van still had nightmares about the horrors of Chosin. He would wake up, bathed in sweat, shivering and hearing those god-damned Chicom tin trumpets screaming like banshees in the cold darkness. It was usually about 3:00 a.m., but there was no going back to sleep. He would get up, put on a pot of coffee, and get in the shower while it brewed. Because of all he had endured and continued to endure, he would take care of these Marines, his boys, and when they were ready to go home, there would be no charge. The beers and anything else they ordered would be on the house.

Larry spent the quiet days with his mother, talking and doing whatever she wanted to do. They visited his dad's grave at Chenango Valley Cemetery on one of the warmer afternoons, and he accepted an invitation from Ralph's social studies teacher at North High School to talk to his class about the work the CAC units were doing with the Vietnamese people. Sgt. Peters arrived at the school in his dress blue uniform and Ralph was thrilled. He was so proud of his brother.

The days flew by, and soon it was time to leave. Upon his arrival back at Da Nang Marine Base, Peters was reassigned to the Military Police Company attached to the 1st Marine Division.

PART 3

Peters's months in Vietnam seemed to be irrevocably linked with the village of Hòa Thành. On June 1, 1967, Delta Company, 3rd Military Police Battalion was assigned duty as the Armed Forces Police Company, Da Nang Marine Base, and on June 8, the battalion commenced civil affairs work in the village of Hòa Thành. During the next month, temporary field clinics were set up, and 360 local villagers were treated by American doctors and nurses through MEDCAP (Medical Civic Action Program). The village elders were delighted to see Sarjah Pete back in Hòa Thành and Peters felt at home. Within a month, Peters and his company started drilling a new well and began construction on the new refugee school he had planned before departing on leave in April.

In July, there was a shortage of experienced NCOs within the rifle companies. Peters was always the first to step forward wherever he was needed, so he volunteered to serve as a squad leader in Mike Company, 3/5th Marines. This was Larry's way of giving back. He had not forgotten the kindness of Frank Van Valen, and this was Van's old outfit, the regiment that had fought at the Pusan Perimeter in 1950—the first to land at Inchon, liberate Seoul, and survive the Battle of Chosin Reservoir. Fourteen Marines had received the Medal of Honor after Chosin Reservoir.

In early August, the 1st Marine Division turned its attention to the Quế Sơn Valley following several major operations around Đà Nẵng. In an attempt to draw the NVA into another destructive confrontation Operation COCHISE was launched on August 11; however, the NVA largely managed to avoid contact with the three Marine battalions tasked with the operation. COCHISE ended on August 28 with only modest results.

3/5 Marines—Operation COCHISE—August 19, 1967

Sweep operations were initiated to shield the local populace from intimidation during the upcoming South Vietnam elections. Operation SWIFT, which was intended to be the fourth and last of the 1967 operations in the Quế Sơn Valley, began unofficially on the morning of September 4.

Delta Company, 1/5th Marines was attacked at about 4:30 a.m. by a superior NVA force while in a night defensive perimeter near the village of Đông Sơn. Delta had been attacked by the NVA 2nd Division, and by 8:30 a.m., with twenty-nine Marines dead, the company was under threat of being overrun, so 1st Battalion sent Bravo Company to assist them. The US companies were each composed of about 180 Marines. The NVA had some three thousand troops in the area.

At 9:30 a.m., the 5th Marine Regiment ordered the 3/5th to aid Bravo and Delta. They had only Kilo Company and Mike Company available. The company commanders were told to prepare for a helicopter lift to the area of Đông Sơn.

September 4 was Labor Day in the States. People were looking forward to visiting the beaches and enjoying late summer barbecues, but a world away in Vietnam, the war raged on.

Cpl. Roy Hardin of 2nd Squad, 2nd Platoon, Mike Company, said, "Sgt. Pete came and woke us up before daylight on Monday morning. He told us we were heading out. Another Marine unit had run into trouble, and we were to get ready for the choppers. We got our shit together and headed out—then waited a long time. Hurry up and wait—some things never change. We finally boarded around noon. Sgt. Pete had a funny look on his face when he gave us the scoop. He looked more concerned than usual. I think his gut told him we might be in for a long, bad day."

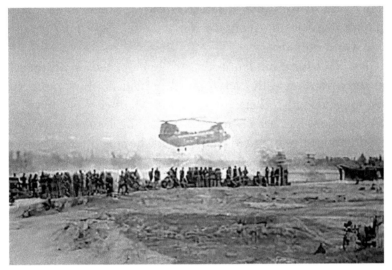

Mike Company at Hill 63—Operation SWIFT

With Mike Company on board, the choppers headed toward the battle, but the LZs nearest the fight were "too hot" for them to land. Enemy gunfire in the area was too heavy to risk attempting to deliver the loads of Marines. The choppers finally discharged the company in some dry rice paddies about 1.5 miles northeast of Bravo and Delta. Kilo Company landed a half-mile further west.

"The weather was hot and very humid," Peters said. "The breeze while we were flying in on the choppers was great, but as soon as we hit the ground, we could hardly breathe. It was miserable, and the flak vests we were wearing made it even worse. My platoon downloaded without incident. We quickly got organized and the company moved out in a wedge formation. We headed into a lightly wooded area, and it was surprisingly peaceful—almost too peaceful."

"It was midafternoon, and we heard scattered gunfire," Cpl. Hardin said. "We stopped close to a small hill. Sgt. Pete came running up and told us 1st Battalion had been hit hard and we were going to help them. We ran some and walked some. Man, it was so damned hot."

The Mike Company Marines arrived at another expanse of dry rice paddies and one of the 1st Platoon squad leaders told the commander he had seen one of the trees move. The commander told him if it moved again, "shoot the son of a bitch," so he did, and their whole world exploded.

An NVA force hidden in the tree line opened up on the Mike Company Marines with everything they had: machine guns, small arms, mortars and rockets, and a dozen Marines went down. Five NVA battalions had been lying in wait to ambush them. Each battalion held about five hundred troops. Had the squad leader not spotted the "moving tree" when he did, the NVA would have slaughtered all of the Americans as they moved across the rice paddies without cover and no place to run. "It would have been Custer at the Little Big Horn all over again," Peters said.

Just before the battle commenced, 2nd Platoon had passed some deep bomb craters on their way over the top of a small knoll. As the Marines came over the hill, they were attacked by another group of entrenched NVA soldiers who were hidden in a bamboo thicket. The enemy troops dropped one mortar on the Marines, causing them to pause, and as they began to advance again, more mortars landed on them, and then the heavily camouflaged enemy force opened up with a thunderous barrage of deadly fire. Peters ordered 2nd Squad into the craters.

"Our squad approached the top of the hill," Hardin said, "and the carnage started. I remember Sgt. Pete screaming 'Get that gun!' and I was hit in the left arm. The force of it spun me to the ground, and another shot shattered my rifle. I was screaming, along with other members of 2nd Squad. We were being shot at with every move we made. The machine gun was close, maybe twenty yards away, in a thicket part way down the slope of the knoll. I was fighting to stay conscious, but I remember seeing the NVA troops moving in and coming toward us. There were hundreds of them, and there were Marines lying on the ground all around me. Man, it was so f***in' bad. I was calling for help and my blood was spurting on the ground with every beat of my heart. I heard someone holler 'Corpsman!' I couldn't move. That gun had me and my squad pinned down tight. I knew I was gonna die. The NVA were comin' after me and I wasn't able to defend myself. We were ass-deep in NVA, and I had no weapon. I was scared shitless!"

"Take cover!" Peters yelled, and the Marines on the front line quickly began to pull back up the hill and jump into the comparative safety of the craters. The air was filled with bullets and the roar of the barrage was horrendous.

No one who has not experienced total ground warfare can possibly imagine what it is like. It encompasses every sense and heightens the senses to a point that they scream for release. The oppressive heat and the gut-wrenching fear that makes you shiver with cold sweat streaming down your face; your heart beating out of your chest; the stench of blood and gore, cordite, scorched earth and burning human flesh; the sound of bullets hitting all around you and tearing into the Marine next to you, and the sight of guys being blown apart; the ear-shattering din of mortars and RPGs and automatic weapons and grenades and choppers, combined with the screams of the sergeants—the screams of the dying. The sheer piss-your-pants terror of being eighteen years old and knowing you are going to die and still finding the will and the heart and the courage to do what you were trained to do. It is so damned insane.

Casualties quickly began to mount. Peters understood that if the Marines continued to sit there hunkered down, they would be wiped out. Crouching low, the sergeant began to rally his men, and organized 2nd Squad to knock out one of the machine gun nests that had 2nd Platoon pinned down. As he moved forward, he was hit in the leg and went down. The AK round that struck him was probably a ricochet as it did comparably little damage. He had felt the jolt and the searing heat to his right leg—the bullet had passed through the fleshy part of his calf, missing the tibia by an inch. A direct hit would probably have shattered the bone. Lying face down in the moist, red dirt, Peters closed his eyes. For a split second, he felt an overwhelming desire to sleep—he was exhausted. Maybe he'd wake up and all this would have been just a horrible nightmare. He ran his tongue over his cracked lips—his mouth was so dry. He remembered his mother saying she could "spit cotton," when her mouth was dry, and he smiled. Suddenly the adrenalin kicked in, and he jolted wide-awake. He wiped the muddy sweat from his face with his hand and reached down to check his leg, feeling only a dull ache and numbness. He rose slightly and looked back at his men. Only seconds had elapsed since he had gone down, but they were watching him intently. Refusing medical attention and ignoring his wound, Peters got to his feet, grabbed his M16, and in spite of the intensive enemy fire, continued to lead his men forward

Steve Leroy, a radio operator with 2nd Platoon, was trying to stay low out of the line of fire and lug his heavy equipment back up the knoll with him. Rounds were flying everywhere, and Leroy had been wounded in his right shoulder. Suddenly, Lt. Capodanno, a Catholic Navy chaplain, seemed to appear out of nowhere. Capodanno had jumped aboard one of the helicopters as it departed on the rescue mission to Đông Sơn. The priest grabbed Leroy from behind by the arm holes of his flak vest and dragged him and his radio to safety in a bomb crater.

"I didn't know what was happening," Leroy said. "Suddenly I was being pulled backward. I glanced over my shoulder and caught a glimpse of purple—then I saw a golden cross on it and realized I was being helped by a chaplain. What in hell is a chaplain doing here in the middle of this shit? He dragged me down into a crater, blessed me, called for a corpsman, and was gone. A corpsman showed up to patch up my shoulder, and I was left wondering if I'd dreamed it all."

"Father Capodanno seemed to be everywhere," Peters said. "He was rushing around exposing himself to relentless enemy fire, assisting the wounded, providing last rites for the fallen, and calming those still alive. He was incredible."

Cpl. Jon Danko, was kneeling and firing at NVA soldiers attempting to cross the rice paddy, when the enemy machine gunner opened up again. A bullet went through the leg of Armand Leon, one of the Navy corpsmen, and it cut his femoral artery. Danko attempted to drag Leon up the knoll and into a crater where he could be taken care of by another corpsman. Danko put one finger in Leon's wound to staunch the bleeding and tried to fire at the enemy with the other hand while "muscling" the corpsman up the slope. As Danko struggled with Leon, Lance Cpl. Steve Connelly came down the knoll and tried to help. Connelly was struck in the chest by a bullet and fell on top of Danko and Leon. Pfc. Jim Mackay rose up to help and was also killed. As the dead were pulled back over the crest of the knoll, Father Capodanno rushed to give each of them last rites.

Danko said, "There was a continuous barrage of small arms fire coming from the north tree line as I tried to drag Leon over the top of the knoll."

"Danko saw an NVA machine gunner rise up out of the grass, and he was only fifteen or twenty feet away," Peters said. "Danko momentarily left Leon, crawled a few feet, and aimed his rifle at the man, and *click!* His M16 jammed. The enemy gunner unloaded on Danko, so he jumped into a nearby crater. Leon bled to death as Danko fought to save him. To my left was a squad leader named John Alberti from Texas. His body was slumped over one of his dead Marines. He had jumped out of a crater to aid the man from his squad and was shot in the head. Both men died. It was an absolute bloodbath. We kept firing but were running low on ammo."

Suddenly, like an avenging angel, a Huey gunship appeared above the fracas. The pilot fired rockets into the tree line and door gunners blasted the enemy ground force with their M60 machine guns until their ammo ran out. For a few minutes, there was some respite from the NVA barrage as the enemy kept their heads down and focused their attention on the attacking chopper.

While the gunship was attacking the NVA positions, Peters rallied his men again, urging them forward. However, the machine gun soon resumed firing, and his platoon remained stalled by the unrelenting storm of fire. They had to knock out the gun emplace-

315

ment. As Peters advanced down the forward slope of the knoll, seeking whatever cover he could find, there was a massive explosion. The sergeant was hit in the face and neck by shrapnel from the mortar blast and was knocked to the ground. Lying stunned amid the detritus of the eroded slope, Peters tried to clear his head. He was bleeding from deep cuts on the left side of his face and from his left ear. For a moment, he could hear nothing but a dull roar somewhere in the distance. He had to focus on where he was and what had happened to him. He shook his head, trying to clear the haze from his brain and the fog from his eyes. Peters's vision began to clear, and he looked back toward the crest of the hill. The members of his squad, those still uninjured, were there focused on him and ready to follow him. What had seemed like a lengthy recovery period had actually only been a few minutes. "Now's the time to do what I have to do," Peters said to himself. "It's now or never. Otherwise, those bastards are going to keep us pinned down until they kill us all."

Wiping away the blood, sweat, and tears streaming from his left eye, Peters continued his assault down the slope and stood up fully exposed to enemy fire. He was forcing the camouflaged enemy troops to reveal their positions. As Peters urged his Marines to continue the fight and aimed at the exposed NVA positions, he was struck by machine gun fire in the abdomen and chest, which knocked him to the ground again. Dragging himself to the shattered stump of a tree, the sergeant propped himself up and continued to point with his M16 at where the machine gun nests were located on the adjacent ridge. He was still fully exposed to enemy fire, and as bullets struck all around him, no one dared go near him—except for one.

Ignoring the steady barrage of gunfire and shrapnel, Father Capodanno crawled to Peters. Shrapnel from a mortar round had ripped into the chaplain's right shoulder and hand, rendering the arm and hand useless, but he struggled on to reach the dying sergeant. Summoning every bit of strength he could muster, the priest pulled himself forward with his left arm and knees, pushing through the broken branches and plowed earth. When Capodanno reached Peters, he pulled himself in next to the young sergeant. "God is with you," he said. "He is with us all." A look of peace and a faint light seemed to glow across Peters's face, and he managed a weak smile. Still under fire, Capodanno uttered the Lord's Prayer with Peters and as the Marine breathed his last, Father Capodanno held him in his arms, and continued to pray. Greater love hath no man.

Administering last rites with his left hand, Capodanno eased Peters's body down behind the stump where it was protected and crawled on assisting where he was needed. Cpl. Danko saw him bent low and moving toward another fallen Marine. He called to the chaplain and told him to "watch out for the machine gun!"

Three Marines were attempting to take out the NVA gunner. Two of them were cut down immediately—the third Marine was shot through the thigh and could not move. Capodanno crawled forward to assist the man, but there was another burst of fire from the gun. Throwing himself between the Marine and the gunner, the chaplain cradled the wounded man to his chest and used his own body to try and shield him from the deadly fire. Capodanno was killed instantly, along with the gyrene he had sought to save.

A short time later, another Marine was able to crawl close enough to toss a grenade into the machine gun nest, taking out the gun crew, but the battle raged on for several more hours. Fighting desperately, and with repeated air support from F4 Phantoms, A4 Skyhawks, and Huey gunships, the Leathernecks held on until dark. In addition to Sgt. Peters, Lt. Capodanno, and the Navy corpsman, thirteen other Mike Company Marines died that day, and there were scores of wounded. Of the 165 Marines who went into battle on September 4, only sixty-three were physically unscathed as fighting ceased with the arrival of darkness. When scouts were deployed the following morning, they counted 137 NVA bodies surrounding the Mike Company position, and they were the ones the enemy had not retrieved during the night. Over the course of the next ten days, the fighting continued in an effort to secure the valley. Operation SWIFT concluded with a total of 127 Marines and Navy corpsmen dead and 362 wounded. Official accounts at the time listed over fourteen hundred enemy troops killed, but post-war records indicate the total number was several times that. US intelligence agencies later determined the NVA 2nd Division and the VC 1st Regiment, the units most involved, were subsequently unfit for combat due to their losses, were recalled back north across the DMZ, and were not available to participate in the Tet Offensive of 1968.

PART 4

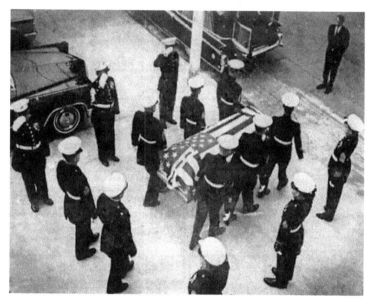

A Marine honor guard carries Peters's flag-draped coffin as it is moved to St. Andrews Catholic Church for funeral mass

The solemn high requiem funeral mass for Sgt. Lawrence Peters was offered on September 21, 1967. The service was followed by burial next to his father at Chenango Valley Cemetery. Mildred Peters had all of her children home. It was obviously not the kind of joyous reunion she and Larry had discussed and planned when he was home in May, but it was good to see everyone and she was so proud of Larry and all he had accomplished in his short twenty years.

While serving with the Fleet Marine Force in Hòa Thành, Peters had financially supported two Vietnamese orphans, a nine-year-old boy and an eleven-year-old girl. Peters's sister, Lt. Shirley Peters, said members of the Peters family would take responsibility for the youngsters since her brother's death. The family also requested "in lieu of flowers" please contribute to the Marine Corps Civic Action Fund for Vietnam, a fund administered by CARE and used by the 3rd Marine Amphibious Group to aid Vietnamese villages. Larry Peters's work with the people of Vietnam would live on after his death.

On April 20, 1970, Mildred Peters and her family met with VP Spiro Agnew in Washington, DC, and were presented with Larry's Medal of Honor for "his outstanding valor, indomitable fighting spirit and tenacious determination in the face of overwhelming odds."

In addition to the Medal of Honor, Peters's other awards included the Bronze Star Medal, the Purple Heart, National Defense Service Medal, Vietnam Service Medal with three bronze stars, Republic of Vietnam Campaign Medal, and the Vietnamese Cross of Gallantry with Palm. On Memorial Day 2017, fifty years after Peters's death, the Peters family donated his Medal of Honor, along with his other medals, scrapbooks and citations to the Broome County Historical Society in Binghamton, New York. The items are now on display at the Broome County Public Library. A spokesman said the display "will give people a chance to see an important life that was lost— someone who had a future ahead of them that was cut short by the Vietnam War."

AUTHOR'S NOTE:

Aside from Sgt. Peters and Father Capodanno, fictitious names were used for the Mike Company Marines and Navy corpsman in the story. Here are the actual names of those who died on the first day of Operation SWIFT, listed alphabetically, by rank and award received.

September 4, 1967, Navy Lt. (Father) Vincent Capodanno (MOH), Honolulu, Hawaii.

September 4, 1967, Sgt. Lawrence David Peters (MOH), Binghamton, New York.

September 4, 1967, Lance Cpl. Thomas W. Fisher (Navy Cross), Allentown, Pennsylvania.

September 4, 1967, Hospitalman Armando G. Leal (Navy Cross), San Antonio, Texas

September 4, 1967, Lance Cpl. Andrew Mix Giordano (Silver Star), Smithtown, New York.

September 4, 1967, Lance Cpl. Jack Albert Berry, Lubbock, Texas

September 4, 1967, Lance Cpl. Steven Thomas Cornell, New York, New York.

September 4, 1967, Lance Cpl. Richard Guerrero Jr., Corpus Christi, Texas

September 4, 1967, Lance Cpl. Albert Willard Santos, Fall River, Massachusetts.

September 4, 1967, Pfc. Dennis Franklin Fisher, Alta Loma, California.

September 4, 1967, Pfc. Tony Gabaldon, Reedley, California.

September 4, 1967, Pfc. Raymond George Hengels, Downers Grove, Illinois.

September 4, 1967, Pfc. Charles Frederick Martin, Littleton, Colorado.

September 4, 1967, Pfc. James Calvin McKenzie, Yorba Linda, California.

September 4, 1967, Pfc. Gene Al Mortensen, Salt Lake City, Utah,

September 4, 1967, Pfc. Steven James Wright, Norco, California.

We were too young
To possess such old souls.
Looked from eyes
That had seen more than one should.
Walked without the cane,
Yet carried the crutch.
Old Souls
In such young men.
Lay with skeletons,
Thought as one.
Thirteen months under the gun.
Wept blood
At the visions that come.
Watched the eclipse;
Saw the moon eat the sun
As old souls
Devoured the young.

"Old Souls"
Lief Ericson

CHAPTER 15

VINCENT ROBERT CAPODANNO

The Grunt Padre

Lt. Vincent Capodanno, USN

In New York City, Labor Day 1967 seemed to be just like many that had gone before—a national holiday with cold beer, grilled burgers and hotdogs in the backyard. Banks and stores were all closed. South Beach and Midland Beach on Staten Island were crowded with tourists and kids dreading the start of the new school year. But some 13,600 miles west of the Hudson River Valley, in the Quế Sơn Valley of South Vietnam, there was little to celebrate.

In the midst of the horrific maelstrom that is total war, the kind of muddy, bloody, meat-grinder war only Marines, Army infantry, and some special operations units have experienced—amid the deafening din of machine guns, grenades and mortars, the nonstop bursts of M16s and AK47s, and the thump-thump of medevac choppers, a Navy chaplain from Staten Island was somehow able to hear the cries of his wounded and dying Marines and bring them comfort.

During Operation SWIFT in Quảng Nam Province, South Vietnam, September 4, 1967, Father Vincent Capodanno's unit, Mike Company of the legendary 3rd Battalion, 5th Marines, was pinned down in an NVA ambush. The Marines were outnumbered five to one, and after hours of intense battle, Capodanno was severely wounded. A bullet had badly mangled his right hand and shrapnel from an exploding mortar had inflicted serious wounds to his right shoulder. The priest had refused medevac and would accept only minimal care so medical supplies could go to his injured Marines. "Others need it worse," Capodanno told the corpsman trying to assist him.

Marine Uh-34 medevac helicopter

PART 2

Vincent Robert Capodanno Jr. was born February 13, 1929, on Staten Island. He was the youngest of ten children born to Vincent Robert Capodanno Sr., an Italian immigrant from Gaeta, Italy, and Rachel (Basile) Capodanno, who was born in Brooklyn of Italian ancestry. Growing up as the "bambino" in a large Italian-American household, life was good and generally happy for "Junior." Like his mother, he was known to have a wonderful sense of humor, and when he laughed, his entire body shook. He attended grammar school and Curtis High School, graduating in 1947. He also attended one year of evening school at Fordham University. During the day, he worked for a New York insurance firm in order to pay his tuition. He entered the Maryknoll religious order in Ossining, New York, in 1949 and was ordained a Catholic priest by New York's Francis Cardinal Spellman on June 14, 1958.

Father Capodanno's first assignment was as a missionary in Miaoli, Taiwan—about one hundred miles off the coast of Communist China. He studied the Chinese language while doing parish work, taught native catechists, distributed food and medicine to the Taiwanese aboriginal people, and directed a youth hostel. Capodanno spent several years in Taiwan and then was reassigned to teach at a Maryknoll school in Hong Kong. He served in the mission field from 1958 to 1965.

On March 8, 1965, Lyndon Johnson deployed thirty-five hundred Marines to South Vietnam in response to the Gulf of Tonkin Incident of August 1964. The Johnson administration blamed North Vietnam for confrontations with US Navy forces off the coast of Vietnam. That was followed by a nationally televised speech on July 28, 1965, in which Johnson announced his decision to send an additional fifty thousand U.S troops to South Vietnam. That would increase the number of personnel there by two-thirds and bring the US commitment there to one hundred twenty-five thousand men.

Observing the escalating war, Capodanno felt drawn to serve his county as his three older brothers had done during WWII. Responding to the need for Catholic chaplains, Father Capodanno requested and eventually received permission from Maryknoll to enlist in the Navy Chaplain Corps. Upon finishing Officer Candidate School, which was tough both mentally and physically for the 36-year-old priest, Capodanno was commissioned a Navy lieutenant and assigned to serve as chaplain of a US Marine battalion. He arrived in Vietnam during Holy Week, April 1966.

Because of Lt. Capodanno's personality and charisma, the younger enlisted Marines gravitated to him as a person, and they quickly figured out how much he cared for them, both individually and as a group. He was fifteen to eighteen years older than most of them, so he became a father figure for many, as well as their counselor, their friend, their confidant, and their priest. One moment he would be quietly praying by himself, and minutes later, he would be surrounded by young Marines joining him in prayer. He seemed to have an innate ability to know when one of his men needed to talk, and he would sit and wait until the Marine was ready. Then, the conversation might go on for hours. It never concluded until Capodanno was sure he had provided comfort or consolation for the man who needed him. "He understood things about us we didn't even understand about ourselves," one eighteen-year-old Marine said.

Capodanno spent hours each day counseling, reassuring the disillusioned, consoling the grieving who had lost friends, instructing converts, hearing confessions, saying mass and serving communion. At heart, the Maryknoll priest would always be a missionary. He established a reading library for his men and contacted friends and organizations in the States to send books, candy, cigarettes, and St. Christopher medals for his Marines. At Christmas time, he made sure no Marine was without a gift. He shared his rations and salary with anyone who needed it and wrote countless letters of support and condolence to the families of wounded and dead Marines. He also attracted and served Protestants, many of whom attended his masses. His services were well attended, and he had no problem drawing crowds on short notice. His sermons were concise but always on target and comforting to Marines of any faith or no faith at all. And before heading out on a combat operation, he would always tell his Marines, "Try not to lose your humanity."

Ministering to Catholic and non-Catholic alike

Lt. Capodanno also counseled and mentored some of the younger officers. He would take meals in the mess tent with other lieutenants and listen to their problems. "He was unlike any other chaplain I had ever met during my years in the Corps," one senior officer said. He was very personal, very approachable—he was never shocked by whatever subject the young officers discussed. One day while having our noon meal, one of the Marine lieutenants rushed into the tent, and upon reaching our table said, 'What kind of f***in' soup have we got today?' He had not seen the chaplain, who was sitting at our table. All of us, without saying a word, sat up, and looked straight at Father Capodanno. You could have heard a pin drop. Father, without missing a beat, finished his bite, then looked at the rest of us and said, 'If that's the kind of soup he wants, let him have it,' and everyone broke out laughing. He was just a great guy to be around. He would put himself where he knew others would be. He'd relax with other officers smoking his Camel cigarettes and sipping a couple cans of Shlitz beer. He'd walk around the area where the enlisted men were billeted. He'd stuff his pockets full of chewing gum and candy bars for the men. Everyone loved to see the Padre coming their way."

Capodanno often participated in combat operations, although he was discouraged from doing so by his superiors. His chaplain duties did not require him to serve on the front lines, but he was determined to be wherever his Marines were deployed. He lived the life of a Marine "grunt"—he worked, ate, and slept under the same conditions as the Marines in his charge. Wherever the men went, he went. He would sneak on board one of the departing helicopters and arrive in full battle gear (without a weapon) in the midst of whatever operation his company was embarking on. The commanders would assign someone to watch him and keep him on base, but he seemed to always find a way to get past the watchers. He gained a reputation for putting the well-being of his Marines above his own safety, moving among those wounded and dying on the battlefield. The Marines referred to him as "the Grunt Padre," and they loved him. "Wherever the Marines were, Father Capodanno was there," one Marine observed. "Whether it was knee-deep in swamp water or in mud up to his ass, the Padre was always there with us Marines." For eight months, Capodanno went on combat missions. In November he received a Bronze Star with "V" device for valor after rescuing wounded men under fire near Chu Lai. In December, Capodanno was transferred to the 1st Medical Battalion at Da Nang but still caught rides on supply helicopters to be with the Marines in the field. He requested a six-month extension of his tour and, after a thirty-day leave in June 1967, he was moved to the 5th Marine Regiment.

Father Capodanno offering communion to his Marines

Capodanno had been with Mike Company 3/5th Marines for three weeks when he was ordered to go help set up a battalion aid station for the wounded and dying during Operation SWIFT. The Padre hopped aboard a helicopter with a team of Mike Company Marines, but they did not make it to their destination. The chopper was shot down in the middle of a rice paddy near where the battle was taking place. Capodanno and his crew evacuated the wrecked chopper and set up a command post on a small hill. They could hear gunfire and explosions and knew they were near to the action. Then Capodanno heard a Mike Company radio operator calling back to the command post: "We've been overrun," the RTO yelled. "We can't hold out much longer."

Father Capodanno had been in Vietnam long enough to know where his men needed him most, and it was not on the safe side of that hill. Grabbing his helmet, the priest slung a bag holding his sacraments over his shoulder, tucked his purple silken priest's stole in around his neck, and took off running up over the crest of the hill and into the violent madhouse on the other side. Spotting the wounded radio op who was struggling with his heavy equipment, Capodanno grabbed him by his flak vest and dragged him up and into the relative safety of a bomb crater. The average lifespan of a radio operator during a battle in Vietnam was five seconds, but the chaplain bought him a little more time. Summoning a corpsman for the radioman, the priest moved on to help wherever he was needed. And help was needed everywhere.

Again and again, during the next several hours, amid the stifling heat and the vicious storm of bullets and shrapnel, Capodanno performed the same service with the wounded and dying. The noise was horrendous with the roar of the weapons punctuated by the yells of Marine sergeants and the screams of the wounded. He soothed, calmed, and encouraged all he could reach. He administered last rites for the dead, directed Navy corpsmen to assist those still alive, and helped move them to safer locations. "The Padre seemed to have an aura around him," one of the Marines said. "We just knew that during the tough times, God was with him."

The chaplain's first wound was a bullet through his right hand which disabled his fingers. He was bandaged by a corpsman but refused to leave the battlefield. "I need to be where my Marines need me most," he insisted. "My boys need me here." Tugging a towel from around his neck, the priest wrapped it around his mangled hand and cinched it tight to help staunch the flow of blood. Then, crouching low, he hurried on across the smoky, gouged hillside, aiding the injured to the best of his ability, blessing and anointing the dying and the dead with his left hand. The scene was a bloodbath, and there were bodies everywhere he looked.

On several occasions, the Marines were ordered to withdraw in order to avoid being overrun. This left the dead and wounded outside the perimeter and whatever little protection that offered, but the chaplain continued to minister to his boys. Capodanno was choking in the midst of a cloud of CS tear gas which had been deployed by the Americans to make the NVA force disperse when he was wounded the second time. The wind direction had changed, blowing the choking irritant back over the Marine position, and the chaplain had given his gas mask to a young Marine who did not have one.

"We were getting gassed and taking fire," the eighteen-year-old Marine said. "I hadn't brought my gas mask because I had never needed one before. I was coughing and gagging, and then I felt a tap on my shoulder. I turned my head, and a guy is handing me a mask. I looked back and the first thing I thought was 'Man, this guy's old!' Then I saw the cross—a chaplain—what the hell is a chaplain doing out here? I took the mask, got it on, took a few breaths to get my lungs cleared, and then handed it back to him. I never saw him again."

In the ensuing chaos, a mortar shell exploded near Capodanno, and he was hit by a hail of shrapnel which disabled his right arm and shoulder. He was bandaged up and once again refused to leave the battle. "Stay calm," he told the struggling corpsman. "Someone will come to help." Placing his left hand on the young sailor's shoulder, he said, "God is with all of us this day."

"The chaplain squeezed my shoulder," the corpsman said, "and for a brief moment, I felt a sense of peace wash over me in the middle of all the carnage. I have no words to explain it."

As the battle continued, Capodanno caught sight of a Marine who was wounded and pinned down by an NVA machine gunner. The man had been attempting to reach other wounded Marines when he was hit in the thigh. His femur was shattered, and he could not move. He was in intense pain and crying for help. Rushing to his side, the chaplain called for a corpsman and began to assess the young man's wounds just as the gunner resumed firing. Without hesitation, he threw himself on top of the man, trying to shield him from the machine gun with his own body. Father Capodanno died performing his final act of love, the victim of twenty-seven bullet wounds to his back, neck, and head.

Operation SWIFT, 3/5 Marines

Operation SWIFT continued on Tuesday. A fresh Marine company arrived at dawn and launched a counterattack that forced the NVA regiments to break contact. With all engaged companies now relieved, 1/5 and 3/5 Marines were ordered to pursue the withdrawing NVA. In the afternoon of September 6, two battalions of the VC 1st Regiment attacked Company B, lead company of the 1/5 Marines. Company B was isolated and nearly overrun but held when Marine artillery fired tear gas canisters around their position. The

3/5 Marines were also heavily engaged a few hours later. Early on the morning of September 12, two NVA companies attacked Company I, 3/5 Marines' night defensive position, but the attack was repulsed. Operation SWIFT concluded on September 15.

As word spread that Capodanno had been killed, young Marines wept openly, and a pall of deep sadness descended over the entire division. A memorial service and requiem mass for Chaplain Capodanno was held at 1st Marine Division headquarters, Da Nang, on September 13, 1967, and it was packed with officers and enlisted men—both Catholic and non-Catholic—and all Marines who could be spared were in attendance. The mass was celebrated by US Navy Capt. (Father) John Keeley, 1st Division Chaplain. The Presbyterian Regimental Chaplain, 5th Marines, Lt. Cmdr. Eli Takesian, delivered Father Capodanno's eulogy:

"Capodanno had deep, gentle, hurting eyes; compassionate eyes that ignited people; eyes that had seen an awful lot; eyes that would embrace you. He had the courage of a lion and the faith of a martyr. He lived the Christian life. He laid down his life for his people and changed a lot of lives. Father Capodanno emulated Christ as much or more than anyone I ever knew. We used to joke that troops shot in the back were often running away," Takesian continued, "but that certainly was not so with Chaplain Capodanno, a courageous man, whose sacrificial act truly emulated Jesus Christ."

Takesian said later, "I remember one young Marine who came to me immediately after hearing the news of Chaplain Capodanno's death. He was so choked up, and he asked how Chaplain Capodanno could allow his own life to be taken when he loved life so much. I told him it was precisely because he loved life—the lives of others— that he freely gave his own." Vincent Capodanno was thirty-eight years old.

PART 3

Back in the States, the requiem mass for Vincent Capodanno took place at Queen of Peace Church in North Arlington, New Jersey, on September 19, 1967. Interment followed with full military honors in the family plot at St. Peter's Cemetery, Staten Island, New York.

Funeral procession for Lt. *Capodanno*

On December 27, 1968, the Capodanno family was invited to Washington, DC, and on January 7, 1969, Mr. and Mrs. Vincent Capodanno Sr. were presented with their son's Medal of Honor by the Secretary of the US Navy Paul R. Ignatius.

In less than eighteen months, Lt. Capodanno, a "non-combatant," had been awarded the Bronze Star Medal with "V" device for valor; the Purple Heart Medal with two stars; the Combat Action Ribbon; the National Defense Service Medal; the Vietnam Service Medal with Fleet Marine Force Combat Operations Insignia and three bronze service stars; the Vietnamese Cross of Gallantry with silver star (November 1966, as a result of heroic service to both American and South Vietnamese troops); the Vietnamese Service Medal with bronze star, the Republic of Vietnam Campaign Medal with 1960 device, and the Medal of Honor. He was the first Navy chaplain to lose his life in Vietnam and the first chaplain to be awarded the Medal of Honor in Vietnam.

In January 1969, Maryknoll Missions received a letter from a Navy doctor who had served with Capodanno and the Marines. Here is a portion of the letter from the Maryknoll Archives:

We had a chaplain, a Maryknoll priest named Capodanno, who had been over here for sixteen months. Usual tour of duty in Vietnam is twelve months, but the good padre had it extended on condition that he would be allowed to continue with the "grunts" (Marine infantrymen). He appeared, in spite of his quiet unpretentious manner, to be a veritable thorn in the Division Chaplain's bald head. The DC wanted Fr. C. to live at Headquarters from where he could "spoke" out to all the battalions in the division—but Fr. C. would have none of that. His mission was to the grunts fighting in the front lines whom he felt really needed a chaplain. His audience was always a small group of 20-40 Marines gathered together on a hill or behind some rocks, hearing confessions, saying mass. It was almost as though he had decided to leave the "other 99" in a safe area and go after the one who had gotten in trouble. Over here there is a written policy that if you get three Purple Hearts you go home within forty-eight hours. On Labor Day our battalion ran into a world of trouble. When Fr. C. arrived on the scene it was 500 Marines against 2500 N. Vietnamese. We were constantly on the verge of being overrun, and the Marines on several occasions had to "advance in a retrograde movement." This left the dead and wounded outside the perimeter as they slowly withdrew. Early in the day he was shot in the right hand—one corpsman patched him up and tried to evacuate him to the rear, but Fr. C. declined, saying he had work to do. A few hours later a mortar shell landed near him and left his right arm hanging in shreds. Once again he was patched up and again he refused evacuation. There he was, moving slowly from wounded to dead to wounded, using his left arm to support his right as he gave absolution, when he suddenly spied a corpsman get knocked down by a burst from an automatic weapon. The man was shot in the leg and couldn't move. Fr. C. ran out to him and positioned himself between the injured boy and the weapon. The weapon opened up again and this time riddled Fr. C. completely, and—with his third Purple Heart of the day—Father went Home. And that…is my Christmas message to you—the one conveyed to me by Fr. Capodanno, the message of love.

And there was a seemingly endless stream of honors and memorials:

- Soon after his death, the first chapel bearing Father Capodanno's name was dedicated on Hill 51 in the Quế Sơn Valley, RVN.
- Within four months after his death in 1967, almost $4,000 (equivalent to about $34,000 in 2022) had been raised by organizations such as The American Legion, The VFW, the Knights of Columbus, and the Marine Corps League for the purpose of building the Saint Vincent Chapel, in Capodanno's Taiwanese mission territory. This was his family's first choice as a memorial to his life and his mission work. After various delays, the chapel was completed in 1995 in the small mountain town of Thiankou with the help of Father Daniel Dolan, another Maryknoller and Capodanno's former pastor in Taiwan.
- The San Francisco Bay Naval Shipyard (Hunters Point, 1941–1994) dedicated Capodanno Hall on November 3, 1969. The hall served as a Bachelor Officers' Quarters.

Philip Capodanno unveiled the dedication plaque that described his brother's heroism.

- In March 1971, the Knights of Columbus, Madonna Council in Staten Island began a campaign for a permanent memorial honoring Father Capodanno in his home borough.
- The USS *Capodanno* (FF-1093) was commissioned in honor of Lt. Capodanno on November 17, 1973, and became the first ship in the US fleet to receive a Papal Blessing when blessed by John Paul II on September 4, 1981, the fourteenth anniversary of the chaplain's death.
- On July 4, 1974, Seaside Boulevard on the East Shore was renamed for Father Capodanno.
- For the United States Bicentennial weekend, the city of New York declared July 3, 1976, "Father Capodanno Day," and a memorial mass was followed by a parade that included the US Marine Corps Color Guard, marching bands, and many other groups.
- Near the midpoint of Staten Island's Father Capodanno Boulevard, at the corner of Sand Lane, a granite monument with a plaque was erected in the chaplain's honor. Near the end of the boulevard, alongside Fort Wadsworth's Father Capodanno Memorial Chapel, stands a 1977 statue of the chaplain praying for a fallen corpsman during their final battle.
- In 2002, the former Chaplain of the Year Award was renamed the Father Vincent Capodanno Chaplain of the Year Award.
- The South Beach neighborhood on Staten Island is the location of Father Vincent Capodanno Catholic Academy, formed by the merger of two parish schools in 2020.
- Further memorials to Vincent Capodanno were noted in his published biography:
- Capodanno Memorial Chapel, Naval Station Newport, Rhode Island
- Capodanno Drive, Naval Station Newport, Rhode Island

- Capodanno Chapel, Naval Hospital, Oakland, California
- Lt. Capodanno Chapel, Camp Pendleton, California
- Vincent Robert Capodanno Naval Clinic, Gaeta, Italy
- Piazza Vincent Capodanno, Gaeta, Italy
- Capodanno Building, Navy Personnel Command, Millington, Tennessee
- Capodanno Chapel, Marine Corps Air Station, Iwakuni, Japan
- Catholic Chaplains Memorial, Arlington National Cemetery, Arlington, Virginia
- Capodanno Chapel, The Basic School, Marine Corps Base Quantico, Virginia
- Capodanno Memorial Chapel, Al-Taqaddum (TQ) Air Base, Iraq
- Vincent Capodanno Memorial, National Shrine-Our Lady of Good Help, Champion, Wisconsin
- Father Vincent Capodanno High School, Southern Pines, North Carolina
- Capodanno Chapel, USS *Mount Whitney* (LCC 20)
- Chaplain Vincent R. Capodanno Shelter for Homeless Veterans, in Boston, Massachusetts

PART 4

As a chaplain candidate in the US Navy in the 1980s, Daniel Mode was captivated by the story of Vincent Capodanno. Over the next few years, Mode researched Capodanno's life, used that material for his master's thesis at Mount Saint Mary's Seminary, and turned it into a book titled *The Grunt Padre*, which he published in 2000.

Working with a group called Catholics in the Military, Mode used his research to initiate a "cause for canonization" application to Rome for Capodanno. Rev. Timothy P. Broglio, JCD, Archbishop for the Military Services, USA, cleared the way for the cause to go forward, and Capodanno was declared a "Servant of God" by the Congregation for the Causes of Saints.

Mode followed in Capodanno's footsteps, serving as a Navy chaplain for thirty years. He deployed on active duty in several war zones, including the Persian Gulf for Operation IRAQI FREEDOM and Bagram, Afghanistan, for Operation ENDURING FREEDOM. [As a result,] "I identify with [Capodanno] more," Mode said. "It has brought a realism to my study of his life."

Archbishop Broglio formally opened the Cause on October 1, 2013, when he appointed a tribunal to conduct an inquiry into whether Father Capodanno lived a "life of heroic virtue." Over the next three and a half years, the tribunal gathered facts on Capodanno, interviewing those who knew him and other witnesses as well as collecting documents. The tribunal appointed a theological commission, composed of three theologians, who poured over his writings, and a historical commission, which pieced together the details of his biography and life history. On May 23, 2017, the archdiocesan tribunal wrapped up its nearly four-year inquiry, and Reverend Broglio declared the archdiocesan phase of the Cause closed. That decision cleared the way for the tribunal's findings to go to the Holy See's Congregation for the Causes of Saints for review and a possible decision on whether to advance the Cause to the next stage of consideration.

There was also an additional development on July 11, 2017. Prior to that date, there had been only three paths to sainthood: martyrdom, living the virtues of Christian life to a heroic degree, and "exceptional case," based on the confirmation of an ancient tradition of veneration of the saintliness of a person. Pope Francis now established a fourth path for sainthood for people who died prematurely by offering their lives "for the love of God and neighbor." The Pope began his announcement by quoting John 15:13, "No one has greater love than this, that someone would lay down his life for his friends." Francis went on to say, "Those Christians are worthy of special consideration and honor who, following in the footsteps and teaching of Jesus, have offered their life voluntarily and freely for others and have persevered in this to death." Father Capodanno is the first to be considered for this new path to sainthood.

In March 2020, the Vatican announced Capodanno's postulator (promoter, Reverend Daniel Mode) had finished writing the formal position for the Cause for Sainthood. The position was formally printed and submitted for distribution among the Congregation for the Causes of Saints, and should the good priest be deemed worthy to carry on with canonization by the Congregation for the Causes of Saints, he will next be beatified, and then declared a saint.

Father Vincent R. Capodanno

O Divine Master,
Grant that I may not so much
Seek to be consoled, as to console;
To be understood, as to understand;
To be loved, as to love;
For it is in giving that we receive,
It is in pardoning that we are pardoned,
And it is in dying that we are born to eternal life.

"A Prayer of St. Francis of Assisi"
Anonymous

EPILOGUE

FATHER VINCE

After Chaplain Capodanno's death, one of the senior Marine officers said, "When Father Vince died, one of my duties was to inventory all of his personal belongings and ship them back to his family. Having known him, I decided not to return two things he had left behind, because I knew that's what he would have wanted me to do, and I knew he would have approved of my decision. One was a footlocker full of candy bars and chewing gum. He always carried a pocketful of those treats and passed them on to the young Marines who had not enjoyed a sweet since their arrival in Vietnam. The other was a bag full of St. Christopher medals. During his visits to the Marine billets, he'd give them to the men to pray and carry for protection, and the guys treasured them because they recalled who had given the medals to them. I gave all those items to the new chaplain so hopefully he would be as well received and appreciated as Father Capodanno was. I will never forget Father Capodanno. I will always think of him and thank him for his service. Semper Fidelis Padre—to us Marines, you will always be a Saint."

ABBREVIATIONS

AIT: Advanced Individual Training
AO: Area of Operations
APC: Armored Personnel Carrier, M113
ARDF: Airborne Radio Direction Finding
ARVN: South Vietnamese Army
ASA: Army Security Agency
BNR: Body Not Recovered
CIDG: Civilian Irregular Defense Group
CP: Command Post
DEROS: Date Estimated Return from Overseas
DLIWC: Defense Language Institute—West Coast Branch
DMZ: Demilitarized Zone
FAC: Forward Air Controller
FNG: F*cking New Guy
H&S: Headquarters and Service
KIA: Killed in Action
LLBD: Lực Lượng Đặc Biệt (South Vietnamese Special Forces)
LVT: Amphibious Vehicle-Tracked
LZ: Landing Zone
M113: Armored Personnel Carrier, APC
MAG: Military Assistance Group
MACV: Military Assistance Command—Vietnam
MCAS: Marine Corps Air Station
MCB: Marine Combat Base
MCRD: Marine Corps Recruit Depot (boot camp)

MEDCAP: Medical Civic Action Program (US doctors treating local population)
NAS: Naval Air Station
NCOIC: Non-Commissioned Officer in Charge
NSA: National Security Agency
NSG: Naval Security Group
NVA: North Vietnamese Army
RFPF: South Vietnamese Regional Forces ("Ruff-Puffs")
RRD: Radio Research Detachment
RPG: Rocket Propelled Grenade
RRFS: Radio Research Field Station
RRU: Radio Research Unit
RVN: Republic of South Vietnam
SOG: Special Operations Group
USAFSS: US Air Force Security Service
VC: Viet Cong
WIA: Wounded in Action
XO: Executive Officer

REFERENCES

Foreword

The Banksy quote is thought to have originated with Irvin D. Yalom, an existential psychiatrist, author, and professor of psychiatry, and can be found in his book *Love's Executioner and Other Tales of Psychotherapy.*

Tribute to Two Gentle Heroes

Based on Chapter 30, *UNLIKELY WARRIORS: The Army Security Agency's Secret War in Vietnam 1961–1973,* by Lonnie M. Long and Gary B. Blackburn—iUniverse, Inc. 2013
"Kontum: The Battle to Save South Vietnam," by Thomas P. McKenna, 2011 https://uknowledge.uky.edu/upk_military_history
https://smallwarsjournal.com/jrnl/art/army-intel-navy-gunfire-and-marine-mission-execution-saved-many
https://magazine.washington.edu/feature/a-soldiers-promise-we-will-come-back-for-you/March 2014

Chapter 1
Benedict Maher Davan

SIXTEENTH CENSUS OF THE UNITED STATES: 1940, BUREAU OF THE CENSUS
https://www.ar15.com/forums/general/Vietnam-Experts

https://www.quora.com/How-were-American-soldiers-transported-to-Vietnam-i-e-which-route-did-they-take

https://cherrieswriter.com/2012/03/08/vietnam-freedom-bird-why-cant-i-remember-the-ride/

Maine Baseball Hall of Fame President's Award—1994

Maine sports hall of fame 1996—John "Paddy" Davan

Westbrook High School yearbook, 1964, Westbrook, Maine

https://en.wikisource.org/wiki/Writings_of_Henry_David_Thoreau_(1906)/Volume_7/Chapter_2

https://digitalcommons.lesley.edu/cgi/viewcontent.cgi?article=1008&context=newspaper_archiv2

https://www.bhg.com/gardening/trees-shrubs-vines/trees/japanese-maples/

Operational Reports—Lessons. Learned, Headquarters, Fifth Special Forces Group (Airborne) First Special Forces, Period Ending 30 April 1967

http://paulowniadevelopment.ro/en/paulownia-plantation/

http://www.specialforcesbooks.com/B55.htm

Po Dharma, Vietnamese-Cham activist leader of FULRO, Cham cultural historian

http://www.findagrave.com/cgi-bin/fg.cgi?page=gr&GRid=162829515

Citation for Posthumous Award of the Distinguished Service Cross

Coffeltdatabase.org

MilitaryHallofHonor.com

SERVICE OCCUPATIONAL CODE, 11F4C, Undefined Code

https://www.almanac.com/weather/history

Nha Trang Mike Force History

"NUI COTO and the MIKE FORCE ASSAULT on TUK CHUP"—March 1969, Copyright © 2014 Gary B. Blackburn

https://www.pressherald.com/2017/12/28/looking-back-352/

https://www.pressherald.com/2020/01/28/the-universal-notebook-living-among-the-dead/

Combat After Action Interview Report, Battle of Nui Coto, March and April 1969, Department of the Army, Twenty-First

Military Detachment, Fifth Special Forces Group (Airborne), First Special Forces, 1969

"F.J. Kelly, Green Beret Leader In Vietnam War, is Dead at 78," *New York Times*, New York, New York, Section 1, p.23 of the National edition, January 4, 1998

US Army Special Forces 1961–1971 by Col. Francis J. Kelly, Dept. of the US Army

http://www.westbrookhistoricalsociety.org/Cemeteries/St.Hyacinth Cem.pdf

http://www.thewall-usa.com/guest.asp?recid=12014

Letters from Maj. Hampton Dews III

Letters from Edward L. Woody

"Maine Pair Get DSC for GI Son," *Portsmouth Herald*, Portsmouth, New Hampshire., July 30, 1969

"The cry of the cicada," Matsuo Basho, 1690, translated by William George Aston, Public Domain

"A Terrible Conflict—The Cambodian-Vietnamese War," War History Online, November 4, 2016

Chapter 2
Emilio De La Garza Jr.

Letters, photographs and documents from Lee De La Garza

Ask Tom: What can you tell us about the 1948 New Year's Day https://www.chicagotribune.com/weather/ct-wea-1231-asktom-20161230-column.html

"Sliding into 1948: New Year's Day ice storm cripples Chicago," by Steve Kahn and Jennifer M. Kohnke/WGN-TV, Frank Wachowski, National Weather Service Archives

"Marines Rites Set," *The Times*, East Chicago, Ind., April 17, 1970

https://www.tapatalk.com/groups/brownwaternavyanddelta-armyvietnamveterans/r-r-t16416.html

US Marines In Vietnam Vietnamization and Redeployment 1970–1971 PCN 19000309600

"Medal of Honor, Lance Cpl. Emilio De La Garza Jr. (Medal of Honor citation)," *Marines Awarded the Medal of Honor*, History Division, USMC

1201021027, US Marine Corps History Division, Vietnam War Documents Collection, The Vietnam Center and Sam Johnson Vietnam Archive, Texas Tech University, Lubbock, Texas

Col. Bob Fawcett, USMC (Ret.), 2/1 Vietnam Era Reunion Speech, San Diego, California, November 11, 2012

"American Heroes: Grunts, Pilots & "Docs," Book I, Chapter 23, by Michael Dan Kellum, Navarro-Hill Pub. Group, January 1, 2011

"E.C. man gave his life to save platoon," by Lu Ann Franklin, *The Times*, East Chicago, Ind., May 30, 2016

"Man killed saving fellow Marines honored," by ABC11, WTVD-TV, Munster, Ind., 2020

https://www.tourofdutyinfo.com/notebook/essay4-r&r/

"R & R in Honolulu a Six-Day Moment of Peace for Soldiers and Their Wives" by Wallace Turner, *The New York Times*, New York, New York, April 13, 1970

"Emilio Albert De La Garza Jr., Lance Corporal USMC—All Gave Some, Some Gave All" by Duane Vachon, February 14, 2014

"Memorial for Lance Corporal Emilio De La Garza Jr., Second Battalion First Marines, Echo Company, 1970" by Corpsman Sam Lyles

Obituary of Fr. Peter Miller, SCJ, Milwaukee, Wis., October 3, 2000

Obituary of Carmen Castaneda De La Garza, *The Times*, East Chicago, Ind., April 13, 2004

Obituary of Emilio A. De La Garza Sr., Vancouver, Wash., February 9, 2016

"Vaya con Dios," Larry Russell/Inez James/Buddy Pepper, 1952, Ⓒ Creative Commons Deed

Chapter 3
Sharon Ann Lane

Notes from family, friends, and brother and sister Vietnam veterans

Lane, Sharon Ann—"Citation For Posthumous Award of the Bronze Star Medal with 'V' for Valor Device"—Army General Orders NUMBER 598

"The Women of the Army Nurse Corps During the Vietnam War" re: nurses uniforms www.vietnamwomensmemorial.org

Ohio Society of Military History, Massilon, Ohio

"How the Vietnam Generation was Robbed of its Heroes and its History" by B. G. Burkett and Glenna Whitley, published by Verity Press, Inc., Dallas, Texas, 1998, ISBN I, 56530, 284–2

"Cong Rocket Kills Beloved Canton Nurse," Jack Leggett, *Canton Repository*, Canton, Ohio, June 10, 1969

"Hostile Fire: The Life and Death of First Lieutenant Sharon Lane," by Phillip Bigler, Vandamere Press, 1996

"Sharon Lane Was The Only Woman Killed By Direct Fire In Vietnam," by Dan Doyle, *Canton Repository*.com

"Searching for answers to Sharon Lane's death in Vietnam," by Lou Filardo, *Canton Repository*, 2016

"Nurse Sharon Lane Paid the Highest Price in Vietnam," By Robert F. Dorr, June 30, 2013, https://www.defensemedianetwork.com/stories/nurse-sharon-lane-paid-the-highest-price-in-vietnam/

The Vietnam Women's Memorial Photo by Rudi Williams, American Forces Press Service, Public Domain

https://armyhistory.org/first-lieutenant-sharon-ann-lane/

"Veterans Voice: A nurse in Vietnam, she's still paying the price," by Mary K. Talbot, *The Providence Journal*

"Blood smells the same, but for Vietnam nurses, the war never ends," by Dana DiFilippo, *The Vietnam War*, September 8, 2017

"The Best and Worst of Times: American Nurses in Vietnam," by Paula Bailey, MSE Henderson State University

"Does Anyone Care? About the Health of Women Who Served in Vietnam," Sharon Rice-Grant, Master's Thesis, California State University, Sacramento, California, 1986

"Women Vietnam Veterans" from "The Trauma of War: Stress and Recovery in Vietnam Veterans," by Janet Ott, edited by Stephen M. Sonnenberg, Arthur S. Blank and John A. Talbott, Washington, DC, American Psychiatric Press, 1985

"Friends recall only nurse killed by hostile fire in Vietnam," by Dake Kang, www.morningjournalnews.com, May 30, 2017

"In Country: US Nurses During the Vietnam War," by Aaron Severson and Lorilea Johnson, RN, MSN, FNP-BC, October 5, 2020

"Ohio Nurse 1st Slain Female 'GI,'" *Dayton Daily News*, Dayton, Ohio, June 10, 1969

"Enemy Rocket Kills 1st US Army Nurse," *Deseret News*, Salt Lake City, Utah, June 10, 1969

"Canton Nurse Killed in Viet," by Edwin Q. White, *Canton News Journal*, Canton, Ohio, June 10, 1969

"Rocket blast fatal to Army nurse in Saigon," *Redlands Daily Facts*, Redlands, California, June 10, 1969

"First US Army Nurse Killed in Vietnam War," *Reno Gazette Journal*, Reno, Nev., June 10, 1969

"Canton Nurse Dead in Chu Lai Shelling," *The Marion Star*, Marion, Ohio, June 10, 1969

"1st Nurse Killed," by Edwin Q. White, *Corpus Christi Caller Times*, Corpus Christi, Texas, June 10, 1969

"She Wanted to Stay in Vietnam," *Akron Beacon Journal*, Akron, Ohio, June 10, 1969

"Suite Memory of Sharon," *Akron Beacon Journal*, Akron, Ohio, November 4, 1969

Mary Kathleen "Kay" Lane Obituary, www.sandersfuneralhomes.com, August 15, 2015

"The Healers," Laurence Binyon, 1914, Public Domain

Chapter 4
Paul Wayne Anthony

Notes from family and friends

STANDARD CERTIFICATE OF DEATH: Joseph D. Anthony, February 25, 1956

NC Vietnam KIA/MIA's gravesites

http://www.homestead.com/6924SS/

www.virtualwall.org/da/AnthonyPW01a.htm and www.findagrave.com/memorial/17833624/paul-wayne-anthony

http://www.geocities.com/rjcooper_2005

6924th Scty Sqd, Http://www.homestead.com/6924SS/

FOREVER YOUNG, Number 10 of a Series, "In honor of Memorial Day and Paul Anthony's birthday—a tribute: Paul Wayne Anthony—Carolina Boy," Copyright © 2014 Gary B. Blackburn

"A/1C Paul W. Anthony Obituary," *The Charlotte News*, Charlotte, North Carolina, April 14, 1970

6924th Security Squadron Assoc., AFROTC Scholarship, University of North Carolina-Charlotte

"Sunburnt Boys," John Charles McNeill, *North Carolina Poems* by E. C. Brooks, Published by North Carolina Education, Raleigh, North Carolina, 1912, Public Domain

Chapter 5
Henry Nicholas Heide II

Letters and notes from David Hewitt

Letter and photographs from Col. Carlos Collat

Interview and notes from Richard Schlies

https://www.almanac.com/weather/history/FL#

Body of Secrets: Anatomy of the Ultra-Secret National Security Agency, by James Bamford, New York, New York, Random House, 2007

Cryptologic Almanac (PDF), National Security Agency, Archived from the original (PDF) on September 18, 2013

Guide to Cryptologic Acronyms & Abbreviations, 1940–1980, p.27, October 2002

"CRYPTOLOGIC HISTORY SERIES—TOP SECRET UMBRA—NOFORN," *National Security Agency: Focus on Cambodia, Parts 1 and 2*, Cryptologic History Series, Southeast Asia, January 1974 Previously Released 2004 by NSA in Freedom of Information Act Case #: 3058

UNLIKELY WARRIORS: The Army Security Agency's Secret War in Vietnam 1961–1973 Chapter 23, Pages 314–326, by Lonnie M. Long and Gary B. Blackburn, iUniverse, 2013

My Story of Vietnam, by Gene Hutchins, https://stories.ninepbs.org/viewstories/gene-hutchins-2/

Defense Intelligence Agency Helicopter Loss database: Helicopter UH-1H 68–15246

"2 S. Florida GIs killed in Viet," *The Miami News*, Miami, Florida, January 27, 1970

"Father Of Killed GI Is Bitter Over Nightmare Of Unknown," by Dave Harrison, *Fort Lauderdale News,* Fort Lauderdale, Florida, January 28, 1970

"GI Dies—Father Lives Nightmare," by Dave Harrison, *Fort Lauderdale News*, Fort Lauderdale, Florida, January 28; 1970

"Picture Reminder Of Snarl Arising In Death Of GI," by Dave Harrison, *Fort Lauderdale News*, Fort Lauderdale, Florida, February 4, 1970

"Purchasing Managers Hold Annual Election," *Fort Lauderdale News*, Fort Lauderdale, Florida, May 21, 1970

"Hollywood Hero," *Fort Lauderdale News*, Fort Lauderdale, Florida, September 3, 1970

"Evelyn M. Heide Obituary," *Tallahassee Democrat*, Tallahassee, Florida, February 16, 2012

"Two Pairs Are Wed," *The Daily Oklahoman*, Oklahoma City, Oklahoma, December 27, 1968

"Services of Spec. 4 James Ronald Smith," *The Daily Oklahoman*, Oklahoma City, Oklahoma, December 7, 1969

"City Officer War Victim," *The Daily Oklahoman*, Oklahoma City, Oklahoma, January 27, 1970

"A Nation Praises One of Its War Heroes," *The Daily Oklahoman*, Oklahoma City, Oklahoma, May 26, 1970

"'Copter Pilot's Parents Given Decoration," *The Daily Oklahoman*, Oklahoma City, Oklahoma, May 6, 1970

"The Fallen Subaltern," Lt. Herbert Dixon Asquith, 1916, Public Domain

The story of "Jaguar Yellow Bird" is based on Chapter 28, *UNLIKELY WARRIORS: The Army Security Agency's Secret War in Vietnam 1961–1973* by Lonnie M. Long and Gary B. Blackburn, iUniverse, Inc., 2013

Chapter 6
Hilliard Almond Wilbanks

www.fac-assoc.org

Medal of Honor Citation—Hilliard A. Wilbanks,

"Bird Dog's Last Battle," by John T. Correll, *Air Force Magazine*, March 1, 2007

Hilliard A Wilbanks Foundation, Inc.

https://sofrep.com/fightersweep/f-105-thud-mechanic-recalls-vietnam-days/

https://aircommando.org/wp-content/uploads/2019/03/Air%20Commando%20Journal%20Vol%202%20Issue%204.pdf

Air Force Heroes in Vietnam, Chapter II, "The Forward Air Controllers," Published under the auspices of the Airpower Research Institute, Air War College, Maxwell Air Force Base, Ala., Maj. Donald K. Schneider, 1979

https://www.warhistoryonline.com/instant-articles/vietnam-bird-dog-pilot-hilliard-wilbanks.html, Jeff Edwards, Guest Author, July 6, 2018

https://www.thisdayinaviation.com/tag/hilliard-a-wilbanks/

Museum of Aviation, Robins Air Force Base, Warner Robins, Georgia

"Capt. Hilliard Wilbanks," *Air Commando Journal*, Vol. 2, Issue 2, Fall Edition 2013

"Once you have tasted flight," John H. Secondari, 1965

Chapter 7
John Andrew Barnes, III

Notes from family and friends

"John Andrew Barnes III," by Molly Strakosch, Needham High School

"Barnes," *The Boston Globe*, p.36, Boston, Massachusetts, November 21, 1967

https://www.almanac.com/weather/history

"An Interview with Carson Barnes Fleming," *The Dedham Times*, p.6, Dedham, Massachusetts, November 10, 2017

"Dedham Soldier Receives Posthumous Medal of Honor," *The Dedham Times*, Dedham, Massachusetts, November 10, 2017

"Needham Man to Receive Medal of Honor for Son," *The Boston Globe*, p.3, Boston, Massachusetts, November 4, 1969

"Reflections," Dedham High School, p.29, 1964

"2 Dedham Heroes—John A. Barnes III & Henry Farnsworth," by James Parr, May 31, 2010

"Veteran's Monuments and Memorials in the Town of Dedham: Three Self-guided Walking Tours around Dedham," Troop 1, Dedham, Boy Scouts of America, Timothy Cunningham, 2014

"PFC John A. Barnes III," *Medal of Honor recipients*, 173rd Airborne Brigade, US Army

https://www.army.mil/article/37660/operation_power_pack_u_s_military_intervention_in_the_dominican_republic

Eighty-Second Airborne Division War Memorial Museum

Military Editor Drew Brooks, *Fayetteville Observer*, Fayetteville, North Carolina.

http://www.psywarrior.com/DomRepublicPsyop.html

https://www.historynet.com/going-to-war-in-1965-with-the-army-you-have.htm

Medal of Honor Official Citation for John A. Barnes, III

"Vietnam Fighting Grows in Highlands with Two New Battles," Associated Press, Saigon, South Vietnam, November 11, 1967

United States Army Center of Military History

"The Battle of Hill 875, Dak To, Vietnam 1967," Leonard B. Scott, Army War College, 1988

"Dak To: America's Sky Soldiers in South Vietnam's Central Highlands," p.325, Edward F. Murphy, Ballantine Publishing, 2007

"Firefights in Vietnam," Washington, DC, United States Army Center of Military History

"Dak To 1967: 33 Days of Violent, Sustained Combat," by Tim Dyhouse, *VFW Magazine*, March 2006

"A Soldier's Story/Battles at Dak To," by Jeffrey Nordahl, *VFW Magazine*, March 2006

"The battle of Dak To," by Tom Hebert

"Miss Carson Barnes is Engaged to Lt James Fleming of Brookline," *The Boston Globe*, Boston, Massachusetts, June 1, 1952

"Medal of Honor For Dead GI," *The Boston Globe*, Boston, Massachusetts, November 5, 1969

"John A. Barnes Jr. Obituary," *The Boston Globe*, Boston, Massachusetts, June 13, 1973

"Katherine (Hermes) Barnes Obituary," *The Boston Globe*, Boston, Massachusetts, May 6, 1976

"James S. Fleming Obituary," *The Boston Globe*, Boston, Massachusetts, November 25, 2008

"Carson (Barnes) Fleming Obituary," *The Boston Globe*, Boston, Massachusetts, September 15, 2014

"Before Action," Lt. William Noel Hodgson, 1916, Public Domain

Chapter 8
John Paul Bobo

Notes from family and friends

"Second Lieutenant John Paul Bobo, USMC," *Who's Who in Marine Corps History*, History Division, United States Marine Corps

"General characteristics, 2nd Lt. John P. Bobo Class, Maritime Prepositioning Ships, T-AK," The United States Navy—Fact File, US Navy, August 22, 2007

"Medal of Honor, 2dLt John P. Bobo (Medal of Honor citation)," *Marines Awarded the Medal of Honor*, History Division, USMC

https://www.msc.navy.mil/sealift/2003/October/bobo.htm

"Honoring John P. Bobo," by Katie Lange, *Department of Defense News*, May 18, 2020

"Honoring 2nd Lt. John Paul Bobo's supreme sacrifice," by James Neiss, *The Niagara Gazette*, Niagara, New York, March 31, 2017

"VOICES: Remembering a remarkable act of heroism," by Jim Michaels, *USA Today*

http://www.geraldgillis.com/usmc-lt-john-bobo-medal-of-honor/

https://getlinscorner.org/learn/the-battle-of-getlins-corner/

Navy Cross citation to First Sgt. Raymond G. Rogers, Jr

Navy Cross citation (Posthumously) to Cpl. John Leon Loweranitis

Navy Cross citation to Hospital Corpsman Third Class Kenneth R. Braun

"Shootout on Hill 70," *US News and World Report*

"Marine Hero's Medal of Honor Given to His Parents," p.22, *The New York Times*, New York, New York, September 5, 1968

"Marine Officer is Killed in War," *The Niagara Gazette*, Niagara, New York, March 30, 1967

"Falls War Victim Given Top Honor," *The Niagara Gazette*, Niagara, New York, August 27, 1968

"Great-Heart," Rudyard Kipling, 1919, Public Domain

Chapter 9
Samuel Swann Linville

Notes from family and friends

Vanderbilt Magazine PMB 357737 2301 Vanderbilt Place, Nashville, Tenn., 37235–7737

vanderbiltmagazine@vanderbilt.edu

https://charliecompany.org/charlie-company-troops/stories-of-vietnam-experiences/fred-childs/ait/

coffeltdatabase.org

https://www.almanac.com/weather/history

"Raymond H. Davis Obituary," *High Point Enterprise*, High Point, North Carolina, December 26, 1953

The Turning: A History of Vietnam Veterans Against the War, by Andrew E. Hunt, New York University Press, p.5, 1999

"The Veterans Antiwar Movement in Fact and Memory," by John Prados, *A Companion to the Vietnam War*, John Wiley & Sons, p.403, 2008

Hargrave Military Academy, Chatham, Virginia, 1960 and 1961 yearbooks

"The First Battalion (Mechanized) Fifth Infantry Twenty-fifth Infantry Division In The Viet Nam War—February to December 1967," compiled by First Battalion (M) Fifth Infantry Society of Vietnam Combat Veterans, Inc.

"The First Battalion (Mechanized) Fifth Infantry Twenty-fifth Infantry Division In The Viet Nam War—1966 to 1971," compiled by First Battalion (M) Fifth Infantry Society of Vietnam Combat Veterans, Inc., January to May 1968

https://www.vietnamwar50th.com/assets/1/7/Vietnam_War_ Commemoration_Map_2.pdf

"The Call of the Stream," Charles H. Crandall, 1919, Public Domain

Chapter 10
Michael David Helmstetler

Notes from family and friends

"Marine Aviation Cadet Michael D. Helmstetler," *High Point Enterprise*, High Point, North Carolina, April 4, 1966

"Dorothy Haney Helmstetler Obituary," *High Point Enterprise*, High Point, North Carolina, March 8, 1992

"Larry Charles Helmstetler Obituary," *High Point Enterprise*, High Point, North Carolina, April 19, 1996

"Helmstetler-Spell Couple Says Vows," *High Point Enterprise*, High Point, North Carolina

"Lt. Anthony J. Schultheis Receives Navy Cross," https://valor. defense.gov/Portals/24/Documents/ServiceCross/NavyCross-WWII.pdf

https://www.almanac.com/weather/history

"A History of Marine Medium Helicopter Squadron 161," by Lt. Col. Gary W. Parker, USMC, 2014

https://www.stripes.com/news/special-reports/vietnam-sto-ries/1966/after-5-decades-marine-officers-reunite-reminisce-about-the-basic-school-1.483723

https://www.vhpa.org/KIA/K10889.HTM

http://www.popasmoke.com/kia/conflicts/usmc-reserve/
incidents/19680428

"The Final Formation," by Rev. Ray Stubbe, Special Edition, *Khe Sanh Veteran Magazine*, 1995

http://www.popasmoke.com/kia/conflicts/vietnam/
incidents/19680619

"Marine Corps could barely maintain Helicopter Pilots," George Curtis, Popasmoke.com

11-04-2003

http://vandvreader.org/report-from-vietnam-february-27-1968/

US Marines In Vietnam The Defining Year 1968 PCN 19000313800_5

https://www.marines.mil/Portals/1/Publications/US%20
Marines%20In%20Vietnam%20The%20Defining%20
Year%201968%20%20PCN%2019000313800_5.pdf

"*Last Stand at Khe Sanh: The US Marines' Finest Hour in Vietnam*," by Gregg Jones, Da Capo Press, April 2014

https://www.marines.mil/portals/1/publications/the%20battle%20
for%20khe%20sanh%20pcn%2019000411000_1.pdf

"Schultheis, Helmstetler Plans Told," *Pensacola News Journal Sun*, Pensacola, Florida, March 26, 1967

"Sue Schultheis Is Bride Of Lt. M. D. Helmstetler," *Pensacola News Journal Sun*, Pensacola, Florida, July 2, 1967

"First Lt. Michael David Helmstetler Obituary," *High Point Enterprise*, High Point, North Carolina, July 3, 1968

"Warm Summer Sun," Mark Twain, 1896, Public Domain

Chapter 11
Marvin Glenn Shields

Notes from family and friends

https://www.almanac.com/weather/history

"Marvin Shields killed in Viet Nam," *Port Townsend Leader*, Port Townsend, Wash., June 17, 1965

"Marvin Shields laid to rest at Gardiner," by Mrs. Peter Jorgenson, *Port Townsend Leader*, Port Townsend, Wash., January, 24 1965

"Honor Medal Awarded," *Bremerton Sun*, Bremerton Wash., September, 14, 1966

"USS *Marvin Shields*: The 'Can Do' Ship," by Julius J. Lacano. Historian, US Navy Seabee Museum, https://seabeemuseum.wordpress.com/

https://seabeemuseum.wordpress.com/tag/marvin-g-shields/

https://www.navytimes.com/news/your-navy/2020/03/03/what-this-seabee-did-to-earn-the-medal-of-honor/

Medal of Honor Citation—Marvin Glen Shields, Construction Mechanic Third Class, US Navy

Naval Historical Center

"Obituary of Barbara Diane Shields Rote," http://obits.dignitymemorial.com/dignity-memorial/obituary.aspx?n=Barbara-Rote&lc=6893&pid=157374316&mid=5086804, 2012

Dana Brenner, *Vietnam Magazine,* October 2018

Southeast Asia: Building The Bases The History Of Construction In Southeast Asia: Vietnam Construction, by Richard Tregaskis, April, 20, 2011

President Lyndon B. Johnson awards Marvin Glenn Shields the Medal of Honor posthumously on September 13, 1966, by Duane Colt Denfeld, Ph.D., HistoryLink.org Essay 10928, December 30, 2014

"Marvin Shields: Only Seabee Awarded Medal of Honor," by Doug Sterner, Curator, Military Times Hall of Valor

"Honoring Marvin Shields' Legacy," by PO2 Ryan Batchelder, Navy Public Affairs Support Element, Det. Northwest

"This Is How Marvin G. Shields Became The Only Seabee Ever To Receive The Medal Of Honor," by Dan Doyle

"Remember Dong Xoai!" by Richard Fournier, *VFW Magazine*, June/July 2015

"Dong Xoai Battle Ends, Hundreds Killed," Associated Press (AP) press release, Saigon, June 11, 1965

"Jets Smash Barracks; VC Ambush Battalion," *Tri-City Herald*, Pasco, Kennewick, Richland, Washington, June 14, 1965

"Attack on Dong Xoai Special Forces Camp—June 9–10, 1965," *The Military Engineer*, November to December 1965

"Gets Father's Medal," *The Chronicle*, October 12, 1965

"Dong Xoai, Vietnam 1965," written and illustrated by Joe Kubert

Dong Xoai Incident Report

Dong Xoai After Action Report

Dong Xoai Lessons Learned and Recommendations

"The Mariner's Dream," William Dimond, 1822, Public Domain

Chapter 12
John Charles Yates

Notes from family and friends

"Yates Family trip to New Mexico," *The Daily Journal*, Fergus Falls, Minn., July 16, 1962

https://www.thoughtco.com/farming-post-world-war-ii-1146852, by Mike Moffatt, January 27, 2020

https://www.usmcu.edu/Research/Marine-Corps-History-Division/Brief-Histories/History-of-Marine-Corps-Recruit-Training/

"Lance Cpl. John Yates visited by mother and grandmother at Camp LeJeune, North Carolina," May 1964

Silver Star Medal Citation, Sgt. John Charles Yates (MCSN: 108133), USMC

http://www.hiddenkona.com/349/SeaStoriesProsise2.html

https://www.wikiwand.com/en/Operation_Napoleon/Saline#/Battle_of_Dai_Do, public domain material from documents of the USMC

U.S. Marines in Vietnam: 1968 The Defining Year, by Jack Shulimson, History and Museums Division, Headquarters, USMC, ISBN 0-16-049125-8, 1997, Public Domain

U.S. Marines in Vietnam: Fighting the North Vietnamese 1967, by Gary Telfer, History and Museums Division, Headquarters, USMC, ISBN 978-1494285449, 1984, Public Domain.

Where we were in Vietnam, by Michael Kelley, Hellgate Press, ISBN 978-, p5–484, 2002

"Operation Hickory II Part B—The View from the Ground," Summarized by Hugh Connelly, with input from P. Martin Johnson, Lt. Col., USMC (Ret.), who was the Battalion S-3

Officer and later Commanding Officer of "A" Co, Leo R. Jamieson, Lt. Col., USMC (Ret.) (Commanding Officer of "A" Company and field commander for First Amtracs in Hickory II) and several fellow participants, enhanced by official USMC records of the Operation, including the Command Chronology of the First Amphibian Tractor Battalion, the most relevant parts of which are the S-2/S-3 logs, http://www.amtrac.org/1atbn/Battles/OpHickory02B.asp,

Company Roster, Company B, First Amphibian Tractor Battalion, FIRST Marine Division (Rein.), FMF, October 1968

Silver Star Medal Citation, Gunnery Sgt. John Mark Avery (MCSN: 1518220), USMC, October 1968

Navy Cross Citation, 2nd Lt. John Charles Yates (MCSN: 0-108133), USMC

"Fergus Falls Marine Awarded Silver Star," *The Minneapolis Star*, Minneapolis, Minn., November 25, 1967

"Yates Awarded Cross of Gallantry," *The Daily Journal*, Fergus Falls, Minn., September 18, 1968

"Fergus Falls Man Cited for Bravery in Vietnam War," *The Daily Journal*, Fergus Falls, Minn., November 24, 1967

"Fergus Falls Marine Killed," *Star Tribune*, Minneapolis, Minn., October 22, 1968

"Fergus Falls Marine Dies in Vietnam," *The Minneapolis Star*, Minneapolis, Minn., October 22, 1968

"City Plans to Honor War Casualties," *The Daily Journal*, Fergus Falls, Minn., October 22, 1968

"Killed In Vietnam," *The Minneapolis Star*, Minneapolis, Minn., October 24, 1968

"Yates Family Prefers Memorials," *The Daily Journal*, Fergus Falls, Minn., October 22, 1968

"Funeral For John Yates Set Friday," *The Daily Journal*, Fergus Falls, Minn., November 6, 1968

"John Yates Posthumously Awarded Vietnam Honors," *The Daily Journal*, Fergus Falls, Minn., April 15, 1970

"Vietnam Awards Given to John Yates' Parents," *The Daily Journal*, Fergus Falls, Minn., July 28, 1971 https://www.almanac.com/weather/history

"Obituary for Louis Edgar Yates," Laporte, Minn., September 2007

"Obituary for Mariana McKnight Yates," LaPorte, Minn., August 2008

"How to Die," by Siegfried Loraine Sassoon, April 1919, Public Domain

Chapter 13
Delbert Ray Peterson

Notes from family and friends

https://www.almanac.com/weather/history

https://www.mu.iastate.edu/gold-star-hall-kiosk/all-by-name/delbert-peterson/

Delbert Ray Peterson Biography, Copyright © 1995–2020, Iowa State Memorial Union

"AC-47 Factsheet," Archived from the original on 2014-10-11-USAF

Shulimson, Jack, *US Marines in Vietnam: 1966, an Expanding War.* History and Museums Division, USMC, p56, 1982

https://www.catkillers.org/history-1966-Battle-of-A-Shau.pdf

https://www.airforcemag.com/article/valor-valor-in-two-dimensions/

Air Force Cross Citation: Peterson, Delbert Ray (MIA-KIA) Department of the Air Force, Special Order GB-189, July 13, 1966

Homecoming II Project October 15, 1990

https://dpaa.secure.force.com/dpaaProfile?id=a0Jt0000000KYl-ZEAW, MAJ DELBERT RAY PETERSON

https://www.ac47-gunships.com/ac47_history.htm

"ISU Gold Star Hall ceremony honors fallen Vietnam soldier from Manson," by Teddi Barron, *News Service*, November 3, 2010

"You will not be forgotten," by Christinia Crippes, *The Courier*, Waterloo, Iowa, September 18, 2015

"Museum honors 25 Iowans missing in action," *Sioux City Journal*, Sioux City, Iowa

Denzil "Denny" Peterson Obituary, *Messenger News*, https://www.messengernews.net, 713 Central Ave, Fort Dodge, Iowa, 50501

http://www.specialoperations.net/Spooky.htm

"When I Come Home Again," *From an outpost, and other poems*, Sgt. Leslie Coulson, 1917, Public Domain

Chapter 14
Lawrence David Peters

https://www.boyscouttrail.com/content/ceremony/eagle_scout-1673.asp
https://usmccap139.com/general/usmccaposcar/cap-history, by R. E. Hays (MSGT, USMC, Ret)
https://cherrieswriter.com/2020/08/01/operation-hastings-a-marine-hell-hole/
https://libertyyes.homestead.com/Operations/Operation-Hastings-1966.htm
"U.S. Marines in Vietnam: An Expanding War, 1966," *Marine Corps Vietnam Operational Historical Series*, Marine Corps Association, ASIN B000L34A0C, by Jack Shulimson, 1982, Public Domain
"U.S. Marines in Vietnam: Fighting the North Vietnamese 1967," by Gary Telfer, History and Museums Division, Headquarters, US Marine Corps. ISBN 978-1494285449, 1984, Public Domain
"The War in the Northern Provinces: 1966–1968," by Lt. Gen. Willard Pearson, US Government Printing Office, Washington, DC, 1975
https://www.almanac.com/weather/history/NY/Binghamton/1967-04-10#
https://flybgm.com/
Medal of Honor Citation—Lawrence David Peters—Posthumously awarded to his family by Vice-President Spiro Agnew on April 20, 1970.
"Old Souls," Lief Ericson, 2022, Used by permission of author

Chapter 15
Vincent Robert Capodanno

Letter and notes from family, friends, and fellow Vietnam veterans
Letter written to Father Vincent Capodanno's Brother, James, by 3/5 Navy Corpsman Vic Perez

The Father Vincent Capodanno Guild www.capodannoguild.org

Maryknoll Mission Archives

Memorial to Father Vincent Capodanno, Fort Wadsworth, New York.

USS *Capodanno* (FF-1093) named in honor of Lieutenant Capodanno

Certificate of Papal Blessing

Father Capodanno's Medal of Honor citation; awarded January 7, 1969, Washington, DC

https://www.combatrosariesforheroes.com/capodanno-kapaun/

https://catholicherald.org/local/devils-advocate-sainthood-cause-explains-process/

https://www.catholicworldreport.com/2020/05/24/the-dramatic-story-of-the-priest-who-died-on-a-south-vietnam-battlefield

https://www.milarch.org/father-capodanno-bio/

https://cherrieswriter.com/2021/09/26/remembering-father-vincent-capodanno-54-years-since-death-of-staten-islands-fearless-grunt-padre/

"Two Canteens and a Bible—the Chaplain's Legacy," *The Marine Corps League Magazine*, Autumn Edition, P.22, 2001

"Marines at Outpost Mourn For Chaplain Killed in Battle," The Philadelphia Bulletin, Philadelphia, Penna., September, 1967

"The Grunt Padre: The Service and Sacrifice of Father Vincent Capodanno, Vietnam 1967," by Father Daniel Lawrence Mode; All royalties from sales support the Father Vincent Robert Capodanno Foundation

"Charity by Proxy," by Peter Duffy, *The Wall Street Journal*, New York, New York, March 7, 2008

https://thechaplainkit.com/history/stories/chaplain-vincent-capodanno-moh-winner/

"Vincent R. Capodanno, the Padre who gave all for wounded Marines," by Doug Sterner, *Vietnam magazine,* April 2020, https://www.historynet.com/vincent-r-capodanno-the-padre-who-gave-his-all-for-wounded-marines.htm

http://www.securenet.net/3rdbn5th/mike35/capodanno1.htm

Public Domain material from websites or documents of the United States Marine Corps.

"U.S. Marines in Vietnam: Fighting the North Vietnamese 1967," by
    Gary Telfer, History and Museums Division, Headquarters, US
    Marine Corps. ISBN 978-1494285449, 1984, Public Domain
https://www.maryknollmagazine.org/2017/09/capodanno-
    grunt-padre-50-years-later/
"A prayer of St. Francis of Assisi," Anonymous, Public Domain

Photographic Sources

Dedication
    a: M. Mitchell
    b: M. Mitchell
    c: M. Mitchell

Thank you
    a: G. Blackburn

Tribute
    a: US Army
    b: US Army
    c: J. Mastro
    d: D. Ward
    e: Associated Press
    f: D. Ward
    g: R. Carlson

Chapter 1—Davan
    a: E. Woody
    b: E. Woody
    c: E. Woody
    d: E. Woody
    e: H. Belisle
    f: H. Dews
    g: E. Woody
    h: E. Woody
    ·: E. Woody

    j: H. Dews
    k: E. Woody
    l: E. Woody
    m: H. Dews
    n: H. Dews

Chapter 2—De La Garza
    a: USMC
    b: L. De La Garza
    c: L. De La Garza
    d: L. De La Garza
    e: L. De La Garza
    f: L. De La Garza
    g: L. De La Garza
    h: L. De La Garza
    i: S. Lyles
    j: L. De La Garza
    k: L. De La Garza

Chapter 3—Lane
    a: Lane Family
    b: US Army
    c: US Army
    d: US Army
    e: US Army
    f: US Army/B. Kramer
    g: US Army

Chapter 4—Anthony
a: US Air Force
b: A. Plumstead
c: US Air Force
d: USAFSS

Chapter 5—Heide
a: Heide Family
b: USASA
c: USASA
d: Heide Family
e: Smith Family
f: C. Collat
g: US Army
h: B. Barrera
i: D. Hewitt
j: D. Hewitt
k: M. Likens
l: D. Hewitt
m: US Army
n: C. Collat
o: Unknown
p: USASA
q: Black Family
r: US Army
s: US Army:

Chapter 6—Wilbanks
a: US Air Force
b: US Air Force
c: US Air Force
d: US Air Force

Chapter 7—Barnes
a: US Army
b: Barnes Family

c: US Army
d: US Army
e: J. Nordahl
f: DOD
g: DOD

Chapter 8—Bobo
a: USMC
b: Bobo Family
c: US Navy
d: USMC
e: USMC
f: US Navy
g: US Navy

Chapter 9—Linville
a: F. Goins
b: Hargrave
c: Hargrave
d: Hargrave
e: Hargrave
f: US Army
g: D. McDonough
h: US Army
i: US Army
j: Linville Family
k: DOD
l: Linville Family

Chapter 10—Helmstetler
a: Helmstetler Family
b: *High Point Enterprise*
c: USMC
d: US Navy
e: Helmstetler Family
f: USMC

g: USMC
h: US Navy
i. DOD
j: USMC

Chapter 11—Shields
a: US Navy
b: US Navy
c: US Navy
d: US Navy
e: US Army
f: US Army
g: US Army
h: US Army
i: US Navy
j: *Sea Bee Magazine*

Chapter 12—Yates
a: USMC
b: Yates Family
c: Unknown
d: Yates Family
e: A. Brown
f: H. Connelly
g: M. Jamieson
h: D. Law
i: Unknown
j: USMC
k: USMC
l: T. Soliz

Chapter 13—Peterson
a: US Air Force
b: Peterson Family
c: Peterson Family
d: US Air Force

e: US Air Force
f: US Air Force
g: US Air Force

Chapter 14—Peters
a: USMC
b: Peters Family
c: USMC
d: USMC
e: USMC

Chapter 15—Capodanno
a: USMC
b: USMC
c: USMC
d: USMC
e: USMC
f: *Staten Is. Advance*/B. Schwartz
g: Maryknoll Archives

Author
a: US Air Force
b: L. Long

ABOUT THE AUTHOR

Gary B. Blackburn is a native Iowan and served with the US Air Force Security Service, a subordinate of the National Security Agency, from April 1961 to October 1964. As a member of USAFSS, Blackburn studied Mandarin Chinese at the Institute of Far Eastern Languages, Yale University, and Technical Chinese at Goodfellow AFB, San Angelo, Texas, Blackburn's first overseas deployment was to the 6922nd Radio Group Mobile, Kadena AB, Okinawa. He worked directly under NSA supervision at the Joint Sobe Processing Center, Torii Station, Sobe, Okinawa, processing and distributing top-secret intelligence reports coming in from all over Asia. In January 1963, Blackburn was reassigned to the 6987th Security Group, Shu Lin Kou Air Station, Taiwan, where he was employed as a Communist Chinese Air Force voice intercept processing specialist. After his Asian tour was complete, he returned to Goodfellow AFB as a member of the elite 6948th Security Squadron (Mobile) to finish his military commitment.

Gary is a graduate of John Wesley University in High Point, North Carolina. He is retired from Eastern Air Lines, Inc. and the US Department of Homeland Security. He served as commandant of cadets, vice president of development, and director of public relations/alumni affairs at Oak Ridge Military Academy, Oak Ridge, North Carolina, over a span of ten years.

Gary's writing career began when he was approached by an old friend from his military days. Lonnie Long and Gary Blackburn met in Taiwan in 1963, when Long, who was a member of the Army Security Agency, was assigned to work with the Air Force for several months, and they became friends. Long had been collecting research materials for over a dozen years on the mostly top-secret (and therefore unknown) history and accomplishments of ASA, but he was not a writer. Blackburn had done extensive journalistic writing and editing but had never written a book. Lonnie's proposal: If Gary would do the writing, he would provide the research and they would split any profits that might come from the project. The result three years later was *Unlikely Warriors: The Army Security Agency's Secret War in Vietnam 1961–1973*, which has become the definitive work on secret efforts to gather communications intelligence in Vietnam by the US Army (ASA), Air Force (USAFSS), Navy, and Marine Corps (NSG).

During the pandemic year of 2020, Blackburn finished his second book *Those Gentle Heroes: A Tribute*. In 2023, responding to demand, he published his third book, *More Gentle Heroes*, and he continues to write.

"I love doing it," he says, "These are stories that need to be told—these are heroes who need to be remembered."

CPSIA information can be obtained
at www.ICGtesting.com
Printed in the USA
JSHW012019260423
40793JS00001B/3